# Fannie Hardy Eckstorm

# Short Stories

# and

# Essays

edited and annotated
by

Tommy Carbone

Burnt Jacket Publishing, LLC
copyright, 2023

# BURNT JACKET
# PUBLISHING

# MAINE

**Books from Tommy Carbone**

The Lobster Lake Bandits
Mystery at Moosehead

The Elephant Mountain Gang
Mystery at Maine's Moosehead Lake

I Am Penobscot - A Novel

Woods and Lakes of Maine - Annotated Edition:
A Trip from Moosehead Lake to New Brunswick in a Birch-
Bark Canoe

Hubbard's Guide to Moosehead Lake and Northern Maine
Annotated Edition

Exploring the Maine Woods
The Hardy Family Expedition to the Machias Lakes

David Stone Libbey – He was Penobscot

The Penobscot Man – Life and Death on a Maine River

Katahdin, Pamola, & Whiskey Jack – Stories & Legends from
The Maine Woods

# FANNIE HARDY ECKSTORM
## SHORT STORIES AND ESSAYS
### ANNOTATED

Cover photo and interior illustrations, and photos from the editor's collection, or as otherwise noted.

Book design, author of new material, and edition editor, Tommy Carbone. Use of all newly added material (text and photos) from this book, other than short passages for review purposes or used within quotations, requires prior written permission be obtained by contacting the publisher at info@tommycarbone.com. Thank you for your support.

Material from Eckstorm's journals is courtesy of Special Collections Raymond H. Fogler Library, Univ. of Maine, with acknowledgments to Desirée Butterfield-Nagy, M.L.I.S., for her research assistance.

Cover Photo, Ripogenus Gorge from the dam.

Back cover Photo, Ripogenus Gorge from the "putting in place."

***Burnt Jacket Publishing, LLC***
Maine
*copyright 2023*

ISBN: 978-1-954048-32-4
20231201ISPBK

www.tommycarbone.com

1. Maine woods - 2. Short Stories - 3. Lumbering - 4. Creative non-fiction - 5. Maine history - 6. Naturalist - 7. Hunting and fishing. - 8. Woodsmen – 9. 19th Century History - 10. Northwoods Maine.

# EXPLORING THE MAINE WOODS
## The Hardy Family Expedition to the Machias Lakes

"I was just mesmerized by Fannie Hardy Eckstorm.
She took me completely by surprise.
She and her father go off on this passage, and it might as well
be the *Odyssey*!
There are passages in here which are just distillate, they are just
perfect descriptions of something I may have seen, but never
could have articulated with the imagery that she has used."

**review by**

## Peter Neill

*host*, **Conversations from the Pointed Firs**

Maine lumbering and river-driving history is kept alive by several organizations in Maine. The stories in this book will come alive should the reader visit these wonderful museums.

These photos were taken by the editor at the
Chesuncook Boom House Museum.

*Editor's Photos*
*Courtesy of the West Branch Historical Preservation Committee*

# INTRODUCTION

**Fannie Hardy Eckstorm** was an interpreter of nature, an ornithologist, and an expert on early Maine history. She had a mind for detail and applied scientific habits in her writing research. Her father, expert Maine woodsman Manly Hardy, educated her on woodlore during their extended trips into the deep Maine woods. The education she received at Smith College formed her writing habits and developed her ability to see connections. Following her time as the superintendent of Brewer, Maine schools, she spent decades writing about the lumbermen and Maine Native Americans. She documented their stories to preserve history and to teach on the ways of the woods, those who worked there, and most importantly the lives they lived.

For over seventy-five years, most all of the short stories in the first half of this book have been read by only a few, who like myself, have opened the boxes held at the Special Collections Department at the University of Maine Fogler Library. While Eckstorm submitted numerous stories to magazines and newspapers, it is thought that only two of the included short stories have been published before. On her typed notes for the story, "In the Maine Woods," Eckstorm herself was not sure if it had been printed. This is understandable. Eckstorm had many parallel projects and compiled her journal archives some years after she wrote the tales to paper. A few of the stories included were complete in content, but never polished to completion; and one is only her preface to what was to be an epic Maine woods adventure. It is my hope that through this annotated edition others will enjoy the fantastic writing from Eckstorm.

The stories are based on accounts she was told from her father, woods-guides, woodsmen, lumbermen, and river-drivers. Eckstorm was serious and factual in her published writing. She had little patience for someone who got their facts incorrect about Maine places or Maine people. Some of the included stories are lighter than her other works and even have a bit of humor. While she didn't write fiction per se, these tales certainly pass for creative non-fiction. However, she steered away from applying fictionalized elements to the real people she wrote about. From this, we can then believe that stories like the included *Spike-Sole Shoes* and *A River Tale - Life Gulliver* are stories based on real men and she relays the true words others told her.

Even as Eckstorm was a skilled interviewer and listener, she acknowledged where she was required to add *interpretation* to the oration by river-driver Dan Golden. She noted, *in Danny's excitement of reliving the drive, he became too eloquent to follow understandingly*. Golden also could not have told her what his partner in crime, Boney Davis, was thinking as he fought the West Branch to keep clear of boulders; but she included the realistic thoughts to enhance the story. Eckstorm rounded out Golden's recited history with what she knew of Grand Falls on the West Branch of the Penobscot River and of men of the trade. From the scribing of Golden's words, and through her descriptive writing, the reader will be swept down the falls with Golden and Davis as they commanded their batteau along the rushing river current <u>wearing nothing</u> but their spike-soled river-driving boots.

Whenever Eckstorm may have had a question about a story, she usually sought two or more sources. For Golden's story, Eckstorm admits to not having verified with others. Her saying so, hints slightly at the grandness of the story, or the tale-bearer, but it was too good a story for her not to document. In her portfolio of river-driver stories, it reads closely possible to have occurred.

Over the years, Eckstorm listened to numerous rivermen telling of running falls with their batteaus. When her father took her to the Maine north woods above Moosehead Lake in 1891, she lugged along her heavy camera, glass plates, and wooden stand (when there were no roads to be conveyed upon) to photograph the river-drivers in action at Ripogenus Gorge. Her photo of the drivers picking a jam is included so the reader may appreciate the remoteness of the woods and the laboring done there. Additionally, the editor would ask the reader to also consider the dedication it took, more than 130 years ago, with the camera equipment being what it was, to achieve such a crisp historic photo. We might add *photographer* to Eckstorm's accomplishments.

In the evening hours, the drivers sat around their campfires, as lumbermen and river-drivers will do, and Fannie was welcomed into their circle. With the flicker of firelight illuminating the men's patched pants and worn red shirts, she absorbed their recollections, their sayings, and their mannerisms. It is no wonder then that her stories read as if she was there with the men during their adventures and perils, because, for a time, she had been. In her capturing of Dan Golden's words about his glorious moment of rebellion from a quarter century earlier against river-driver boss John Ross, she skillfully adds details as if she herself was along the river that day.

Although Eckstorm had annotated her typed sheets with sparse handwritten corrections, the stories required modest editing and formatting to bring them to completion. While I wish Eckstorm could have discussed the edits, I trust she would have appreciated bringing the stories of these men out of the boxes to be read. The intent of her stories, the character portrayals, and outcomes are unchanged and are as Eckstorm had written them—including in some, where the reader must figure what Eckstorm had hinted in the end.

To Eckstorm's writing of dialogue, I have made the most edits. She often wrote as pronunciations were made by the speaker. The effect, while authentic to the time, caused the text to be unwieldy to decipher in parts. Likewise, there are pronunciations and nuances of speech that remain in the text as she wrote them; whether speech from the lumbermen or her Penobscot Indian friends. For example, when an Indian made reference to a person or place, no matter masculine or feminine in nature, Eckstorm wrote as the person labeled their subjects. When her storyteller described Big Sebattis Mitchell, she wrote their words as they were spoken: *"S'battis, she big man an' she clever man an' she slow but when reached it McDougall Falls she mos' hot."* Eckstorm also wrote many words as they were pronounced: 'dribe' for drive, as in river **drive**; and 'berry' for **very**. The text of this edition has been somewhat adjusted for readability in several cases.

I would not have been able to edit and annotate these stories had I not studied Eckstorm's writing and notes for years. There are numerous connections in these stories to her other work which made the project even more satisfying as I discovered new historical details left by Eckstorm. In these tales, the readers of my prior annotated works from Fannie Hardy Eckstorm will find recognizable characters in her theme to preserve Maine's early river-driving history. And while these short stories are wonderful stand-alone pieces on Maine history, I recommend the following annotated books in order to fully experience Eckstorm's writing style and the period of time she captured:

o *The Penobscot Man - Life and Death on a Maine River (2022).*
o *Exploring the Maine Woods - The Hardy Family Expedition to the Machias Lakes (2021).*
o *Katahdin, Pamola, and Whiskey Jack - Stories and Legends from the Maine Woods (2021).*

The second half of this book, Part II, includes Eckstorm's essays on resident opinions, as well as legal cases over the unequal enforcement of the Maine Game Laws during the second half of the 1800s. These articles were published in *Forest and Stream* between March and August of 1891. They followed directly her series titled, "In the Region Around Nicatowis," essays which are annotated in, *Exploring the Maine Woods – The Hardy Family Expedition to the Machias Lakes.*

The topic and the factual presentation of these essays are quite the opposite of the sometimes humorous stories of Part I. The ideas may seem old and played over the near century-and-a-half since written. Yet, the reader is advised to look for the connection between the essays and other Eckstorm stories. Of course, debates still are had on hunting practices in Maine in the current day, and will continue into the future. The sportsmen still debate with the legislature and the Department of Fisheries and Wildlife over game matters; whether over Sunday hunting, bass-fishing tournaments, bear-baiting, or the coyote season; likewise, poaching still occurs, as evidenced on a popular game warden television show. Thankfully, most all wardens now have stellar reputations. The characters today may be new, but the accusations are old: too much protection of the game, not enough protection; meddling by outside groups lobbying for legislation; support of hunting for tourism money (and this goes for fishing as well), but unfair to the residents (or those from away); and on and on.

As a woman of twenty-six years of age when she wrote the game law essays, she was well versed in the current state of game affairs. This was in part due to the coaching from her father and his many hunter friends. She also was well educated and had a circle of friends in public matters. The articles were written, as Eckstorm so plainly states, to give the position of the more rural residents. She is very clear that the positions she presents were not her own, but she took on the task of writing the opinions of the rural population due to her close understanding of those residents and the particular region of Maine they inhabited or hunted. She wrote to explain the situation to those who she stated failed to understand, or were not able to get to the heart of the matter. Eckstorm wrote the articles to shed light on the felt emotions of the people in order to affect a change in statute clarity and enforcement equality. In doing so, Eckstorm subjected herself to criticism in the periodicals, and on the streets, for her writing on the topic. In the woods near Ripogenus Dam the situation became even more serious for her and her father.

When first published, there were disagreements over her statements. A few example responses are included to paint the full picture. The essays are republished in this volume to assist readers who may search out Eckstorm's original words. In engineering, we talk of 'Going to the Gemba.' That is a Japanese technique advising to go to the place where the work or action is done, for that is where you will find the truth. I advise you, when wanting to understand the positions of Fannie Hardy Eckstorm on people, traditions, or the game laws, to go to her own writing as the source, and not academic papers, opinion pieces, websites, or books written to analyze her in order to critique her positions, without regard for the time period of history in which she lived; especially when some writers it appears disregard her actual words, words in which she states exactly what she stood for and why.

Eckstorm spoke and visited with the lumbermen, in their woods; she went *to the gemba*. For her research on the game laws, she talked with the accused, the lawmakers, the courts, and the people. She reported on the situation through investigation and with diligence.

The Game Law Essays section may be of interest to the Maine hunter, but this section is as important to those interested in Eckstorm as a Maine writer and historian. For while she took on the Game Commission, poachers, wardens, and the justice system in this eloquent series, it is equally interesting as a view into her writing abilities. For why would a woman, in 1890 and 1891, who had penned naturalist pieces on the chickadee, the sapsucker, and the Canada Jay, take on such a controversial subject? The essays were certainly not casual pieces to write. She spent numerous hours in reading articles, doing interviews, and going over court records. Her interests were, at the time, birds and lumbering history, but here she was, investigating how wardens, detectives, and even the railroads were unable to follow the letter of the Maine laws. She did this because something was not right. In taking her stand, she named names and her life was threatened for it.

On the back cover of *The Penobscot Man - Life and Death on a Maine River*, I included a quote from Eckstorm. It reads:

"It is lovely to be beautiful, but it is essential to be true."

The pursuit of truth, I believe, is one reason why Eckstorm tackled the difficult subject of the game laws. By doing so, she was criticized then in print and threated in the woods. Even today, the meaning of her words in the essays are misconstrued by some writers and historians. In all she did, she pursued the truth and what she felt was right for the people of Maine. If a law was being unfairly executed or misunderstood, she could be counted on to teach about the wrong. This theme of being true, to those who read her other stories, will be apparent.

History is, as history was. It is not my intent in this book to analyze Eckstorm's words or the words she used through today's lens. The lover of history, those who wish to learn about it, will enjoy these stories and essays for what they are. Eckstorm knew the days of the river-driver, and the habits of the woodsmen from her younger years were changing and on the point of extinction. She wrote these stories to pass along the history and the character of those people. I've found no other writer from that period in Maine history who wrote as descriptively as Fannie Pearson Hardy Eckstorm.

Tommy Carbone, PhD
Maine — 2023

# FANNIE HARDY ECKSTORM

### (1865 – 1946)

The photo on the right was taken in 1888, the year of Eckstorm's college graduation, and two years prior to her writing the series of game law essays that are presented in this book.
*Images courtesy of Special Collections*
*Raymond H. Fogler Library, University of Maine*

\* \* \*

**As** the editor has written biographical sketches of Eckstorm in the books, *Exploring the Maine Woods – The Hardy Family to the Machias Lakes* and *The Penobscot Man – Life and Death on a Maine River*, in this book, words about her were written by her own pen. The following autobiographical note is from the April 1901 issue of the *Forest and Stream* magazine and was prefaced by a note from the periodical's editor.

## From the editors of Forest and Stream
## April 1901

**Our** older readers must still have a warm personal interest in the writer who, as Fannie Hardy, a few years ago contributed to the *Forest and Stream* a notable series, of papers on the Maine woods. Her vivacious letters descriptive of canoeing excursions with her father, Manly Hardy, were characterized by a rare knowledge of woodcraft; and when she wrote of the vexed and perplexing problems of Maine game protection, there was shown throughout such a sympathetic insight into actual conditions as to command respect. The man of the Maine woods—the hunter, trapper, guide, who was confronted by a fast coming changed order of things, who found it hard to give up the old ways and to face the new, who held stoutly to what he believed were his natural and inalienable rights, who was misunderstood or perhaps willfully slandered by the outside world—this man who could not speak for himself, found a friend and an advocate and champion of Fannie Hardy. No one may know the real history of those times who shall not have read her letters then published.[1]

It is because of this interest in one so well known to *Forest and Stream* readers that we have asked permission to print the following personal notes (which were) written by Mrs. Eckstorm at the request of her publishers, Messrs. Houghton, Mifflin & Co.[2]

---

[1] The essays in Part II of this book.
[2] The publisher utilized for the publication of Eckstorm's books, *The Bird Book* and *The Woodpeckers*.

## Written by Fannie Hardy Eckstorm:

I **was** born in Maine some thirty-five years ago, and remained here on intimate terms with all outdoors until I went to school and college. From Smith College I carried away with my degree some of the rewards of hard work and some of the satisfaction of profitable leisure. Among the latter are to be numbered long and usually solitary walks in the woods and over the mountains; the organizing of the Smith College Audubon Society with Miss Florence Merriam, as recently related by her in "Bird Lore," when John Burroughs came to help us, and the rummaging of all of the old historical collections and old French narrations that were accessible.

Returning home, I acted two years as superintendent of schools, and then went into a publishing house to see what it was like. And in the course of time I went to the Pacific coast and was married.

As a clergyman's wife in the far West and later in the East again, I had little leisure for any of my old avocations, though my husband enjoyed them all and encouraged the preparation of the books about to be issued. He was an excellent naturalist, and our few outings were spent in woods and fields, trout fishing and watching the birds. Since his death, I have once more come back to my old haunts in Maine.

Yet it is the first period of my life that accounts for my tastes. As I recall it, it seems to me that few could have enjoyed a childhood so nearly ideal. It was all fairy land and romance, out of school hours. Most of the people I knew had met adventures or done large things—sea captains, hunters, trappers, missionaries, travelers to all lands. Each one told his story and went his way. The books on the shelves were books of adventure—Capt. Cook, Moffat, Livingstone, Sir Samuel Baker, Kane, Hall, and every other notable Northern voyage and African exploration as it appeared. And before I could read, Virgil was a nursery tale and Homer a fairy story. All the time a world as wild as theirs lay just outside, and men built on these large epic lines—trappers, moose hunters, deer stalkers, scalers, lumbermen, river drivers, crack watermen—were coming and going and breaking bread with us. When I teased for a story, I got, it might be, the "Trojan Horse," or Ulysses bending his great bow, or Thoreau's guide, Joe Aitteon, going to his own death in the rush and welter of Island Falls to save his boat's crew.[3] Everything was of heroic size. King Arthur and Jack Mann, Robin Hood and Jock Darling were names of about equal weight and vividness, with the odds somewhat in favor of the one who could walk in to dinner and speak for himself as an abler man than the one who, for all his valiant deeds, had yielded and become a ghost.

It was my father's business that brought such a diversity of woods life to our doors. He and his father before him had dealt in all the products of the woods; had hunted, fished and trapped all over the Maine forests and knew most intimately everything that lived in the woods. With sixty years of such life behind me, it was impossible not to appreciate all the fine points of a bear

------

[3] In, *The Penobscot Man - Life and Death on a Maine River* in the chapter, *Rescue*, Eckstorm clarifies the location, "as one leaves Quakish Lake, is Rhine's Pitch of about ten feet; then Island Falls of two miles of very strong water with a heavy fall,—twenty feet in twenty rods in one place,—and Grand Falls, a mile long, with the Grand Pitch, twenty feet perpendicular, just before the river enters Shad Pond." On Maine's Penobscot waters, a waterfall 'cliff' is termed a *pitch*, and the falls are the run of fast water. Thus, you carry around a pitch, and *maybe* run falls—all depending.

skin, a moose hide, a snowshoe, or a canoe. Such knowledge was my inheritance. And I was taught as well the tricks of woodcraft that all hunters use; to know how to tell who caught a lot of fur by the way the skins were stretched and handled; and something of the differences almost inconceivably fine, but which my father could tell with all but magical correctness, the very section of country where a given mink or sable skin was taken.

Then there were the Indians, who came constantly, often a score of them in a day. They told me stories, brought me baskets and little birch bark or carved cedar canoes, and made a pet and plaything of me. I loved them all, without regard to comeliness, though perhaps my favorite was one of a scarred countenance, who explained that "She 'n' I 'n 'nother fellow we b'en fight; she bit it my nose off," meaning thereby that only two had joined battle, and that the nose was still in evidence, though very much damaged.[4] With all the white hunters I was the daughter of the regiment. I levied tribute of spruce gum, and if my doll needed furs some lonely trapper far in the wilderness was sure to remember to save the skins of the weasels that entered his traps for a gift to me.

When I played school, it was with fox skins stuffed with hay for my pupils. I remember how their black legs used to hang down and their pointed noses would stick up as they were ranged in line. I was permitted to play with all the skins except the black and silver foxes. Mink, sable with orange throats, otter, fisher, beaver, lynx and bear, I could roll and tumble among them as much as I desired, though the best fun was to slide down a great pile of foxes—a thousand or more in a heap sometimes—as they lay waiting the semi-annual shipment to London. And in all the

---

[4] This Indian was Peol (Piel) Molly Nicola, son of Molly Molasses.

packing, pressing and finishing of the bales I was permitted to help.

So my earliest associations were chiefly with the mammals. Birds came later. It was not till I was ten years old or so that my father began to collect and study birds. As I was his inseparable companion and adoring follower, it was inevitable that I should do as he did. For many years we worked together, making a representative collection of North American birds, doing most of the taxidermal work ourselves. And continually we were driving, walking or canoeing all through the woods near home and in the deep woods gathering notes of their habits. To grow up with a science under the tutelage of an accomplished naturalist and in surroundings adapted to one's pursuits is a good fortune that comes to few. So I had a childhood rarely happy and complete,[5] nor can I think of anything more likely to gratify that "healthy curiosity" of which you speak than an account of these earlier years.

-----

\*\* In 1929, the University of Maine conferred to Eckstorm a Master of Arts degree in *honoris causa*.

---

[5] Of course, we have an old use, as in, 'to have a rare old time,' for with much enjoyment.

# ECKSTORM'S MAINE TRAVELS

On this Maine map image are noted some of the areas Fannie Hardy Eckstorm explored during multi-week canoe trips with her father, Manly Hardy.

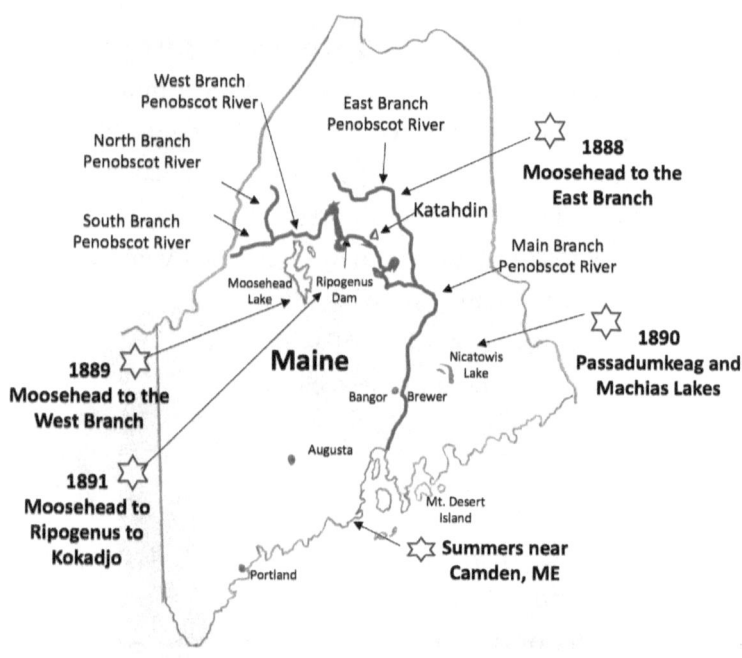

The 1890 trip down the Passadumkeag River to the Machias Lakes is covered in, *Exploring the Maine Woods - The Hardy Family Expedition to the Machias Lakes.*

The 1891 trip from Moosehead to Ripogenus Dam to Kokadjo is covered in, *The Penobscot Man - Life and Death on a Maine River.*

# PART I - SHORT STORIES

These selected short stories are a collection of mostly never before published tales from Fannie Hardy Eckstorm. In her handwriting on the original typed pages, there were some modest corrections in the margins; mostly grammatical or word changes. The editor has included those corrections along with modest edits to complete the stories for publication.

As some of these stories were not fully developed for publication when first written by Eckstorm, they were not as complete for story as Eckstorm's other works. In a few instances, I have played manuscript editor and corrected or added a sentence here and there to fill out the story. In addition, I have given the dialogue more life and other formatting necessities.

Footnotes for explanation, historical context, or information have been added. If Eckstorm had included an original footnote, it is prefaced with her initials.

Insets of historical information are included where appropriate for context and background. The photographs added by the editor within the chapters were not part of the original writings, and are included to add to the story or clarify a concept.

# SPIKE-SOLE SHOES

**When** one has a visitor who wishes to see the sights the proper thing to do is to take him to Oldtown to see the Indians.

On the whole the Indians do not seem to mind it much. It is the unhappy showman who finds it an impossible situation. It puts one in a savage mood to have to stand between a seasoned friend and a green acquaintance and, with an introductory wave of the hand, announce, "This, sir, is one who tended me as a baby; it is called an Indian; at its best it is no much darker than yourself and at its worst it is very nearly as white as yourself; you will perceive, however, that it is of different flesh and blood, not endowed with the same noble feelings; look, observe, acquire the local color of the phenomenon and see if you cannot pick up enough to write a newspaper article telling us what to do with the red man."

I confess that when I take a stranger thus with me, I go to see my old friends as friends, not as curiosities, and our talk is carried on without much regard for the stranger's impressions. Sometimes he observes that an Indian is more human than he had anticipated. Sometimes too he catches a glimpse of the heroism, the self-devotion, the humane and lovely pity that make both red and white brothers beneath the skin, and when he comes away he says, "After all, these Indian of yours are more men than I had imagined." That is what the good showman ought to be able to show to the visitor to Indian Island.[6]

---

[6] Eckstorm certainly felt strongly about her friends of the Penobscot nation. She took offense to the mischaracterizations of them from

With such a one I went some years ago to see the Indians. He was a youngster fresh from the city, most amazingly untutored in everything outside of paved streets but responding with coltish delight to the stimulus of this new free life which he felt, but could not catalogue. Something was different from New York; he thought it must be the air. Many who summer here attribute all their refreshment to the air. But it is deeper than that; it is the 'freigeist'[7] of the people, their open-air spirit, which is so tonic; to explain the difference as only a higher charge of ozone is to over-look entirely its spiritual balm.

But the youngster was not analytic; he was so densely ignorant, so sweetly receptive of correction, so ardently curious about all he saw that to play Mentor to his Telemachus[8] was all too flattering to one's self-esteem. And he did have a pretty eye for differences. With a little instruction he was able to pick out the types indicated to him, to see that an axeman is a different man from the river-driver; that the head-lumberman is a marked man in feature and bearing; that the hunter is no more plainly revealed by his features than by his voice; that the trapper is unlike the still-hunter; that we are infinite in our varieties by the finest differences which yet are distinct. And he came to have a little notion of the River, what it means to us, how it affects all grades of life, what it is to work "on the river," why men love it,

---

the curiosity seekers, the casual visitors, all the way to the likes of Henry David Thoreau, whom she felt missed opportunities during his conversations with Penobscot guides, Joseph Attean and Joe Polis. See appendix in, *Exploring the Maine Woods. The Hardy Family Expedition to the Machias Lakes.*

[7] German, with a meaning of free spirit, free-thinker.

[8] Telemachus was the son of Odysseus and Penelope in Greek mythology. Athena disguised herself as a mentor to help him for his task.

and die by it—and feel lost when they are separated from it. But all this came in time.

When we went to Oldtown he was in the springtime freshness of his verdancy; it was all strange to him, as indeed Oldtown must be strange to anyone who has insight but no acquaintance with this kind of life.

"Oh, see the little prick-holes in the side-walk!" he exclaimed with the interest of a child.

"The calks in the drivers' shoes do that," I started to explain.

"Corks? What do they have corks on their boots for? To keep them light, so they won't sink?"

"To help them in sticking to the logs. They have to wear them in picking jams."

He showed his perplexity in his face. "Why—I don't see –"

I laughed at him, though he was not the first I had seen in distress of understanding our technicalities; an enormously learned professoress who knew Sanskrit and could read the Rig Veda[9] once admitted that she supposed that "picking a jam" had something to do with getting berries for supper.

"We'll talk about jams when we see the men at work on one," said I. "But if you want to know all about spike-sole shoes, Oldtown is the place to learn it in."

So once more I called his attention to the plank side-walk pricked full of holes, now filled with dirt from passing feet and showing merely as black speckles.

"They were sharp," said he, examining them attentively.

There was an old batteau in a vacant lot nearby and I bade him examine how the bottom-boards and sides had been peppered

---

9 The Rig Veda (or Rigveda) – an ancient Indian collection of Sanskrit hymns.

with holes the size of bird-shot. He saw how the inside rails and knees[10] had been torn by the boatmen's shoes.

A tree trunk and root dug from the ground to be sawed into boat bracing, or knees.

*Image courtesy of*

*J.W. Swan & Sons*
*Boats - Timber - Workshops*

"And they must be quite long," said he reflecting. And again, "They must have a good many of them in their boots."

But I wasted no breath on descriptions. There was a little cobbler's shop nearby and I led him up to it and showed him the strings of shoes hanging before the door.

There they were, the spike-soled drivers' shoes, each one with its soles and heel bristling with steel calks sharpened to a point, an inch long before insertion, three quarters of an inch afterwards (for then they did not use the brush-ended patent calks such as are worn today). The youngster looked at them, felt their points, examined the buckled strap at the top which keeps the shoe

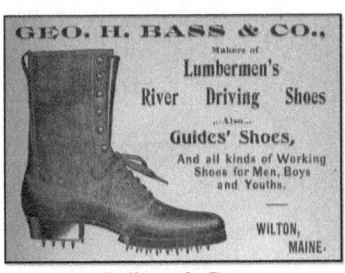

Spike-sole Boots.
Also called Corks, Caulks, or Calks.
*Advertisement For River Driver Boots*
*from the year 1900.*

---

[10] Knees are braces along the bottom and sides of a boat. They are fashioned from the angled portion of a tree's lowest portion of the trunk and root. The sections are dug and cut from the ground.

from being torn from the foot when the calks stick deep. He studied the double row of spikes and counted them.

"Forty in the sole, eight in the heel," he stated, definitively, but then thought about it. "Do they always wear such a pile of them?" he inquired.

"That is what is called a full set now," I answered. "Men have their preferences. Old Isaiah Morey never used to wear but one row unless the place he was going into was very bad and then, it is said, he had been known to put in two. But styles have changed from time to time. Of the old "pounded-out" calks they used twenty-five ball and four heel calks; then a full set was thirty-ball and five heel; now it is forty-ball and six or eight heel to a shoe; that's the ordinary wear."[11]

"Jolly!" said he, "but it must make a fellow happy to have a man dance on his corns with those things on! Those are the cruelest-looking things in the way of spikes that ever I came across."

Then I told him how the floors of all camps and up-river taverns were picked to pieces by them; how much damage the drivers sometimes did when they got into a drunken row on a train and kicked the upholstery into ribbons; how finally it had been forbidden by state law to wear calked shoes on cars so that we no longer saw them as once upon a time.[12]

And then it came to me to tell a story. The best time for telling a story is when you are on the spot where it happened, as we were then. It was a little story of spike-sole shoes, but I thought to myself to put him off the scent, to try the fineness of his instincts.

---

[11] Eckstorm noted in her journal edits, "Since then we have added eight more to the ball."

[12] Maine at one time had statutes dealing with wearing spiked boots and shoes in public places.

From my mentorship, I tested whether he could appreciate the best there is in our men.[13]

So, I led him across the road to the back of the great woolen mill where, looking out, we could see the rush and hear the clamor of Oldtown Falls. I took my time and pointed it all out to him, with little side excursions after topics of interest that the falls might grow upon him; for one unaccustomed to water never appreciates its force. There were the piers of the old railroad bridge that once led across to Milford, the second railroad in New England, begun in 1832. On that bridge it was Saul Ninepence, an Indian, went to bed one night when he was drunk imagining he was safe at home, and falling through the ties he was killed.

I pointed out the place where, in order to save a drunken fool, who having started one cold winter night from Milford side to paddle a batteau across with nothing but a fence picket had been miraculously borne upon the head of Goat Island. The best men of Indian Island had risked their lives in a most desperate adventure.

I tried to make felt the clear starlight of that night. With deliberate explanation, I imparted to him the chill of a river mist over the quick water. He was told of the crowds of whites who had gathered first to watch, and then to help, and who giving up the task unaided, summoned the Indians across by swinging lanterns from the ferry landing; how these men, having brought their boats down opposite the island where the ship-wrecked sot was lying, pushed out into the current but time after time were swept downstream. I relayed how they were wet with the sweat of their exertions as if it were mid-summer and yet it was so cold that the ice froze on their setting poles until only by turning them end-for-end could they hold their grip. The youngster stared,

---

[13] Eckstorm playing the mentor, Athena.

wide-eyed as I explained how half the people of the town waited through the moiety of that bitter night watching in frightened expectation of worse disaster of their efforts to save a drunken man whom at last they rescued on the point of freezing.

"It was rum did it and *Debble* steered him," was the sententious summing-up of Big Sebattis.[14]

With a slight turn to my left, I pointed out the Indian Island with its white church spire and clustered houses, telling him in detail bits of old lore; the story of swinging the ice-cake to form a winter bridge to the island; the story of the great winter freshet when, for a week though supplies of all sorts were running low, not even the boldest of them dared venture to come over to town because the great ice-cakes ran so thick and swiftly; the tales of men who had been swept over the falls and of others saved by strenuous exertions. And all the time I was letting the water drum into his ears some respect for it. My youngster was coming to an understanding that Oldtown Falls is not to be played with; that the man who gets caught on the lip of that tugging, roaring, rushing torrent is a dead man whose friends say, '*good-by to him*' when they see him going over.

"So nobody ever went over that place and came out alive?" he asked sobered.

"There was one–once. One river-driver I was told did it." (But there are two parts to that story and I was wondering if he would be keen enough to see that the other was the better half; the other was the story I meant to tell.)

"It happened years ago, right here. A log jam, as bad as they are, had formed." I pointed. "The river-drivers picking the jam were Indians from the Island—you can see where they lived and

---

[14] Big Sebattis Mitchell, his story is told in a chapter after his own name later in this book.

there's ledgy island on the lip of the falls where the logs were jammed. Now, imagine just how the boat was hovering along the upper edge of the jam waiting for the men who were picking it." I motioned for him to follow and we walked closer to the riverbank. "They had a full crew, and a full crew for working on logs is seven men—bowman and steersman, four midshipmen at the oars and one on the lazy seat. Sometimes they will all be out on the jam, less the one who is tending the boat. Usually the two in the ends stay in their places, but when the moment is critical and the jam is expected to "haul," that is to start, then all are in their places but one or two of the most active fellows.

"This time it was Louis Ketchum[15] and Sam Newell who were left to put the last touches on the jam and the boat lay just above with her oars fanned out like a fish's fins all ready to dart upstream on the instant. Big Frank Nicolai, the steersman, was standing out-board on the logs, holding her stern so as to give the boys a better chance to jump in when they had to run for their lives.

Breaking a Jam on the
West Branch.

Fannie Hardy Eckstorm
photo.

*Courtesy of University of Maine
Fogler Library
Special Collections.*

---

[15] This is but one of a few writings in which Eckstorm uses Louis, and not her familiar, Lewey.

"It is an ugly place to be holding a boat there just above Oldtown Falls, but Big Nicolai was a clear-headed man, a fine figure of a man, splendidly built and in his prime. It was summertime and he had on white canvas trousers—no, nothing to do with the story or his task, but I happen to remember that fact, as you will hear why. You can almost see him up there holding his boat by its pointed stern, responsible for the lives of the four men in the boat, but as deeply concerned to save the two on the logs if he could.

"And there were Louis and Sam on the logs below yanking and hacking and working like demons to loosen the last binding logs and set the whole mass tumbling over the falls. Nothing but a fire calls for any such exertion as breaking a jam. They pulled and pried and jumped like cats. Wherever they leaped they stuck of course, for they had on their spike-soled shoes.

"Then of a sudden they get at the sticks that bind the jam. Through the whole mass runs a tremor, like the quiver that jars the unlaunched ship before she takes the ways. A little premonitory yawn runs through the log jam, as if it was just waking up. For a second it stretches itself. Then, on the moment, it is wide awake—a heaving, rolling, grinding mass. Logs fight with other logs and with the current in a panic, making a blind rush for the falls. The men caught out on a log jam when she hauls are not considered a good risk in insurance circles."

"What about these?" the young man asked.

"Well, to this day, I remember Louis's telling the story. They were caught with the logs and farther from the boat than they wished they had been. They ran." I motioned to have the youngster consider the water.

"It is not easy running over the backs of slippery, plunging logs rearing to leap a twelve-foot fall. Louis told me this story while shaking his head slowly from time to time; as he couldn't

believe he'd lived to tell about it. In his contemplative way, he
said,

    'You ought to have seen Sam run. I declare I never saw
anything so funny in all my life. It made me laugh so to see
him that I tumbled down myself and pretty near went under.
And Sam he did get caught; he went over the falls along with
the whole jam, just an awful mass of logs and water. I just
barely made the boat. You see the crew, they was holding
on till the last minute—waiting on me—but the logs were
spreading and the current was sucking her down and I was
some ways off. It wouldn't do to drown five men on the
chance of saving one, with one already given up for dead.
But Big Nicolai was holding on to the last second, standing
on some loose logs by her stern, and they were all yelling to
me to run. Seemed to me as if I was doing some running
right then, but as I got near, the logs swung free. I was too
far to make the boat and there was only one chance left. Big
Nicolai saw it.

    'Don't mind me, Louis; Jump! Jump anywhere!' he yelled.
'I tell you it did look like a wicked thing to do, but it was
that or go over the falls along with Sam. So I sprung for all
I was worth and landed one foot square on Nicolai's hip and
tumbled into the boat over him; he in after me. We just
barely pulled out. I could see the blood spurting through
those white canvas pants he had on, where every one of a
full set of calks went in their whole length. He wiped at the
blood with his hand, but he never said a word. And then we
got out of it. All but Sam.'"

    My words dropped off, and I looked down towards the end of
the pitch.

    "Say, you don't mean it?" whispered the youngster.

"Sure," I said. "Louis said so."

"But Big Nicolai? What about those spikes?"

"Oh, he was laid up for a month and lost his work. Those boatmen were getting three or four dollars a day then, perhaps more for good men like Big Nicolai. But that was nothing more than he expected when he told Louis to jump. They'd—any of them—do that much the same."

"You don't mean it," said the youngster, but this he said under his breath and not at all as if he were doubting my word. It was a new breed of men to him.

"But you are missing the main part of the story," said I. "It was about Sam Newell who was the only man who went over Oldtown Falls and came out alive, that is that I ever knew of."

He was looking at the falls intently; thinking. He felt the pause of my talk. "What about Sam Newell? I thought you said...?"

This he said in a monotone and so remotely that it showed he had not the least curiosity about a feat without precedent or post-sequent.

"Oh, the boys all turned in at the landing and went down solemn enough to look for Sam's body. It comes a little hard to lose one man out of a crew. And to know that it might just as easily been any other one of them. A thing like that, well, it brings it home closer than ordinary.

"The first thing they saw almost was the corpse. He was walking out of a French house with a bottle of rum in his hand. They might just as well, so far as thin nerves went, have seen his ghost, but he was very wet and he smiled too broadly for a ghost and the rum looked substantial.[16]

---

[16] Eckstorm had crossed out the word, *whiskey*, and corrected the libation to be *rum*. In the margin, she wrote, "On looking up my notes, I find this was rum, not whiskey; I don't know the difference

So they took him for granted as the real thing and asked him how he made it.

'O,' says Sam, 'pretty good; two times I got my breath knocked out; one time a big log struck me in the back, knocked me clear out of the water. Another time I hit a ledge with my feet and knocked my head.' He took a swig of the rum. 'Made a pretty good run as a log, I guess.'

But the boy was still looking at the falls and thinking. I figured he might want to hear a story or two for himself from someone who was there.

"What say," said I, "we go over to the Island and call on Louis? I hear he's at home now."

The boy followed me to the landing. We crossed in the batteau ferry-boat and walked up the quiet street where the bright-eyed Indian children, who remembered former largesse, smiled in expectation.

We made our call on Louis; one of those pleasant visits full to the brim of reminiscence and wood's-lore and friendly chaffer such as we always enjoyed together. I was talking with Louis as fast as we could about fisher killing deer and the changes in the range of caribou and how the bear had taken to hunting moose, when the youngster nudged my elbow.

In an undertone, he asked, "Why don't you ask him about Big Nicolai?"

---

myself, but the boys would never forgive if I made a mistake on an important point like this." And this is yet another example of her exactitude.

# THE ULTIMATE JEWEL

## At the Hunting Camp of Joe Saul

**The** hunting camp of Joe Saul, the half-breed, sat low in the swale, a place untenantable in summer season; but it was warm in winter and near a spring and he liked to see the red of sunset through the bare birch twigs as he could not do among the pines. Besides, the birch was good for camp wood. Joe's aesthetic tastes did not hinder him from knowing what was personally profitable to himself, and, being a half-breed, he might be said to have no one but himself to consider.

He had no father; his mother was worse than none; if he had brothers and sisters, he could make no boast of them; and he had no country either, for like his Indian associates he lived on a reservation, was without vote or civil rights, without even the duties of citizenship which before now have made life tolerable to those defrauded not only of birthright but of the very right to be born. You cannot create a man more alone in the world than was Joe Saul.

But Joe Saul had created a comrade for himself. "I'm Injun, but I'm honest," he used to say.

This meant that he knew the voice of Honor, that he had observed her face and followed her, but did not as yet (being but a poor and unlettered man), know her name.

He thought her name was Reputation and would have said, with the poet he never heard of:

**"Good name in man and woman, dear my lord,**
**Is the immediate jewel of their souls."[17]**

So when he threw up his head and said, as proudly as if forty generations stood behind him, "I'm Injun, but I'm honest," he thought he was speaking of something too uniquely his to be taken from him.

He had always been a trusted man, the head man of whatever crew he happened to be in, provided it was one of Eben Morrison's, a lumberman of considerable fortune and reputation. The very fact that this winter he had a hunting camp by himself and had placed it where he could see the sunset, argued that life was more than usually lonely with him, that he was not facing a morning prospect of hope and cheerfulness. Not that Joe put it thus; with hard-headed common sense he decided that it would be easier to get water from his spring if his camp faced westward.

When the word first came to him that he was not wanted as head man of one of Morrison's lumber crews that winter, he wondered why his employer had taken another man without hearing from him, but he had not brooded over the matter. He loved Eben Morrison with the unreasoned affection of a dog, and though it hurt him not to be head man in one of the camps, still he bore no grudge against Eben Morrison. Yet, the slight hurt him so much that he would not ask any lower place, but went off into the big woods all alone, trapping and hunting.

---

[17] A line by Iago in Shakespeare's *Othello*; after Proverbs 22:1; and thus Eckstorm's choice of story title.

Then came something which hurt him more, which showed him that Morrison was done with him. Joe up and outright asked (by way of a letter someone took down for him) for his customary place at the place of Morrison's brook drive, which was almost his by right—had not Morrison said over and over again that while Joe Saul was himself, Morrison would never have any other man take his logs out to the main drive—and he had met a curt refusal. Well, here he was, the same Joe Saul, quick, capable, faithful, dogged in his devotion, sure of his own real worth and secure in the good name he bore. This hurt his pride and hurt still his love for Eben Morrison, but still he was not resentful. Places belong to the man who own them, and his only claim upon Eben Morrison was what he could do for him. He was not pricked in his Honor yet.

Then came Bill Fields and changed all what Joe had reconciled with his feelings.

It was just evening, one day the last of February while the sunset still hung red and golden in tangled birch tops, when Bill Fields made his appearance at the door of Joe Saul's hunting camp. Always ragged, always shiftless, always "spring poor," but never needy enough to work much, Bill Fields existed chiefly as a hanger-on at lumber camps, carrying mail and gossip from camp to camp and sure of a welcome while his budget of news lasted, then moving on. To a man spending the winter alone, even Bill Field's company was welcome, provided he did not have to entertain too much of it.

So Bill made himself at home, hung his three pairs of ragged stockings on sticks before the fire, spread his ragged coat out on the bunk, and deposited the rest of his ragged clothes upon the block which served as a chair. Joe waited upon him frying venison over the open fire in his one battered tin plate. In return, Bill Fields, opened his whole budget of news and told all the latest in his most obliging manner. He told of floods and fires, deaths and weddings, but before that and first of all, he selected such items as would interest every lumberman, even those unemployed. He told Joe of what every crew was doing, who had lost horses, the latest failure, who had been killed by rolling logs or falling trees, what game had been seized and how the wardens lost a larger lot in securing this.

The evening was passing pleasantly when from somewhere between his ragged shirts, he produced a flat, black bottle which he polished with affectionate care upon his dirty shirtsleeve before he offered it to Joe.

"Do you ever smile?" asked he, tendering it with excess of courtesy.

"No, I don't drink," answered Joe.

"Ye'd better," said Fields with a knowing look. "It's good."

"Not for me," replied Joe, his eyes on the fire.

Fields looked at him with a look of low cunning, only one grade above the intelligence of a woodchuck.

"I won't tell on ye," said he confidentially.

"But I don't drink, I tell ye," responded Joe, exasperated by his assurance.

"Come now," said Fields, "there ain't no need of bluffin' no longer, everybody knows all about it now. It's out. Might's well enjoy yourself." Bill Fields proceeded to enjoy himself, after which he had less to offer.

Joe took his eyes off the fire. He watched as Fields swallowed. "What's out?" demanded Joe. "What d'ye mean?"

"Oh, nothin' in partic'ler, only that little spree of yourn last fall."

"What?" challenged Joe, presenting a well-knuckled fist very near Bill Field's nose.

Fields discovered then that he had made a mistake, but the only way out was to go ahead. "Why, that time you come to Eb Morrison's house drunk. Sam Harris heard Eb tellin' John Davis about it not three weeks ago."

"Wha-a-at?" demanded Joe, feeling his jaws grow weak with astonishment.

"Just what I'm a-tellin' ye, God's truth," asseverated Fields. "Eb says you come to his house dead drunk last fall to get a pair of snowshoes."

"You lie!" remarked Joe bluntly.

"Nary bit! Them's jest the words Sam Harris heard Eb Morrison tell John Davis."

"You lie!" repeated Joe for lack of anything better to say.

"I don't!" protested Fields, and, anxious to prove himself in the right, he went on and told more. "Sam Harris, he heard Eb say that he wan't goin' to have you run his drive this year and that's the why of it. He give it to John Goldie and you'll find out so if you ask."

Joe was convinced. He had found out about Goldie himself. The lumberman who brought in Eben Morrison's answer to his application had read to him the contents of the note, for Joe was scant of the learning which interprets the written word, and it was Goldie's name the lumberman had read through his somber look.

"Ah-h-gh!" he said, beginning with an Indian grunt, "John Goldie—white man, Frenchman—where, my soul, live it dat man?"

"Shirley," suggested his visitor. Fields gnawed at the piece of meat pierced with a pointed stick.

"Yas-sa, Shirley," assented Joe and kept on frying his venison. He sat before the fire with his chin in his hand trying to make out how Morrison could say that of him; Morrison who had always been his friend and protector. He had owed so many kindnesses to Morrison. Not able to eat himself, he handed Fields another stick of venison.

At length he jumped to his feet, declaiming to himself, "He lies. I tell you Eb Morrison lies. I don't drink an' he knows it! If he didn't want me drive for him, let him say so! I'm man. I can stan' it. I ain't goin' to quarrel with him. If he don't want me he can bounce me an' not go lyin' about me to get rid o' me, but I wouldn't thought it of Eben. Not of Eben Morrison."

In his heart of hearts he added, "I'd give a thousand dollars in a minute not to have it turn out so." (That wasn't a Joe Saul expression; he'd borrowed it from another Penobscot man.) He added quietly, "If ever I had it."

This last Bill Fields of course was in no condition to hear. The prior he paid no attention to, for the heat after being out in the cold, the hearty meal, and especially his liquor, combined to make him rather inattentive to news items, which really was all Fields was good for in the woods. He'd be of no help to Joe in spreading how he took the news, or the oath he added.

As for Eben Morrison, he would have understood if Saul's words had been repeated, carried along by Fields camp to camp. But before he went to sleep that night, Joe Saul had crushed out all the affection he had felt for Eben Morrison. He was an honest man and he could not love a scoundrel. This time he was mortally wounded.

The painful part of this difference was that Eben Morrison was a man of honor, too. His word was as good as his bond. It passed for current coin among those who knew him. What Eben Morrison had said, he had asserted upon the evidence of his own eyes, backed and fully certified by John Davis, another good man, who testified to having seen enough, if not as much. Eben Morrison knew Joe Saul as well as one man may know another, so that if he declared Joe Saul came to him drunk to buy snowshoes, it made it a fact.

Who is going to take the word of a poor Indian who can neither read nor write when his employer, a well-known, respected, well-to-do, influential lumber boss swears to the diametrical opposite? Other things being unequal the word of one powerful boss of men is not as good as the word of another if he is a mere worker; it would not be optimism to deny this, even if the worker had occupied head man positions.

### On the street in front of the Belt, Buckle & Button Company

What Eben Morrison had said that he had seen, Samuel Harris, junior clerk for Belt, Buckle & Button Company, a ship stores and lumbermen's supplier, knew and could testify. He had been out in front of the store one day early in February—and though he was averse to his job (shoveling off the path after a heavy snowfall and picking more or less diligently at the three inches of accumulated ice and hard-packed snow which covered the bricks of the sidewalk, and would continue to cover them until the sun, a more diligent worker than Samuel Harris, had exposed them)—it did not suit him ill that Providence had seen fit to place him where he could listen to such advantage. He was there that morning when up one side of the sidewalk came Eben Morrison and on the other, John Davis, a brother lumberman.

"How are ye, Eb?" asked Davis cordially, pulling off his mitten to shake hands.

"Middlin'-smart, thank you, John.' He shook Davis's hand, then pointed skywards. "It'd be better if Jehovah would stop pluckin' his geese up there-ah. The teamsters are reportin' the horses are getting all tired out."

Davis nodded; knowing snow was good for running sleds, but the horses could only manage so much of it.

Then they stood together, just outside of the dripping eaves, just inside the line where the great avalanches, as they came plunging down from the sloping roofs might be expected to hit the hardest.

"This fall must have given 'em another good fifteen inches up river," remarked Davis looking critically at the new snow.

"Yes, we are likely to have a good driving pitch come spring," replied Morrison, looking on the brighter side of a thick winter snow pack.

"You're operatin' Great Scott this year, ain't ye, Eb?"

"Six in fourteen," promptly returned Eben. In more ways than one, the sea of forest and the wilderness of waters resemble each other.[18]

"Well, look out for the Horse Race;[19] that's where old Anse Smith got hung up in '59; lost his whole drive there. Maybe you remember." Davis knew Morrison would know it, but he went on anyway. "Not havin' any way to hold the water there and such

---

[18] A reference to the Marsden square mapping of the world map and Maine's township maps. Morrison was operating in T6 R14 WELS.

[19] For Horserace Falls see the map later this chapter. This area of Caucomgomoc Stream is a changed water body from that in Anse Smith's time, particularly below Black Pond. Eckstorm knew of A. B. Smith hanging his Drive from her father, Manly Hardy, who'd spent that winter trapping from a half-pitch camp on Round Pond, one township to the north by way of Sis Stream from near the Horserace. Current maps may incorrectly label this stream as 'Ciss Stream.' Round Pond was Caucomgomocsis Pond, the *sis* ending indicating a diminutive. The stream was then logically, 'Sis Stream.' Hardy told his daughter, and she wrote in her journal, '*the logs from Anse Smith's Drive were never gotten out; they blocked the river until they rotted out.*'

a long stretch o' bad water makes it hard; but if you have a good head man—'spose though there ain't any need of sayin' that—seein' you always have Joe Saul."

"No Joe Saul for me this year!" responded Eben emphatically. "Matter of fact, I'm done good with Joe Saul."

"What's that? Joe's always been all right, ain't he?"

"Drinks," said Eben Morrison shortly.

Davis looked at Eben curiously. He'd known Saul for more than a decade. "What's that? You sure somebody's not been trying to poach from ya, Eben? White man, nor Indian, there ain't no sturdier man on the river 'n what Joe Saul is. Joe a drinkin' that's somethin' I've never seen, nor have I heard anyone say." As any good lumber boss, Davis always kept his eyes and ears open about such news, whether about a white man, Indian, or Frenchmen, he was careful of the character he'd put in charge.

Eben glared at Davis. "If it's a lie, I told it myself. I saw him drunk. Dead drunk." He slipped his hand back into his fur-lined mitten. "You know it yourself, John Davis, I always set store by Joe. When he was only a little shaver and I was already a man in the woods, he was always a-taggin' round after me. And there was woods here then. A whole eye-stretch of it. First quality pine, all free from knots. Such pine as you don't see no more." Eben paused and looked up at the snow-covered mountains that rose beyond the river. His statement declared just how long he'd sworn by Joe Saul.

"Well, Joe, he went on the drive for me, when he wan't more 'n seventeen," continued Eben. "That was the first drive he ever made. He's worked for me ever since. Until now." Eben shook his head. "I done my best by him. I put him in as boss when not another man of the river would have trusted an Indian. I said to him, 'You got a head on you, Joe. You know how to head a drive and lead the men.'"

The Old Man's hands rose up. "And he always went ahead all right. Until this blowed up, I couldn't ask more of a man. He was honest and loyal. But when a man goes back on me——." Morrison became silent, listening to the thunder of the snowslides from the roofs as they first rumbled, then rushed, then came slithering down in a great dump of heavy snow.

The men considered the piles that landed a few feet from them. Morrison and Davis stepped under the overhang of the store porch. Samuel Harris began to slowly clear a path through the mound of fallen snow, staying close to the porch so as not to miss overhearing any of the talk.

"But, Eben," urged Davis acting the peacemaker, "ain't you mistaken? I know Joe Saul, an' I never knowed him to drink. He never drunk a drop in his life."

"See here, John Davis," said Morrison turning full towards him, "when'd you ever catch me tellin' things that ain't so? I ain't the man to talk that I don't **know**. He come to my house last fall, early in November, 'twixt daylight an' dark, him an' Peol Lewy—well, you know of Peol Lewy, Joe's cousin, thunderin' old rascal, too—an' a big roan horse with a white scar on his nigh flank.

"'Hullo, boys!' says I, goin' out to meet 'em. Peol sat on the left side of the buggy. They held up their hands in a wave. I went down closer.

"'Hullo, Peol. Hello, Joe. What can I do for you?' says I. I smelt the liquor then from where I stood. Peol, he wasn't as drunk as Joe, he stood as spokesman. He said they wanted some snowshoes to go in the woods with. Then he pointed to Joe, called him *Cousin Susep*, that's Indian for Joseph. But Peol, he stiffened up an' winked at me like and old owl. He whispered so you could hear him two rods off, 'Dem's my cousin, Susep. Too much oc'by (meaning *whiskey*) got it Susep.' Then he told me to charge the snowshoes to the Lord; and right he was, too, so far as he was concerned, for no one ever knew Peol Lewy to pay a debt. Just on the strength of Joe being with him I let him have two pair of snowshoes, caribou, with heads and tails of fall deer."

Morrison paused and shook his head. "Joe never spoke a word. That was about right, thought I. Well, being the state Peol was in, I turned the horse around for them and sent 'em off. And so, you see, no one's passing stories. I guess *I should know*." The last words, Eben Morrison stressed. He concluded, "I ain't set eyes on either one of the rascals since."

John Davis stood silent; listening to the drip from the eaves that the sun was producing from what snow was left after the avalanche. "You're sure?" he asked one last time, really pushing against an honest man such as Morrison, but on account of what he knew of Joe Saul.

Morrison, was agitated at being asked again. All the good years he'd employed Saul coming to his memory, he held his temper. He nodded at his old friend. "John, you know I always liked Joe Saul." Then, of his own accord he returned to the subject. "Joe got someone to write down to me last month, in order to see if I wanted him on the drive this spring. I wrote back pretty short. '*No. Johnnie Goldie had the job.*'" Eben looked at Davis to see his reaction. "I suspect he was galled some, but I couldn't help that none. He knew well enough what to look out for. He'd heard me say time 'n time again to the boys that I wasn't goin' to have no drinkin' men run my concerns for me. He knows all about what I think of that, so he didn't need no more warnin's." Eben stopped abruptly and set his gaze down the snow-covered road. "Hello! Look ah there. Talk of the Devil!" he said with deliberation.

On the opposite side of the street, emerging from the lowest quarter of the city, were two Indians both gloriously drunk. They were trying to keep to the sidewalk assisted by the brick walls on one side and the high snowbanks on the other, but the two tacked from side to side as if the foot-path were as angular as a Virginia fence and they were bound to follow all its windings.

"Sugar!" said John Davis, "I never would have thought it. Of Joe Saul, no sir, not unless I've seen it with my own eyes."

Morrison looked grimly triumphant.

"I supposed he was up in the woods," said Davis.

"So did I," said Morrison. "I didn't think after he got my letter he'd show around here."

"Looks blacker than he use to." Davis narrowed his eyes on the two making their winding way down the straight-as-an-arrow street.

"Oh, he's good and tan," said Morrison. "Snow's blacked him all up on account of the sun and sitting around not lumbering."

"I can't say as I don't think he's looking taller, too," added Davis.

"Ah. Bein' side of such a pudgy, short fellow as Peol is what makes him look tall just now," explained Morrison giving Joe a look over.

"What's that name Peol called him right there? Sounded like, *Brimmertub*." Davis gave Eben a questioning look after picking up some of the loud murmurings between the two over-jolly characters across the street. "I never heard no one call Joe by that name."

"Hmm. I neither," said Eben.

Neither Davis or Morrison knew nothing of the one by the name Joe Shay, whose religious experiences when he posed as a representative of the primitive and persecuted Christians in one of the orthodox prayer meetings, he being too drunk to know where he was or what he was doing, had won for him the epithet of "Brimmertub." Had Eben Morrison ever heard that story he would have understood there was something to question; but as he didn't, and he'd entrenched in his position, he chalked it up to drunken blabbering.

"That's Joe fast enough," said Morrison. Then with a fog in his voice—thinking about how much he had respected Joe Saul—added, "I'd rather give a thousand dollars than have it turn out so." Up and down the West Branch all knew that saying belonged to Eben Morrison. He'd twice stood by his oath with his wallet.

Samuel Harris did not overhear this generous offer, nor did he see Peol Lewy and his cousin when they passed; he'd been called inside the store to wait upon a customer by that time. That was unfortunate for Samuel's wallet, and certainly a misfortune for Joe Saul. For Harris knew the story of "Brimmertub" and who the name had been applied to. Had he been witness to the spectacle on the street and learned of these additional items of interest, he would have imparted such knowledge to Eben Morrison. More so, he'd have told the gossiper Bill Fields on his next round through town. From there, Bill would have passed the facts back to Joe, who quite unimpaired would have understood. For mere logic would have settled the matter, Joe knowing enough of that science to understand that it was impossible for him to be in two places at the same time and that therefore there must have been some ground for Eben Morrison's mistake. And he would have gone to Morrison and settled the matter instead of brooding over it in secret.

### At the Hunting Camp of Joe Saul

Back in the cabin in the deep woods, as things stood just then, Joe Saul felt that a foul and wanton wound had been dealt him in the back by the best friend he ever had. His Indian blood did not render him any less sensitive to injustice than a white man. Indeed, if common tradition is true, there is in that Indian blood a tenaciousness of wrong which outlasts even the white man's memory of injury. It is hardly to be expected that a man who has been defrauded in his birth of all social rights and advantages, of all national ties and personal ambitions, should look lightly upon a great injustice.

Joe Saul was a man as nearly self-made as any man can be, and he was more conscious of his strength than those who, having the tide of circumstance with them, have not been obliged to struggle against a current of prejudice and opposition. He knew his virtue as if she were a person, and when he walked abroad his good fame walked beside him to keep him company.

Then one day he found himself robbed of the one possession which was uniquely his own. When John Davis and several others to whom he had offered his services as head man had successively declined him, he knew that the story must be credited. To lose one's reputation by one's own sin and folly is no light matter; to have it temporarily obscured by the demands of loyalty is hard to bear; but to have it stolen from one is bitter indeed.

What made this insupportable was that it was done by the best friend Joe Saul ever had, the man who for twenty years had stood by him, helped him, trusted him when no one else would; whom he had repaid by the utmost fidelity, by unfailing success in whatever he undertook, by respect that was worth all that Morrison had ever done for him and by affection that no money could have bought.

And now his employer had tired of him. Had he been so urgent for Eben Morrison's interests that it had seemed desirable to be quit of him? Joe Saul bit his lip with anger at the thought.

"Why don't he tell me if he don't want me anymore? Why don't he say 'Go!' Not starve me off like a dog! I can go. I can leave! I won't stay where I ain't wanted." Joe paced across the ten feet of his narrow, low-ceilinged cabin.

And then Joe saw that he had loved a liar, that in his anxiety to be rid of him, his employer had disclosed his real nature and basely and unnecessarily lied. Joe Saul set his nails deep into his palms in the agony; the agony of the thought. When his grip finally relaxed he cared no more for Eben Morrison. Because he was honest himself, he hated himself for having loved a lie. A lie that Eben trusted him and was his friend. And then his heart went out because it had lost its idol.

Joe Saul was left with no man but himself to believe in. When the best was proved worthless, it was logic that the second-best could be no better; therefore, he despised and doubted men. Yet, because he was satisfied of his own integrity, he would still believe in himself though it made all men liars.

He was an untutored man, knowing no metaphysical doubts the existence of virtue, only that men were not what they seemed. A careless, prideless rascal like Peol Lewy might receive the buffets of the world without being hardened, but a man with a reputation white enough to be smirched, comes at last to feel that mud-throwing cannot be all an accident. And so it happens that many a scamp keeps merry and open-hearted, where an honester man becomes embittered against the world.

Joel Saul applied to this one and to that one for the place of boss on their brook drives only to meet with refusal. If Eben Morrison did not want the man, they did not; for Morrison ought to know him by this time. At times he almost doubted whether a good name was worth the toil it cost since it could be lost so easily and through no fault.

In need of money, and maybe more in need of hearing the water pouring over the falls, Joe hired on the drive from Cuxabexis down. It was a small affair compared with Morrison's. And, at that, he went as a common hand. That was the worst of it for Joe. He was forced to swallow his pride after being a head man. It was near as bad as being called a drunk.

## On the Shore of Chesuncook Lake

Both the Cuxabexis and the Caucomgomoc logs come into Chesuncook Lake where logs from the four corners of the horizon meet for the first time. But the Caucomgomoc drive down the stream is long and it debouches at the very head of the lake, while Cuxabexis is short and inlets well down the side into Chesuncook.[20] Therefore it is seldom that, as this year, the Cuxabexis logs are later into Chesuncook than the drives from the long streams up Caucomgomoc way.

But the year had been a prosperous one for Eben Morrison who had met with no reverses, so that his logs entered the lake early and were lying, fat and shining, in the upper waters of "the Cove" two days before the drive Joe Saul hired on, got down lake. Meanwhile, that Cuxabexis Drive being short-handed, tired-out, and dispirited, the logs were later than they had been for years. One positive, one negative, caused both Drives to be at about near the same length down Chesuncook Lake on the same day of that bitter spring.

When at last Joe Saul stood upon the shore of Chesuncook and felt the breeze blowing up the lake, cool on his cheek, almost the first thing that he noticed was a great boom of logs being warped down the lake against the wind. There was the sun,

---

[20] See map later in this chapter.

shining dazzlingly through a loop-hole in the curtain of dark purple cloud which draped the west; there was the low-swelling shore opposite, with its evergreen growth black in the afternoon sunlight and its birch and poplar hazy with their first viridescence; the line where trees met water, no beach being visible with the lake so high; the sparkling sapphire waters of the lake leaping in golden wavelets as far as could be seen to left and right; and there, in the middle foreground of this dark but brilliant scene, wallowing like some Miltonic monster, with a monstrous triangular body and a scarlet-tufted head up-reared, was a great boom of logs. The body was of loose logs, held together by the flexible boom stretched around them; the head was a square platform with a rude upright capstan bristling with pick-handspikes thrust into the great spool that two and thirty men in flaming scarlet shirts might lay their weight upon the warp and wind it round and round the capstan body, drawing the great raft ahead.[21]

Two and thirty men were working–twice the usual number–it was clear that they were expecting the wind would be too much for them and had joined booms, working with two boats and double warps and double anchors that they might get the boom under the lee before the weather roughened. It was a sight to rejoice for a woodsman.

And yet, Joe Saul felt a twinge of jealousy at seeing those logs from one of the upper drives get in before his own. In two or three days more, everybody's logs would be turned over to "The Company" at the dam, and they would all work together.[22] But

---

[21] See inset. The capstan is much smaller than one requiring 'two and thirty men.'
[22] When logs were under the Penobscot Log Driving Company, operating from Ripogenus Dam down the West Branch.

in the days when he had been in charge himself, he had been wont to carry off the honors.

He stood and watched the men on the headworks as they toiled slowly round the spool, stepping the warp which rose a strand higher at each revolution. He saw the batteau, with its sharp prow raking upward. The men rowed to boat-out the spare anchor and drop it a warp's length ahead of the boom, while the anchor underfoot was tripped to become "spare" in its turn. He saw the boom creep ahead, inch by inch; he saw the black logs show their wet sides as they rolled in the sunlight and came up glittering. There were some stray logs out in the lake which had been ridden under by larger logs and had been shot out under the boom. These, the fresh south-west breeze was bearing toward him, and, as he turned to leave the point, the wind caught one and rolled it over. In its black and shining flesh, shone white and clear the log-mark that was cut into bark and wood. Even at that distance he could read "star-girdle"–Eben Morrison's mark.

So those were Eben Morrisn's logs! Joe Saul felt a hatred for them, rolling in the rising wind; he wished that not one of them might ever do good to any man!

That night, when all the others were asleep under the big spreads, he came down to the shore of the lake again. A shift of the weather was apparent, which made him feel uneasy, for that could delay their crossing or make things difficult. If he was head man, he'd have to think it through; as things stood, he didn't. But more uneasy was his mind as he thought of the wrong Eben Morrison had done him. Of what use was a clear conscience if it could not make a man happier than he himself was?

Log-marks were specific to the lumbermen. Eckstorm documented many marks, with a full page included in, *The Penobscot Man - Life and Death on a Maine River (2023)*. Examples:

| | |
|---|---|
| ✱ | Morrison's Star-Girdle |
| ∥ E / | Belt, E, Girdle |
| , E ✱ W . | Notch, E, Star-Girdle, W, notch |

**MEN TURNING A CAPSTAN ON A HEAD-WORKS RAFT**
*Photo Courtesy Maine State Library*

Before steamers operated on the lakes, logs were boomed down the lakes by manpower. To do so, a great boom anchor, weighing over 250 lbs. was boated out ahead of the capstan-raft down the lake. A thick rope, hundreds of feet and weighing hundreds of pounds was run from the anchor back to the raft around the capstan. Another rope extended out behind the raft. To that was connected *the boom* made of logs and chains and ropes that encompassed the logs in a great huge oval. As the men turned the capstan, the raft was pulled towards the anchor. Behind them, the logs were pulled along. When they reach the anchor, it was pulled up and again boated out ahead. This was repeated for miles down the lake. On a lake the size of Chesuncook, it could take three days and three nights, and that's only if no headwind came up and set them back to the beginning. A wonderful story about 'warping boom' by Eckstorm was titled, *Sleeping Nights*, see *The Penobscot Man - Life and Death on a Maine River (2023)*. It is a story memorializing the work ethic of Lewey Ketchum.

He stood by the lakeshore looking out. It was dark, though not so intensely dark. Close to the water there was a glimmering light, and the sky was full of fleecy clouds which were driving northward as the wind backed round, foreboding rain. The lake was disturbed and uneasy, though not as yet very rough, but the wind was rising. He strained his eyes looking out, yet could see nothing. The drifting clouds, the tossing waves, and the bending treetops about him disturbed his brain and let his eyes have no rest, not even the rest of unfathomable darkness. Somewhere on that other lake shore opposite him in the darkness, hauled in behind a point to keep it in the lee, with its anchors off shore and its hawsers inshore to keep it stationary, was the great boom which held half that Eben Morrison was worth. Joe Saul felt a strong desire to know where it was and how it lay.

Joe made his way back to the camp. He walked among the snoring river-drivers. Assured they were asleep, he went back to the tote road, picked up a canoe, and bore it down to the landing place. Then, remembering that a thwart was sprung, he found an ax and concealed by the wind beating the lake against the rocks, he hammered it back so that it might not spring out under the working of the waves. The axe he laid into the canoe again, telling himself he did not want it to be lost or forgotten. Then he made his way through the Cuxabexis Drive's own logs, out beyond their own smaller boom, and into the open lake, steering for a point on the opposite side.

Out there by himself Joe Saul felt better. Tossing in the darkness on waves of which he could see only the white crests, suited his mood. But still he was very bitter toward Eben Morrison; as what man might not be when his prospects had been blighted and his reputation ruined.

He had pulled about three miles when he plainly saw the dark line of black growth which covered Togue Point. As he came into quieter water a little under the influence of land, he could distinguish the great black boom stretched out near the shore. Under the darkness of the trees a red spot glowed like a carbuncle. It was the drivers' fire. Joe Saul knew that near that fire, under slight shelter or none at all, thirty-odd men were lying in a sleep as deep as death. When he saw them that afternoon, he knew by their mechanical stepping of the warp that they had begun to feel the awful weariness of warping boom.

And then he looked at the great boom of logs lying unguarded. It was as much in the lee as Togue Point could shelter it—and that was far more in those days than at present when the dam has been raised; for now the shore there is too straight to give much protection. He watched the logs rolling and riding each other in their narrow quarters while the boom creaked in all its joints. He could hear the logs swash back into the water after an ineffective effort to roll over the boom. Over the sound of the waves, he could hear the boom creaking and working at its bonds as if to chafe them off.

That was Eben Morrison's property doing its best to escape. Why not help it?

Joe Saul pictured to himself what would happen if those logs should burst their boom. Looking out into the gloom which overhung the lake he thought he saw them, thousands upon thousands of logs, drifting off before the wind like a fleet of needles drawn by magnets, straight toward the low, left shore, where, behind the sea-wall crowded up by the ice, the trees of the swamp stood mid-leg in water.

Chesuncook Lake's Togue Point on current-day maps is labeled as Togue Ledge. Togue Cove is where river-drivers used to warp their boom for holding to keep out of the wind and waves. Joe Saul drove with his drive down from Cuxabexis. Morrison's men drove down Caucomgomoc Stream. On this 1899 map, the early dam in those days had raised the level of Chesuncook. In Saul's time, there would have been a much more pronounced *boom cove* at Togue Ledge.

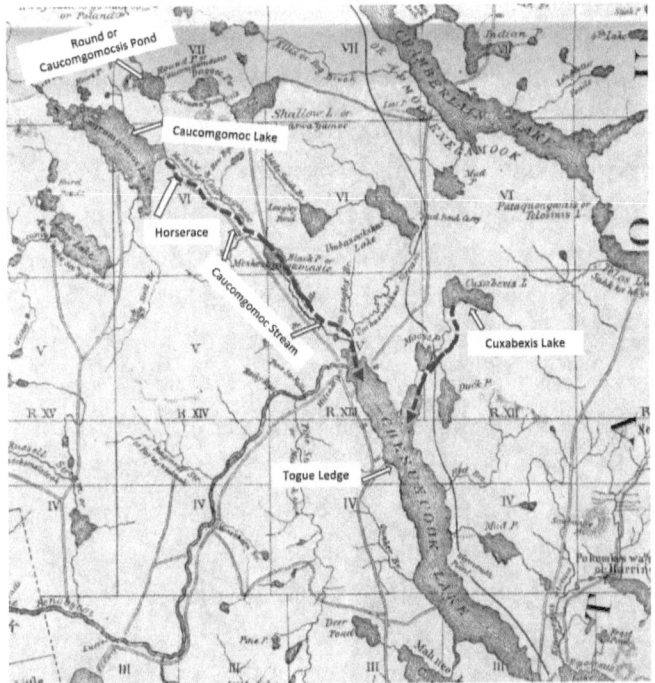

From, Hubbard's 1899 Map, see also, *Hubbard's Guide to Moosehead Lake and Northern Maine – Annotated Edition.*

Joe Saul saw those logs, marked with star-girdle, a mark he himself had been proud to drive in years past, go straight toward the sea-wall, as cattle to the bars in feeding time. There they would wait till the wind and rising waves lifted them over the barrier and gave them the range of the flooded forest beyond, where they would be lost forever. Some would drift up the lake and ground on the low meadows or work their way up the winding Umbazooksus or into the swamps of Caucomgomoc. A thousand men could not recover these logs once scattered; but, here or there, in flooded woods or in natural-meadow, in swamp or behind sea-wall, the water, when it subsided, would leave them stranded, where they would rot for half a century.

Such a loss would ruin Eben Morrison. A half dozen blows of a hatchet would leave him poorer than if he had never carried on large operations and driven great drives down the Maine rivers of the north.

Wrong? Wrong to wrong Eben Morrison? What is wealth beside reputation? What other wrong could off-set the deliberate theft of a man's character? Joe Saul found that his was a hurt which grew sorer with time. There was no balm for it. He smarted afresh under the injury and could not wait for the great Judge, before whom all cases are brought up at last, to award him damages.

He dipped his paddle into the water and moved slowly up to the great boom. It lay there creaking, black and monstrous, and ashore the red-eye of the drivers' camp-fire winked at him, lazily, as if it were not taking notice. He laid a hand on one of the logs of the boom. "Spruce," said he, to himself as he felt the scaly bark. Pulling his canoe along by the side of it, he reached the end of the log. It was double-throughshotted—all booms are on Chesuncook, because the risk is great. "Yellow birch," he commented, feeling of the stout saplings thrust through two great auger holes at the end of each log to tie them fast. (His was a trivial observation, but for the woodsman, wood does not exist as a general concept; it is always some particular kind of wood.)

At last he found his objective. There they were, two sticks the size of a man's wrist, pinning together the links of this log chain. Six strikes of his hatchet, under the cover of darkness, would destroy the whole winter's work of Eben Morrison's crews. It was almost as easy as to rob a man of his reputation!

Joe Saul looked at the stormy, unquiet sky overhead. His gaze took in the lake chafing, yet more restively under the wind, and then he glanced shoreward. The red fire still winked on in the dark; only half awake. He waited a moment, kneeling in the rocking canoe. Then he bent to lift his hatchet from the bottom of the birch canoe.

Before his hand could touch the wooden handle to take up and strike a blow, a sudden revulsion of feeling or else a panic terror fell upon him. He grasped the paddle and pulled with all his might away from the groaning boom and the watchful campfire.

Do bad men see haunts? As Peol Lewy had said? It was as if in the stern of his canoe, perched high on the peak, that his lost reputation, of which he had been so proud, had sat and looked at him over his shoulder. In its presence he could do no evil. He was not a bad man, though men might call him one; he still cared what he did, and what he knew he had done in his past. But yet, though he refrained from the deed, he muttered threats beneath his breath and vowed and unending hostility to Eben Morrison.

It was a rough three mile paddle back across the lake. The bow rode high in the air, facing into a whistling wind and hissing seas. Nor was it without difficulty that, this danger past, Joe Saul stumbled over the loose logs boomed into the cove at the mouth of Cuxabexis Stream. It was long after midnight when he found himself a place beside his river-driver mates. There he rested, though he could not sleep.

All that night the wind blew through the treetops, making them bend and creak. The next morning the lake, instead of being blue, was a dull and ugly grey; white streaks on the leaden water marked the tops of waves otherwise undistinguishable. The sky too, was heavy and the clouds swollen and baggy, like lids that have too long held back unshed tears. A mist hung over the black growth on the farther shore and obscured it, while it added an invisible discomfort to the already numerous disadvantages of the Cuxabexis side.

"Got to hang up, boys," was the announcement of the boss, making the entire crew sulk like the weather. They had been working too hard to be able to enjoy well-earned leisure, and by eight in the morning their resources for entertainment had been exhausted. It was then that the boss proposed going across the lake to visit the crew on the other side. There was no lack of volunteers; even Joe Saul had a curiosity to see what that boom looked like by daylight.

On the other side the men, wearied with their heavy work at the windlass, had been encouraged to sleep late and were still grouped about the fire watching the cook clear away the remnants of the unwonted luxury of flapjacks. A rough but picturesque group they made, of many races and all colors from the oily blackness of the Indian boys to the richest tan that March winds can put upon Saxon fairness. Unshorn and unshaven, hair and beard grew as they willed. The rags that made up their uncouth apparel would have made a stranger to the woods suspicious of their quality. It was like going into a convocation of scare-crows to approach such a crew; but their hearts were all hospitality—and besides, their clothes were no worse than their visitors' apparel.

First, it was a warm welcome. Then, an invitation to eat; though by all appearances the flapjacks, at the remnants of which the visitors, even while they declined the invitation, stared rather hungrily, had met with appreciation long before. The talk therefore naturally enough revolved about the question of "grub."

As if anything was good enough for drivers! "We got measly pork an' weevilly flour with skippers in the biscuit big enough to run clear 'n off to Canady with 'em," grumbled one disheveled malcontent who was seated on a driftwood log, lost from a drive of long ago.

"We seen it walk off ourself, right down the tote road," gravely added an Indian, appreciative of his driver-friends' joke.

"Don't let them misguide you. That ain't Eben Morrison's way," defended one of the visited to be sure there was no misunderstanding about the boss. "He always gives us good as there is a-goin'."

"I ain't great on religion myself," said another of Morrison's men. "Lost all mine when I was little. An' never found no one else's to take its place. But," he forced a pole branch he'd been whittling into the ground, "Eb Morrison's orthodox."

This last was a surpassing compliment; endorsed by all the drivers with nods of their heads.

One man and another spoke of Morrison as men speak of a favorite employer. Through it all, Joe Saul sat silent; at the outer edge of the gathering he contemplated the patches on his pants. He could recall the drives when he worked for Eben Morrison when he'd added each woolen splatch over a hole.

Suddenly, one of Morrison's crew spoke out with an abruptness which showed that the question had long been on his mind. "Why the thunder, Joe Saul, don't you work for Morrison any more? We expected to be under you as head man on the brook drive."

"That's so, why don't ye?" inquired another.

"Exactly what I been meanin' to say," put in a third.

A driver tying his calks, looked up, "Come on, tell us, Joe."

"We's always thought you two, Eb and Saul, was thicker'n witch-grass," remarked a fifth.

On all sides they pressed so that he could not escape. All had known Saul's friendship for Morrison. Some of these men had even worked under Saul when he was one of Morrison's drive-bosses. It was apparent that these men had been too deep in the woods for so long news hadn't reached them. For that, Joe was thankful, but the men wouldn't let up.

"Yes. You'd better told it to us," put in Joe Shay, who was there and who, ever since they landed, had been close by Joe Saul; the two whittling and talking in Indian.

Being thus appealed to, Joe Saul straightened himself up from his lounging position, but refusing to raise his eyes, squinted along the stick he had been whittling, as if to check its straightness. An obstinate expression crossed his face.

All eyes were upon him. Joe had never wanted to speak ill of Eben Morrison, not out loud to others. But here he was, amongst men driving logs that he should have been in charge of. Weeks of discontent weighed upon his mind.

"'Cause I don't like him anymore," he confessed reluctantly. He stared at the ground, indicating he much preferred to be silent on the matter.

"Thought you was great friends with Eben always," said one.

Another spoke up. "And I remember well, the time you knocked me down for sayin' Eben Morrison cheated me on wangan prices! Even though I was just sore and said so as I had lost my spike boot pickin' that jam for him."

Joe remembered that jam. The man had had his leg caught between two logs. He was lucky he lost only a boot and not his leg–or life. Still, Morrison couldn't be held responsible for men's boots and he knew the drivers all knew it. What kind of expense precedent would that allowance drive?

"You hain't gone back on Eben, have ye?" inquired a driver by the name of Murphy, who Joe respected to be a crack man when it came to finding a key log.

On all sides they were Eben Morrison's friends. Joe sat stolid; the center of attention.

"Why don't ye like him no longer?" This quiet request came from his side; from his friend Joe Shay.

"That's it! Just like Brimmer-tub asks. That's what we want to know," spoke up a Morrison man, motioning at Shay.

At last, Joe Saul felt constrained to reply. "He lied 'bout me! That's why," he answered shortly.

There was a chorus of denial. It carried on the wind. It drifted on the waves. Every man who knew Eben Morrison hooted at the notion.

"Vat for he make it lie 'bout you?" asked a Frenchman, arrived by way of Nova Scotia.

"Yes, you must tell us that," chorused several Province men.

The loyal Morrison men gathered closer to Joe. "Tell us what he said," demanded several more.

Joe rose to his feet. He faced his inquisitors. The spikes on his calks dug into the bark strewn about the landing. Staring at their faces he let out the lie. "He said I was drunk!" He waved the naked stick. "Lied. Saying I had come to his house drunk. He told it to John Davis."

Kicking bark aside, he spun to those behind him. "I never. You know me. I don't drink. I didn't go to his house, me'n Peol Lewy. He lies. He knows he does." Saul's voice had gone higher on account of his telling the story, and of the apprehension of telling it to these men, all defenders of Eben Morrison.

Joe Shay, who had risen to stand by his old friend, looked up curiously from beneath his eyebrows at Saul. "Peol Lewy?" he questioned. "What 'bout Peol Lewy you say?"

Saul went on, his tone rising higher. "Eben Morrison said I come to his house with Peol Lewy, drunk, dead drunk, to get snowshoes. Was last fall, he said. I never. I tell you all, I never did. He lied."

Joe Saul sat back down on the log. He was broken from being lied about; lied about from who he considered a friend; lied about something he never did. Not once had he ever been drunk. His voice recovered its pitch. "No man shan't ever tell me I drink, never! I don't! I'm Injun but I'm honest. And Eben Morrison, he knows it." He paused. "Or he's forgotten it."

Joe Shay had sat down beside Saul again. He gave a half glance toward Saul, but kept on whittling deliberately. There was an odd contraction of the corners of his mouth as if he had something to say but did not choose to say it.

The men continued debating among themselves the question of Eben Morrison's veracity. Some believed Joe Saul; for they never saw him touch the mouth of a bottle of liquor. Most were unwilling to condemn Morrison, even when the evidence was so clear on account of Joe Saul's reputation. Small groups formed. With their tin dippers refilled with coffee strong enough to peel paint, they held caucuses below the spruce.

When Joe Saul was again on the point of denouncing Morrison due to being barraged by the inquisitors, Joe Shay spoke up, softly and deliberately. "See here, boys, it's a mistake."

Joe Saul denied it indignantly. "No. No mistake. It's what Morrison said. No doubt. He lied."

Joe Shay said nothing more. He did not want to anger Saul even further.

A driver forced him with encouragement. "Go on, Brimmertub. Out with it."

Shay stated it over. "It's a mistake. This is all a mistake."

"Hurry up, Brimmertub. You said that already," stated the burly river driver.

"Give us the rest of what you know, Brimmertub" demanded one and then another.

They all used the nickname applied to Joe Shay, although most had no understanding why. Brimmertub seemed in no haste to proceed. He shut his clasp-knife and slowly placed it in his hip pocket, as if, that done, he must face the situation.

"Boys," he said, the last excuse for delay being gone, "I tell ye, it's a mistake."

"For the love of moss, we know you said that. Tell us some news," a gruff voice, belonging to the cook, exclaimed.

A pause and then Joe Shay braced himself to talk. "'Twan't Joe Saul with Peol. 'Twas me. Some of you don't know, but Joe and me, we's cousins."

The men stared from Joe to Joe; the two cousins standing next to one another. The drivers had never considered the resemblance on account of relation before; most hadn't given it a thought at all. Now, for sure, they could see it. In build. In facial expression. Even the way the two stood, a little askew.

Joe Shay continued; now his nerves excited to tell all he knew. "Eben Morrison, she don't know me. She ain't seen me since more than ten years, until that day. I was there, 'twas me, with Peol Lewey, both of us drunk, same's as Joe says Eben Morrison said. We went to buy snowshoes."

The men, needing no further evidence, were no longer inclined to talk the matter over. The chief witnesses' past actions, to which they'd seen plenty, were enough to settle the matter.

Joel Saul said nothing. He never looked at his cousin through the speech. He turned abruptly and walked down to the shore to look at the great boom anchored off the cove. There were feelings within him of which he did not know the name. So, Eben Morrison had not lied about him, at least not with intention.

Then he thought, what if Eben Morrison's boom had been broken during the night? What if he had used his hatchet to free those logs and labor of all those men? He saw, standing there on the shore with the rolling of Suncook Lake, that two wrongs do not make one right. He was glad that, whatever the wrong to himself, he knew that Eben Morrison had not lied about *him*.

Behind the grey clouds in the south, the sun was working its way out. At first Joe Saul could not tell whether the new warmth was within him or without. He was pleased that the world was warmer.

"Ah, boys, sun he's comin' t'rough," he exclaimed cheerily as he approached the camp. "In most ways she comes t'rough at last."

"Well, Eben Morrison didn't lie about ye after all," stated the cook with a curiosity to see how Joe was taking it.

"No. He didn't," answered Joe Saul with a heat in his dark face which was as good as a blush. "And I'm glad on it."

He was glad because however much his reputation might be tarnished, however long it might take him to work off those stains which were none of his making, there was no smirch upon his Honor. When the time came that Eben Morrison came to him again, he would find the same old Joe; for he knew the communication among the drive crews would carry the story to Morrison quicker than any letter.

"Some things they can do to us; but some things can't be done only to our own selves," was Joe's own philosophizing as he prepared to follow Honor all the more.

## Editor Note

Fannie Hardy Eckstorm wasn't known to be a writer of fiction. Her writing usually took the form of detailing real-life events and characters. Whether an Eben Morrison and a Joe Saul existed and had such a misunderstanding is unknown. This story certainly reads like a fictional story, but it likely is creative non-fiction. What we do know is that her father, Manly Hardy once misidentified a man who had been drinking.

In Eckstorm's journal notes, there are several pages on Joe Attean and Charles Prouty. Details from those pages can be found in the book, *The Penobscot Man - Life and Death on a Maine River*. The following journal note was not entered verbatim in the prior released book, so I have included it here. It may seem a bit cryptic or out of place if you have not read the chapter, *Death of Thoreau's Guide - Joseph Attien*, in the above noted book. By way of explanation, the note relates to a case of mistaken identity and alcohol use. Keep in mind, this was during the era of the Maine temperance movement. In that book, Eckstorm gives Joe Attean a tribute for being the man he was. The following is one additional example. (The name *Attean* has been spelled as such, or as by Eckstorm as *Attien* and by Thoreau as *Aitteon*.)

**Eckstorm's Journal Note:**

"Father says Joe Attien could not take part in the Fourth of July boat-races because he was governor and it was thought to be beneath the dignity of the governor.

Father tells again the story of Joe and Steve Stanislaus. Steve lived at Lincoln and father was not intimate with him. One day Steve came to buy some traps; bought two otter traps and paid five dollars for them and offered father a drink.

He was just down from the drive and all blacked up and was the image of Joe Attien, his cousin. (They were built similarly and looked a good deal alike.) When elections came on and Joe was the Old Party candidate, father said he wondered why they should put up a candidate who drank.

The tribe said he didn't drink. Father told about buying the otter traps of him. Of course, Joe heard and was sore about it. The next spring at Medway, when a crew of forty men or so, some white, some Indian, Joe said father lied. Three or four spoke up to deny it (editor: *that Joe drank*). Then Steve spoke up and explained that he was the man, that father knew Joe and didn't know him and had intended no harm. Joe never mentioned the affair to father but came around and was good friends. It was not till he was gone that someone present(ly) told father of the incident."

**\* \* \* End of Journal Note \* \* \***
**Editor Note**

From Eckstorm's note, we understand her point that Joe Attean was a man of class. He let bygones be bygones. He did not scrutinize Manly Hardy for misrepresentation. It was let to pass. Steve Stanislaus was also a man of honor to own up to his cousin Joe, and the others, that it was him in the case of mistaken identity. Joseph Attean died July 4, 1870.

# OF BIG SEBATTIS MITCHELL

**"Know** of Big Sebattis Mitchell. Yes, a long time ago. You know 'um Sebattis?"[23]

Assuredly, one need not have grey hairs to remember Sebattis, for it is scarcely ten years since he died. Memories of him, they are not unpleasant; they recalled kindly acts and thoughtful deeds and wise forbearance; seeing only his unwieldy bulk and black Indian face one could hardly have believed that the two were consistent. Sebattis was not a handsome man; he used rather more than the requirement of bear's grease on his big black head; his eyes troubled him, and he had way of filling' up the round hole between upper and lower lip with the tip of his tongue which must have put in danger from the teeth; gentlemen weighing nearly three hundred may be well-groomed but they are not ordinarily captivating.

Those who saw only the exterior of Big Sebattis could not remember him as I did, as a man of serious and generous notions, with a love of justice and a desire to see good instead of evil, solicitous for the best interests of his tribe but a citizen (without rights) of the United States. There was only one point upon

---

[23] Sabattis Mitchell is said to have been born around 1829 in Oldtown, Maine and died around 1893. Eckstorm then would have been writing this story about 1903. Her book, *The Penobscot Man*, was published originally in 1904. Another story about Sabbatis can be read in *Chapter XX Joyfully*, in the new edition, *The Penobscot Man - Life and Death on a Maine River*, Fannie Hardy Eckstorm, annotated edition by Tommy Carbone (Burnt Jacket Publishing, 2022).

which he wavered in his loyalty, and that was whether his loyalty to the country at large would have borne the strain if it had called him to cease being a Penobscot man.

His Indiandhood he might have resigned; his adoptive-rights at Quoddy, where he-married the old governor's daughter and resided sixteen years,[24] he never emphasized; but he was proud that he was born Penobscot. This story turned on that.

# # # # # # # # # # # # # # #

"I have a story of Big Sebat when he was driving for Bradbury on the Magaguadavic which exactly supplements your story of his pride in the superior skill of the Penobscot boatman and I will tell it to you when I come down."

But a pestilent bullet laid him low before we ever met again, and so to get the story I had to go seeking elsewhere.[25]

# # # # # # # # # # # # # # #

"You know 'um Big Sebattis?" A little hush fell upon both of us as we thought of old bygone things.

"Yes—well; well, that time you see she work it ol' Isaac Bradbury. Much as eight years she work for Isaac on Maccadavy river–drivin'. You see S'battis is very good river-driver; she don't go on logs 'cause too heavy, but in boat she been boss number one of the river-drivers. You know she Penobscot man but she marry in Quoddy and cause woman don't want leave she ol' folks an' old gov'ner she blind an' very old, mor'n hunderd years old when died, well, S'battis she stayed

---

[24] Likely, Elizabeth Francis (1831-1917), of Eastport, Maine.

[25] The fence posts surrounding this section are added by the editor. There was a puzzle as to why Eckstorm had added these two sentences and who the quote was attributed to that was killed by a 'pestilent bullet.' The mystery for the editor was revealed within, and the reader will be told as well.

there sixteen years. It was Quoddy she learned it how sail canoe so, she's best man Penobscot tribe sailin' canoe, an' great hand seal shootin' an' porpoise huntin' cause Quoddy folks she get her livin' those ways. But still S'battis she Pencobscot man; she think it more fun runnin' quick water than gettin' drowned out to sea seal shootin,' so when spring come, she ev'ry year gone river-drivin'.

Well, you see, lo-ong time ago was year war broke out, then all white folks she gone war. Injuns gone too 'cause liked it fun an' excitement an' cause good for United States."

It was true enough; our Penobscot Indians served in all three branches of the service, infantry, cavalry and artillery, as well as sharp-shooters; and good men they were too; though a trifle disconcerting to those who were not used to Indians. As witness the story one of them told of himself of the capture of some small defense. The works were ours when someone said he saw a hand waving a newspaper about the logs.

"Well, you see we took good aim an' fired; don't see um hand no more. When we gone up there we found um officer with arm blowed up; hit um elbow, run straight up wrist, smash um arm all pieces. She very mad. *'Don't you see newspaper? We surrender.'* Said we, 'Yes, we seen um newspaper, but when we seen rebel, we shoot!'"

They were good soldiers, but perhaps a trifle over conscientious about putting down the rebellion.

However, Sebattis had no part in that. His nature was pacific, and he was at home at Quoddy all through the war.

"Well, spring war broke out. S'battis Mitchell went on drive in Province for Old Isaac, up Maccadavy River. By jolly those were great times. You see Province man them time hate um Yankee; she want seen um licked bad. She say *'Hope down south she lick you all to hell.'*

## Big Sebattis Mitchell

Sebattis Mitchell was a long-time companion of Manly Hardy. The two spent time on the sea and bays along the coast of Maine hunting seals. Quite assuredly, Manly hired Sebattis as his guide, for Manly often went on trips with hired guides, both white men and Indian. There are three trips noted in Manly Hardy's journal for which Hardy and Sebattis had long excursions.

In 1874, Hardy traveled up the Passadumkeag River and the St. Croix River to Point Pleasant. Today this is the area of the Pleasant Point Reservation lands. This is not far from Quoddy and the location Sebattis was living. The two then sailed a canoe outfitted with a sail, purchased by Hardy, but under the skilled command of Sabattis, down the coast and into Penobscot Bay back to Brewer, Maine. A rough measurement of the possible sea and river voyage would have been over 150 to 170 miles.

From August 21 until September 5, 1874, Hardy again traveled with Sebattis. This trip was down the Penobscot River with a return to Brewer. And Hardy's journal notes a trip in 1878, when the two traveled down the Penobscot River from Brewer, through Penobscot Bay to Little Deer Isle, and then returned, for an eighty mile, or so, round trip, not counting all their side excursions for hunting.

*Photograph from the collection of Fannie Hardy Eckstorm.*
*"Big Sebattis Mitchell - taken 1891."*
*Courtesy Raymond H. Fogler Library, University of Maine.*

The truth of this I knew. Did I not have that little silk United States flag, which the Maine States Survey of 1861 carried down the St. John River with them, making their boats the target of continual insults all the way and almost bringing on bloodshed.[26] It was very true.

My story bearer continued. "Well that time Old Isaac got it his drive down to MacDougall Falls. Jim Lee, he live near that place, and she bad place, by jolly! She wicked ol' hole below there. Don't no one try to run McDougall Falls. Never anybody run that place. Now you see, war been broke out 'bout month by then—"

He was right. Sumter was fired on the 15th of April, and this as I happened to be sure was the 22nd of May.

"—and Province folks he was gettin' cross. S 'battis she big man. An' she clever man. An' she slow! But when she reached it—McDougall Falls she most hot.

Joe Orson he was there that time. He was also Penobscot Injun an' she speak to Sebattis. Said she, 'Spos'n you an' me we run it those falls stop mouth these feller pretty quick! If Yankee run her falls first time, then she can't talk so big.'

Imagine, Sebattis posing as a Yankee!

Yes, you can.

But mark you! these Indians are loyal. Congress gave them medals with Washington's name and face on them for services in the Revolution. Both Penobscot and Quoddy tribes had medals

---

[26] Eckstorm would have this flag because Manly Hardy was assistant naturalist on the 1861 Maine Scientific Survey. Also along on that trip as a guide was Louis Ketchum (character in this book). They went UP the East Branch of the Penobscot River and then down the Allagash to the St. John River.

and earned them fairly. If they had not been loyal, what think you that the British might not have done in 1812 when they held both the St. Croix and the Penobscot? There were almost as many Indians as whites near Bangor then, and had they not been both Christian and friendly, ill would it have happened with the war-whoop and the scalping knife among the scattered settlers of the State of Maine.

So Joe and Sebattis made their way to Bradbury to announce that they were going to run McDougall Falls for the first time. They wanted the loan of a batteau; probably they almost the same as demanded the boat.

Now Isaac Bradbury was their friend and had no reason to wish to see them drowned. He was likewise a head lumberman, and all head lumbermen, whatever the follies of their youth in the way of smashing boats, feel tenderly toward their own batteaus under their responsibility. The boats are to the drive, what the pack train or the wagon train is to an army; without them there is nothing possible. The wangan can't be moved down the river. Men can't be shuttled to the center jams. The crews can't work. The logs don't move. One can almost hear the conversation, and you can imagine it was no whisper.

'Isaac, we want um boat!'

'What do you want a boat for Sebattis?'

'We want to run those there falls.'

'Can't do it.'

'No one ever did try to do it.' Sebattis countered.

'No. I just mean to say, I can't do it to give you a boat.'

'We can do it,' added Orson.

'No one ever did it,' stated Old Isaac.

'Well, we say we can do it, an' we goin' to try. Me an' Yankee Joe.'

'Sebattis, you can't do it; you'll get drowned, both of you, two of my best watermen. And besides, you'll smash my boat in the doin' of it.'

'How 'bout we pay it for boat. You take it pay out of wages,' said Orson, committed without asking Sebattis. 'We give you no reason not. Now s'pose we got drowned an' you lost your boat, you can had it our pay for boat.'

Good for Sebattis and Joe Orson! A boat was worth upwards of seventy dollars—and be sure they would not choose the worst one—and yet here were two poor, illiterate Indians, so sure of the idea they were contending for, so anxious to prove the supremacy of their countrymen, these Indian Yankees, that they bid nearly three week's wages each of them, for the privilege of getting drowned in their own way.

But Isaac only said, 'Tut! Tut!' and turned away He knew all about what fools men were when it came to running boats over falls. The less said the better. He knew too that when a man was determined to run, he would steal a boat if he had to and defy the owner. Oh! there are many things that a man learns when he is head lumberman, and when he'd been a man on the other side.

Perhaps, being a head lumberman he turned away on purpose that if they wished to carry out their plan he might not be forced to interfere. Often times, the Quaker in the head lumberman, waited while the natural man rejoiced.

Then Joe and Sebattis debated in Indian (so as Isaac would not understand)—seriously they conferenced, and it was surmised by Isaac, and all others around, that they intended to brook no interference with their project. There was the boat; they were good for its value; it was *Hey* and *Come on boys*!

"Aw, you ain't the first ones that ever want to run them falls; you needn't feel so big if you not drowned," spoke up a Province man standing by.

"Ugh! What you said?" asked Orson.

"Our falls has been run. Even you don't know." The Province man smirked, glad to have something else to gloat over.

"Haw! You don't mean it! No Province men can do it. She don't got the skill." Big Sebattis stood, feet apart.

"It's true." Said another Province man. "Two days ago."

Then were Joe and Sebattis more than ever excited. It should never be said that if they were the first, that Province men were the only ones who had dared to run McDougall Falls.

But an American river driver standing by asked, "Who was it did it?" Even Old Isaac himself it is said spoke up: "Yes, who did it? One of your men?"

Now the Province men knew they had them. The information was hotter than poplar coals for a biscuit fire.

"Oh, no. Not us. We aren't fools. Not like your Yankees." The Province man leaned on his Peavey.

"Yankees!" exclaimed Orson. He could hardly anticipate it.

"Who? Are they drowned?" asked Sebattis.

"No. They ran them falls and lived."

"Who? Who?" was the chorus of Bradbury's drivers.

"You know them, for certain. Jim White and Dave Libbey. They's been up here digging knees this winter, run it Sunday all right," said the Province man.

# # # # # # # # # # # # # #

Elsewhere I have told how Jim White and his brother-in-law David Libbey ran the falls,[27] and how eight days later, coming

---

[27] Eckstorm's notes on this falls run, and the account of David's death, can be read in, *David Stone Libbey – He Was Penobscot,*

down with another drive of knees, for they had but four men and had to divide their little drive, they generously took in the brother-in-law and cousin to share the fun and ran it a second time with more courage than reason; though it happened to come out all right in the end.

################

Sebattis and Joseph turned slowly and looked at each other. Sebattis grunted deeply. Joe waited the decision of his chief. Slowly it came; for it was a disappointment not to be the first ever to run McDougall's falls, end yet in a way he *was* satisfied.

"Sebattis, she say, 'She's both Penobscot man, David and James are, so that's all right.' Sebattis then turned to Ol' Isaac and the drivers of the American crew, 'You know, s'pos'n been Province man, then we run 'em those falls for sure!' That's what she said! You believe um, Big Sebattis?"

The credit of his country was saved; he had no need to risk their lives—and it was their lives verily that were at stake. But, the question comes, and that is the fine point about the loyalty of, and the ambitions of, Big Sebattis Mitchell—what would he have done if, instead of it being Penobscot men who had run the Province falls, they had been Kennebeckers?[28]

---

writings by Eckstorm and Libbey (Burnt Jacket Publishing, 2022). The story of Libbey and White running McDougall Falls *(or McDougall's Falls)* is fictionalized in the novel, *I Am Penobscot*, by Tommy Carbone (Burnt Jacket Publishing, 2023).

[28] This is Maine 'inside humor' between the rivalry of the Maine river drivers.

# ON OLDTOWN FALLS

Eckstorm prefaced this story with a prelude.
Old Town Falls was a distance of about twenty land-
miles from her home in Brewer, Maine.

**The** rumble and churning of a waterfall, even a great one, is
insistent only for a short time; then everyone near it becomes
accustomed to its undertone and only on Sundays and still clear
evenings of early spring do those who live near to it hear it. At
other times they see the white flash of tumbling water, the suds
and vapor below the falls and it causes neither admiration for its
beauty nor wonder at its strength, it being for six days in the week
the servant of the mill; the strong slave of man. So Oldtown Falls
is now chained to the great woolen mill and turns thousands of
spindles and weaves a web as mysterious to itself as the lady of
Shalott's.[29] Everybody thinks of the web, no one of the growling
slave bound to the wheels below; from it has passed all the
glamor of romance, all the picturesqueness of red shirts and
trooping lumbermen; even the Indians who live just above wear
the cloth of the mill and no longer buckskin and feathers. But
once upon a time—sweep away the woolen mill; destroy all the
habitations of the white man; make the tall pines grow once more

---

[29] *The Lady of Shalott* is a 19th-century ballad by the English poet
Alfred Tennyson.

over road and landing; restore the smooth-edged falls to their primitive raggedness, broke with lodge and island, but steep, impetuous, strong.

It was a cosy nook for the Indian, a good camping ground where shad and salmon ran up in countless numbers, red-fleshed, red- finned, gay in their fishy brightness and glittering like silver; and with net and spear the Indian drew them in, his feast of fatness after the hunger-pains of scanty winters. He loved the place. And here he had his old town.

Today the white men have taken even the name; to the Indian is left only the little island above the falls where the river, parted by it above, joins again before sweeping down over the falls. It is very quiet now; yet, though the loveliness and the picturesqueness of the past is gone, the place is not without interest to the stranger.

Each year many come hither to visit the Indians, to buy a basket or a curio, to have a quiet canoe ride with a real Indian, even to look at the falls by the wool mill.

There is no place about where the stranger more enjoys his brief visit. And so it is there where we conduct our guests.

A great woollen mill has tamed the falls now. They are still there rumbling and churning as in the days when they were the feature of the river that commanded most attention, but they look dwarfed and for six days in the week they toil sullenly at their task of turning spindles. Only on Sundays and clear bright evenings in April do the weary towns folk, sitting in their doorways comment on the sound of the falls which at such times rises over the tumult of the day. There is danger from them still, for ill comes to the boatman who forgets that they are below him.

And yet, a stranger to the river might pass by without ever seeing they were there behind the mill; and that in the old days of logs and lumber, when men lived by the flow of the river could never had happened.

The very carry past them spelled "falls." And the falls meant more to the Indian than they did to the lumberman; they were his fishing place where in the spring he dipped or speared the red-finned shad and the golden-meated salmon; times when the water ran brown with the freshet and the shad-bush flung out its white banners all along the River. Such a place of plenty and of feasting was it, that the Indians here established their old town. Even the name has been preempted by the whites together with the site and the falls and the fishing.

The Indians withdrew to a spot a little less convenient, that smaller island next above the falls which is hugged by the current where the arms of the river lock below it to push downward toward the falls. The current is strong from the Indian Island to the landing on the white man's shore, but he does not mind it, and he probably does not know that his own ancient site and chosen dwelling place, his natural abode is usurped by the great mill beside the falls. He is a patient man this Indian, not prone to dwell upon old injuries or losses; there is no bitterness in him. Yet one thing he does remember, that the falls are there, and not as the slave of the mill, but as the enemy of whoever forgets that from the Indian island to the other shore a man must lay a straight course and hold well against the current and never, never get into the grip of the current that pulls down upon that white curtain of tumbling water, dissolving in mist and foam.

The men who have forgotten have died, well, all but three. Sam Newell went over once with the logs and came out alive. No one was more surprised than himself at his being alive at the end of it. And two men have dared the falls deliberately. Theirs is the greater glory and of them we speak.

Do you know how warm and cosy it can be on Indian Island along in June? That time after the ground is dry enough to lie down on, and yet, before the withering heat of July has driven everyone to the thickest shade. The grass is growing tall then. Buttercups are in bloom. Daisies are budding. The fist wild strawberries are ripening under their leaves.

It was then when Old Tomer Sebattis, black and wrinkled—(it must have been a long time ago, for I find his name on my grandfather's books in 1844 and in his later years, which my father remembers, he was living no longer at Oldtown but at Lincoln)—was building a canoe out under the maple behind his little hut. Squatting against the tree-trunk, with his old stone pipe in his mouth he shaved the cedar ribs for his canoe and laid them by in pairs; each pair of a different length. There was the smell of white cedar freshly cut, a strong romantic fragrance from this sandalwood of the north. In the pile of shavings burrowed and rolled two chubby little Indian boys, with beady black eyes, burrowing through the shavings like big mice at play. They were Louis Porus and Peter Newell; we may name them.

"Oh, Lewy, Lewy, dem's my toes you bit it!" squealed Peter, who just at present was an otter. They were both otters by the way. The shavings were their slide and like the real animal they were gliding down the heap and then wriggling back and up the other side with arms folded on their breasts.

"Dem's my toe!" Peter squealed again.

In a playful mood the other otter had bitten the bare foot of his leader in the game.

"Aw, she so black!" remarked Louis "We thought mus' be she otter tail; she wiggle like otter tail." Louis looked to to the elder at work on the canoe. "Gran-fadder, what for otter she had it long roun' tail? Musquash, she like otter, but she had it little flattin' tail, all scaly like she's fish. What for otter she have the long roun' tail then?"

There's nothing in this world without a reason behind it. The little Indian child is just as prompt as his white brother to ask *What for*? And his elders, wise in generations of unwritten lore, had amassed a hoard of answers that when the question was put to them, they might not be bankrupt.

Two little round black heads, two pairs of round black eyes, like the heads and eyes of seals emerged from the shavings.

"What for, grand-fadder?" Louis held his head up.

Old Tomer Sebattis drew his crooked knife toward him with slow precision, leaving the cedar satin-smooth. He squinted along it before he lay it by its mate to measure and compare.

"Ugh-huh! a long time ago..."—(Thus begin all Indian legends)—"Speak so the very ol' folks, tell us—a long time ago then you see all animals she could talk. Then that time otter she had little tail, like musquash. And musquash she have it her a big fine tail; always she look it over her shoulder, musquash see her nice big tail.

"One day speak so the otter, 'Very nice tail you got it, musquash; very handsome, big tail; we got it little tail, a mean tail. S'pose you took it our tail—for a little while—then let us have it your tail—to see how it look, your own tail for us.'

"Them musquash, she proud had it big animal like the otter talk to him, and otter called it nice tail, that she like the musquash tail. Musquash speak so, 'Yes, we lend it our tail little while.' So she swapped tails with the otter.

"Now otter she gone round playin' all the time, jump all the time, look it at his tail.

"Musquash look round see his now little tail. He's so ashamed. Speaks so to otter, 'Time to swap back.'

"Orter say, 'No, we keep it our new tail.' And he slide away. Now musquash he always look round and see it, his little tail. He ashamed, always he drag it behind him."

The little boys bobbed heads to one another with confirmatory grunts, "Uh-huh! That's so! You seen musquash, she look it behind him. That's so!"

"But musquash tail she's good eat it. Otter she good for nothing!" remarked Peter.

"Pitsonungun!" responded Louis.[30]

"Nah!" remarked his mate in disgust. "Don't hold nothing."

"Do!" remarked Peter, taking a lunge from his heap of shavings, an otter once more, and sliding across Louis's back. It looked like a squabble, rare among Indian children.

"Ha, na!" cautioned the old man. "Don' be like white boy!"

Really, an Indian child could not be as rude as white child; the comparison made them very much ashamed.

"A long time ago," began the elder, to attract their attention. The two little seals came to order at once on their heap of shavings. Then Old Tomer Sebattis put down his tools. He sat on a log and told them all about the Ahlermbaguenosesuc. He animated with his fingers as he explained about the little men who live down under the water, water spirits they are. These are harmless little nixies who are very merry, who dance round and round in Indian dances, stiff-kneed to the music of shotted horns.

"Alumbaguenosis—sis[31] he's little, no-sis, little man Alumbague, lives under water, what called 'em

---

[30] Pitsonungun - a Penobscot word for pouch. Joseph Nicolar (1827-1894) wrote that to carry fire, bound between clam shells, a pitson-ungun was made from the whole skin of the Mo-nim-queh-so—the woodchuck.

[31] The use of 'sis' is the diminutive, as in Sysladobsis Lake, with the meaning of what is now referred to as Lower Dobsy Lake. Read

Oonahgemessuen to Quoddy. She's good little folks; don't hurt men."

"Who seen 'um?" asked the boys.

"We-ell, you see, long time ago, when old folks gone out on water—them look down over canoe—them seen 'um in water all dancin'—all singin'—all makin' great celebration—like Fourth of July." The old man came back to white men's times, after all, for his comparison.

"Where grandfather? Where seen um?"

"In water, in still water, when it cranberry good time she have fun under water."

The boys contemplated the river. They could hear the rush of the water.

"And in falls? She dance in falls too?" asked Peter.

The old man shook his head.

"Why not? For she don't get carried down over falls?" went on his young questioner.

Old Tomer shook his head again.

"Don' little folk live under falls?" Louis's eyes were open wide waiting for an answer.

The old man's head shook vigorously.

Peter examined the look of horror came into the face of the elder. "What? Why you look 'um like that?"

There is one thing, chief among many, that the Indian dreads. More than once his tribe had seen this monster, this great, horned worm rise from the boil and spatter of the surging torrent. The beast was monstrous, insatiate, a destroyer.

---

Eckstorm's full explanation of 'sis' in, *Exploring the Maine Woods - The Hardy Family Expedition to the Machias Lakes*. But here, Alumbague, Tomer is stressing, is a little man, but not a diminutive of someone, or some other.

"Weewilliarmek!" Tomer whispered, hoarsely in a voice that froze them.[32]

The two youngsters, they looked at each other with rising terror, and they were long still, having buried themselves deeper in the yellow shavings. There they hoped no shape of dread might see them, for they knew of the Weewilliarmek, as did all Indian boys fifty years ago.

The old man went back to his work. He shaved his canoe ribs with his crooked knife, bending them about his knee in trial curves. Gradually the little boys regained their speech.

"Ah., grandfather, if not Alumbague folk, ain't ther' never been any man go over Oldtown Falls?"

"Yes," grunted the old man, slowly nodding, but offering no details.

Louis nudged Peter to ask more.

"An' don't he run it all right?" continued the lad eagerly, wanting to know if Weewilliarmek lived near.

"Nah. She come out below." Tomer looked at the boys, and told them how it. was, for there was no safety for them in holding back reality. "Dead. Spos'n she ever found again even."

"Always?" A tremor of horror was heard in Peter's voice. He swallowd hard. "Always she ate 'em, Weewilliarmek did?"

"Always but once," responded the old man, raising a finger to them without turning.

The story was too good, too important for the boys to stay hidden under the shavings. They needed to know more, for they fished and canoed on the river.

Peter slowly crawled out of the pile.

Louis followed.

---

[32] In Eckstorm's work on Indian legends, she notes the spelling by the Penobscots was, *Wiwiliámecq*, the dreaded underwater monster.

They stood by Tomer as he carefully drew the blade across the wood. Peter gently nudged him to draw his attention.

The elder sighed. Even he would not like to be reminded of Weewilliarmek.

They begged the story from him. Slowly he drew himself to it; for the past is not clear to the Indian—a mist hangs before his memory of events gone by from which the vision emerges slowly.

What emerged was a vision of spring time when the water was brown with the spring rains and the current ran full freshet, flooding out the lower foot of the falls, making them a gliddery incline, rather than a straight fall. It was when the coral-red of the maples bloom. When the silvery haze of poplar catkins and the white banner of the shad-bush are flung out. The shad run up the river then; they gather below the falls and men dip them out; the great flat fellows, with sides like silver and bellies pink beneath. One remembers the scales of them dislodged by the dip-net, clinging to its meshes to drop like a drop of silver.

It was at just this time of year, when the shad were running; by this mark, old Tomer Sebattis remembered the incident. It was that morning Sappiel Soccalexis had been dipping shad. Sappiel had to live with the memory of seeing it all; and worse, had to have told everyone, for it was his responsibility to do so.

The old elder motioned the boys to sit next to him on the log. He swept his hand out over the path of the river. "You see in those days there was young men," began the old man; "she's always wantin' done something somebody else hasn't done before. She's always looking chances distinguish himself; This is always so with young men."

He watched their eyes as the two seemed to share a secret wish.

Clearing his throat, he went on. "One day in early spring of the year was two young men, out in canoe. They just paddling for fun. She's nice day, bright sun, but the water very very cold. Snow just melted. The water run high. High pitch over the rocks. But warm sun, make young man feel good." Tomer closed his eyes and let the sun fall on his face.

Peter nudged him.

"Ah. You must have patience, young boy." Tomer patted his knee. "Speak one in bow to the other. *'You s'pose on that pitch water we could run it this canoe o'er Oldtown Falls?'* And the other one he say, *'Yeh, anyone can do that now.'* He said, what you call 'em *brag*. He think the other fellow will say 'No!' I tell you, he miss his guess! By jolly, said that other boy, *'We goin' then.'*"

A small gasp came from Louis.

Tomer shook his head. He cradled his chin with his hand. "So the boys goin' paddle straight for Oldtown Falls." He pointed down river. "That year was great deal she roar those there falls, more than now! She know she got 'em. They can't get away from her pitch. Never was man went over Oldtown Falls and came home to live."

"Did they...die?" Louis stuttered.

"Patience, young man. Learn." Tomer closed his eyes. "Well, other boy, in stern, she don't dare say 'No' 'cause then first boy will tell others, and all laugh at him on island; she can't pull back now if she want to, 'cause current got 'em now. No way out. They must go over. Those two, they was good grit those there boys. Their fathers teach 'um well paddle, but never in pitch."

The old man lighted his pipe. The boys grew impatient waiting.

"They died? Weewilliarmek ate 'em?" Peter asked.

"Both of them?" Louis's head nodded.

"Ah. Listen. Old friend Sappiel seen 'um comin' pullin' the paddle for all she was worth. But they small. Right on head of big pitch of Oldtown Falls, Sappiel holler an holler, *'Don't stop 'em now. Paddle. Paddle!'*" Tomer picked up a stick and paddled over the side of the log.

"Sappiel, he know, they gone. Little hope he had. He seen 'um dark, black hair blow straight out in wind behind 'em. And he speak that he seen 'em laugh, and laugh, just when current took 'em over falls."

Tomer's hand made a pitching motion over the falls.

"They dead?" Peter and Louis spoke as one.

The elder shrugged. "Sappiel, she ain't seen nothing more, cause Oldtown Falls just grab 'um. Right over edge."

"An Weewilliarmek? She there? Old Sappiel see him?"

"Ug," said the old man, losing patience with his pupils' impatience.

"And?" asked the boys. "Them dead?"

"No. Spit' em out!" remarked the old man, with a smile. "Me guess she don't like taste of fools canoe. The good birch all broke, but young men hold fast to canoe bars and they-um stick somehow wheelin' and tumblin' and knockin' 'bout in the rapids. Canoe turned all to spiles, but boys, she's saved."

"So, can do it."

Tomer frowned at them. "No. Listen. Those boys, they says, she knows then somethin' now, what she didn't know before."

"What? About Weewilliarmek? They see him?" asked Louis, nodding his head rapidly.

The elder sighed. "Ug! No. She knows all rocks on Oldtown Falls. An' says never again she go in bad place she can keep out of by thinking." Tomer laughed. "Then, speaks so old men to the fools, *'Maybe now you make it good waterman one these days, cause only fool she willin' to risk his life for nottin' an' only fool, or dead man, can go over Oldtown Falls.'"* Tomer nodded slowly. "That is true. Many ways, true."

"An no one gone over Oldtown Falls since that time?" asked Peter.

The old man shook his head. "Too great risk. She dead man for sure if she a fool."

"But, Grandfather, you'd dare go? You good waterman!" Peter held the elder's arm.

The old man shook his head. "No. And neither you never try."

It might be fine to stand well in the eyes of the rising generation, but he knew that life was still too dear to him to throw it away on Oldtown Falls.

Indian Island from the landing.
Photo by Fannie Hardy Eckstorm 1891.
*Image courtesy of Special Collections, Raymond H. Fogler Library, photo/3208.*

# PENOBSCOT RIVER TALES

Eckstorm wrote three stories under the header Penobscot River Tales. she included this introduction.

**Forty** millions of logs to drive down a thousand-feet of fall,[33] a good three months in which to take them from Seboomook to the boom, a hundred men, then two hundred men, finally three

---

[33] Eckstorm's figure here is likely approximate and to mean forty-million feet of lumber (m-bfl). She was on friendly terms with clerks from the drives and was diligent in her research. Since her direct research at Ripogenus was in 1891, these figures are likely from an average year between the mid-1880s and 1900. Geller documented, typically around those years, 8 million board feet of logs going through the Seboomook Dam each year; with one year noted at 13 million. And from fourteen lumbering operations in 1890, 22.6m board-feet-lumber (bfl) arrived at the head of Chesuncook (*West of Chesuncook & North of Moosehead: Log Drives & Sporting Camps, 1830-1971,* pg. 130-131. *William Geller, 2021, Maine History Documents. avail. from digitalcommons.library.umaine.edu/*). To this 22.6m-bfl example figure would certainly be added the side-drives from many other tributaries that merged along the West Branch below Ripogenus, as well as from the Passadumkeag and other flowages into the main branch of the Penobscot on the way to the Old Town and Bangor booms. In the same reference (pg. 132) for 1905 reported available figures, converting cords to standard board feet, one arrives at 32 m-bfl, to which other drives would need to be added. This is likely how Eckstorm arrived at the 40 millions figure. The thousand feet of fall mentioned is the height above sea level from Seboomook to the booms on the main branch of the Penobscot River.

hundred men to handle the forty million and those that have been added to them. Multiply one hundred days by three hundred men at four hearty meals a day, when one hundred men in one day will eat a barrel of flour and half a barrel of pork and wholesale quantities of other groceries besides, the problem isn't how much food supply is needed, but rather, to calculate how many boats it will require to transport the stuff that feeds this woods-army.

Now complicate it a little more. The annual log-drive operated in enemy country—the woods always was that to the men who work in them. There were no roads then going close to the river—only carry paths out of necessity, and only wide enough for man to carry a batteau. There was no forage, no base of supplies along the route, no communication—no telegraph or telephone (in the old days, at least), no steamers on the lakes then (the boom was warped by hand; the men walking miles around the capstan on a raft), not even horses, or roads (until recent years). There was no anything, but what the boats bringing along in the rear. The distance from the base of supplies along their route is continually increasing. Their main supply camps being at Greenville, Seboomook, Grant Farm, and Chesuncook. Not only that, going down the West Branch of the Penobscot River, there are nine grueling carry-miles in all; miles where not only all the supplies had to be carried, but the boats, those heavy, wooden, thirty-foot, eight-man batteaus, had to be picked up and carried on men's shoulders.

The military man will understand the case. What does the military man think of supporting an army under such conditions? A condition of the cavalry man who can have nothing but what is on their horse's backs and then, upon coming to heavy ground, have to pick up and lug, not only the horses' loads but the horses themselves? For, an average horse weighs close to the same as a large, water-logged, driving boat.

Furthermore, the military man will understand the problem in taking three full companies of men on a three months trip through a hostile country, utterly devoid of food—that is exactly what this river-army had to contend with. He cannot add to the supply he has with him. He must move slowly. He cannot add to the number of his horses, and whenever he comes to difficult ground his troops must not only lug all their food on their shoulders, but in the roughest terrain they all but have to pick up their horses and carry them! An old soldier will admit the difficulty of the proposition.

A hundred men at the beginning of the drive, became three hundred plus at the end of the drive as the side-drives moved into the formation. Each company had to be fed five times a day, all consuming an incredible amount.

Let us say a barrel of flour and half a barrel of pork a day to the hundred men. Tons of food had to be transported and only the boats and men's shoulders to do it.

The problem of the head of the drive is to have enough provided at the start to last down to the Lower Lakes (near to current-day Millinocket, a location where food could be brought in), and not to have too much; too have just boats enough to carry it; and not too many. It was the boats which were at the bottom of all the calculations of the head of the drive. Nothing so upset head man's plans as to lose a boat. If men were drowned, he could resupply their places (cruel as that may seem), but a boat could not be had—short of getting to Oldtown and that would be the easiest of the task. From there the men went against the current rowing, paddling, poling, and shouldering the batteau across carries and around pitches. Replacing a boat meant delay and extra burden on the remaining boats. With all the wood surrounding them, with axes to fell the trees, they could not in the woods build the boat they needed. Therefore nothing touched the head man so deeply as the safety of his boats. They were his scouts, his aides, his cavalry, his baggage train, his main dependence. Such a dependence on boats was never so in other states to the same degree; it is not so here today (1903); but in the old times (up to the 1880s) everything depended upon the boats and the boatmen.

These were the problems of the head-lumberman in the times just closed.[34] Never men solved such grave questions more expertly. They balanced to a nicety that bridge of a hair between crippling their men by providing too little and wearing them out by making them lug too much. It was the boats that did it. Everything depended upon the boats. They provide all the poetry of the Maine log-drives. Jam breaking becomes stale and monotonous, but there is never any repetition in the tales of the boats.

The best men were the boatmen. The deeds of judgment and daring were done chiefly by the boatmen. Rescues were made by them. And no other drives anywhere have ever developed and depended upon the boats as the Maine drives have.

The batteau herself—all the boats are batteaus—and they are all Penobscot. Ira Wallace of Oldtown first shaped her timbers for our rough waters. Hosea Maynard of Bangor refashioned and enlarged her. Vinal built her of such prodigious proportions that she carried six men at the oars besides the boatmen proper.[35] In every line the batteau is Penobscot bred.

What is she like? No one would ever guess her pedigree from her outward appearance; but she is a dory! modified to meet a

---

[34] For reference, Eckstorm in this story is writing of the time in Maine logging history on the West Branch up until the mid-1880s. Horses were first used on Ripogenus Carry in the late 1880s.

[35] 'Boatman proper' refers to the bow man and the stern man.

stationary wave. The dory proper is made light and high-sided; short, to ride a moving wave, to bob on it like a sea-gull. The batteau is built to rise a stationary wave that curls continually in one place; she shoots out over it, is lifted by its shoulders, but she does not rock upon it. She has been lengthened enormously. Her bottom lies all in one plane, unlike the dory's. Her sides flare prodigiously. Her stem and stern both are drawn upward into a taper snout that rake forward many feet from the forefoot. No one but the fisherman can sufficiently admire the virtues of the dory; no one but the man born and bred among them can adequately praise the virtues of the batteau. She is to the river-man what the camel is to the Arab, the mule to the western pioneer; nothing else could have supplied her place in taking logs to market.

It goes without saying that the head man cherished his boats above everything else. It is human nature, too, that the men, not sharing the responsibilities of their chiefs, should not husband them so carefully, and that there should be conflicts between the heads and hands of the drives upon occasions. It was always the boats that they fought over, like Greeks and Trojans contending over the body of Patroclus;[36] and what they did and how, is told is these three true and merry tales of the boats. They have come to me first-handed; my own hand took them from the actors' lips, and if they have a virtue, it is that of authenticity. The first two of them from the lips of those who were in the affairs, the third from one who knew all about it.

---

[36] Patroclus of Greek mythology was friend to Achilles. When Patroclus was struck down at Troy, the Trojans and Greeks fought to secure Petroclus' remains and Achilles' armor which Petroclus had been wearing.

# A RIVER TALE – ISAIAH MOREY'S BLUFF

## How Isaiah Morey bluffed and Alonzo Spearen took him up.

**Isaiah** came very near being a bully. One thing saved him, and that was that he rather liked it when he found a man who was smarter than he was. The old head lumbermen, who had risen from the ranks by sheer will and brawn, were that way. Their men all called them Tom and Dick to their faces,[37] and they in turn bullied those they dared to, and dared those they could not bully. But you couldn't pry it out of them with a peavey that they were not smarter than any other men who ever walked in spike-soled boots. Therein, they were probably right in general and wrong in particular; and therein Isaiah was typical. His faults were buried with him several years ago. It is remembered, however, that he showed his disdain for death and accident by never wearing but one calk in the heel of each boot. Most men want a full set, that is upwards of fifty in a boot, but Isaiah thought one to a boot was a plenty.

"Hmf!" he used to sniff. "When water's very bad I put in two."

---

[37] From the old use of "Every Tom, Dick, and Harry," for everybody, anybody, nobody special or particular; or in this use a put down for persons of not much importance, at least according to the 'working men' of the drive.

And that tells a river-driver what kind of a river-driver Isaiah had been in his days. It was clear that he had a right to brag if he chose.

This is not denying that there were times when Isaiah bragged a little too much. His men did not like to have it rubbed in more than semi-occasionally that they were no good on earth and that all the naturally good river-drivers alive were not much under the age of Isaiah. Going on logs and breaking jams and running boats over quick water were supposed to come as natural as walking to any Penobscot-born boys. It was not soothing to them to be informed otherwise, and there were times when they suspected that Isaiah was hectoring them just to get more work out of them, because when they were mad, they would work harder.

"I tell you, I'll roll him in some day when I get a good chance," threatened Bill Smith. "One calk won't hold him on any log when it comes to rolling. And you just let me see him out on a good crooked log someday. If I can't manage to run and light on that log just long enough to whirl him off into the drink, you can call me Isaac!"

Bill Smith had been particularly called down before the men that morning at breakfast and now at first luncheon time the embers of his wrath were still smoking. They were driving the Passadumkeag Drive, of which Isaiah was the head man that year. They had had rather a hard time across the lake above and now the logs were piling up on Nicatowis Falls. The head man did not like the look of things; they were his logs largely and his loss if anything happened.

While the men lunched at ease on the sloping bank above the falls, he growled around by himself down along the river. It was a clear bank open to the sun and the cook's coffee over his fire smelled good; it stood black and strong in their tin dippers as they drank and ate, with the big beeches behind them all dressed in their little, pink bud-candles slim and taper today, ready to burst into green leaves tomorrow. The wild oats waved in the open space about them. Striped trilliums unclosing in the precincts of the woods behind. They were thirty men, more or less, who had gathered to handle the logs on the falls. In groups they sat or lay about, red-shirted, rough-boarded, trousers cut short at the knee and every foot armored with heavy driving-boots studded with long steel calks. Each of them intended to get a little rest with their meat and drink before their time was called. They watched, with covert amusement, the head man doing sentry, go by the side of the falls as he ate out of his hand.

Isaiah had been more than a little restive that morning When he was farthest from them on his beat they could indulge in personalities; when he was in perihelion to them the subject changed. They were merry fellows, as merry as Robin Hood's men and all but Bill Smith in much the same good humor.

"Isaiah is more proud of that one heel calk of his than a hen is of one chicken," said a Sibley. "You'd think he never could get money enough scraped together at one time to buy him a full set."

"He's too proud of it—pride hath a fall, as Solomon says," returned Bill Smith, shuffling his own full set of spiked-caulkers out of sight behind a log.

"Says where?" asked another one, a Bryant from *the Ridge*.[38]

"Well, had you ever read your Bible full through, maybe you'd have found it," retorted Bill Smith. He explained for the lesser-read. "Solomon, he wrote mostly for the Bible I've heard say."

---

[38] Bryant Ridge - East of Enfield, Maine.

"Well, I can repeat the first five chapters of the Book of Proverbs and it ain't in any one of them," spoke up another named Jim.

"Say, Jim, how'd you come to know all that much of the Bible?" Bryant inquired.

"Had to learn it for goin' in swimmin' Sundays," grinned the bible-memorizing river-driver. He nodded, remembering to himself that his childhood punishment was worth the price of the cooling waters of the Sebois on a summer Sunday. "How'd you learn all the Bible you got stored up?"

"For sassin' Dad mostly, I guess," Bryant confessed. "I had to learn all about the bears eatin' up the little children. You'll recall, all about the bears eatin' up the forty-two little chidren, an' Ananias and Sapphiry. All though, that last was for lyin' though. An' most all 'bout Hell an' that red-horned Devil, so'st I'd know enough to keep out o' the Old Gentleman's claws."

"Well, do ye?" asked Jim.

"We'll, just say, I leave him alone if he'll leave me be. I always treated Old Devil like a gentleman anyways. He ain't got nothin' against me."

"Not so much as Isaiah has on some, I guess." It was only a hazard, but Jim gave a grin to Bryant; assured he was that Bill had heard.

A scowl crossed Bill's face. "Onto that are ye? Well, I did kind of–Oh, never mind! That's what's the matter with him today; and he don't want to own up to it because no one can prove it on him but me." Bill tipped his tin dipper of the already cold coffee to his lips. He couldn't hold back his grimace from the bitter brew. "He's afraid I'll tell on him what it was; but I won't now, honest Injun! You can guess anything you want to, but I ain't told ye anything about it, now have I?" His face was solemn enough but his black eyes danced with mischief; he knew very well that but for what he had said no one would have been put up to guessing anything.

Bill stared down at the riverbank. "Just look at him now, stompin' back an' forth alongs the driver's path, waitin' for us to get through luncheon. He acts like a big panther in a circus cage, slashin' his tail an' walkin', walkin', all the time. Oh! we'll get circus all right on these falls today. That'd be worth the price of a ticket for you all. Somethin's goin' to hum with Isaiah feelin' like that, an' you'll all be blamin' me before the day is out, an' me just as quiet an' mindin' my own biz'ness as much a porky'pine." The fellows' eyes belied his words and his air of weakness, and he knew darn well the trouble a porcupine could make chewing the floor through the bar-room come spring![39]

"Well a porky'pine can sometimes stir up the biggest kind of troule–snarlin' an ki-yi-in'. For a critter that's peaceable an' can't fight, it can make the biggest row of anything that's goin' on four legs," said Jim, who had finished his second plate of beans and was just lighting his pipe.

"Which I ain't got but two, if you mean me, an' I kin' o' guess you do," retorted the black-eyed scamp. "But you better give up guessin' on Isaiah; I'm not tellin' till he does. He ain't got all the quills out o' him yet, n' he feels awful sore." Bill began laughing at his own joke.

Isaiah, once more in perihelion, was near enough to overhear something about "quills." At the same moment black-eyed Bill had tumbled over on his face in the grass and was waving his

---

[39] The lumberman's bar-room is the bunkhouse where the men slept. As lumber camps in Maine were 'dry' with no alcohol (officially) permitted, the name of the room is sometimes misleading. Porcupines will chew through the floors of sheds, camps, or any building as easy as they strip the bark off a pine, girdling it to a faith of death.

heels in laughter as if he had a colic. Isaiah cast a more than
usually long, assessing look at the group. Bill, to him, seemed
too happy for a riverman fed four times a day on beans and coffee
made from reused grinds. There was one who was quick enough
to save the day.

"Say, Lonz, is that true about their shoots? Those porcy'pine
quills? What you were saying earlier. I've heard it is, an' now
I've heard it ain't since you said so. You being a trapper of fisher,
I figure you ought to know." Bryant of the ridge delivered the
question in a voice high enough to carry to Isaiah, who had let
the laughter go for bona-fide porcupine banter, although he was
suspicious.

Lonz was a little fellow, thoroughbred woodsman, as lithe and
nimble a man as ever one who stepped on slick logs being carried
down a mean river. But just then he was busy in stowing away
as much beef and biscuit as the drivers who weighed twice his
weight. He had not seen Isaiah's look. Besides, he considered
porcupine small game whose habits were best left to the concern
of the fisher.

"As I told you when we were lugging over the carry. There's
not a word of truth in it. What? You telling me, you who were
brought up on Bryant's Ridge for not to know that? And named,
Bryant to boot!"

"But I had it straight," ensured Bryant.

"Straight as a horse's hind leg," remarked Lonz, who figured
that was enough to settle the matter. He reached for another
biscuit to sop up the bean juice on his plate before the cookee
came by to clear the tins away.

"Oh, I know all about it," explained the questioner. "I ain't no
more interested in porky'pines more than what you are." He gave
a sideways head nod. "That was all for Isaiah. We might's all
well be lookin' out for squalls from Isaiah this mornin'. Less

somethin' happens to stop him, he's goin' to try an' crowd us. You just watch him."

"And that means somebody stands a chance of getting drowned. The falls ain't very good this morning." Jim's eyes settled on the white water polishing the rocks. "You'd better hope Old Devil plans to leave you be today." He tipped his hat at Bryant.

The falls were not very good that morning, that was a fact. It was rather unlucky that the long-legged scamp with the black eyes had happed to get Isaiah roiled just when they struck this piece of bad water. They'd had it too good since leaving the lake, now the water had turned on them. There is two miles of it on Nicatowis Falls. None of it navigable. Ever! Except to the drive, which by rights cannot go overland. In the summer there is not water enough for canoes. In the spring, when the drive goes down, there is sometimes more water than batteaus can comfortably manage. All on account of the rocks with which nature has bestrewed the stream.

As could be expected of a mean river, it was just then the logs had reefed up and contracted and twisted the channel so that it was pouring down like a sluice, crooked, deep and very ugly. While they had been lunching, the men had been talking over the chances of who'd be put on to pick off those logs and how best to do it. When the cook gave the signal to the cookee to clear away, indicating their lunchtime was over, they got up. Biscuit crumbs fell from their trouser legs as they rose from the ground. Bill picked a few crumbs from his beard and flicked them to a chickadee.

"Might's not wait for him to bellow at us," stated Bryant. "Somebody'll get drowned here 'fore night if he gets any more out of sorts. It's a miracle he let us even eat!"

There was but one opinion, and that was that Isaiah was in a "state of mind." They were curious to know what it was all about. Meanwhile the culprit who had let the cat out of the bag without telling whose it was, blandly refused to share what it was that had so put the head of the drive out of humor; the little he'd ever have until the drive was over anyhow.

"You can all attest, I never told no one," Bill remarked to those around him in a tight circle.

"But we shouldn't have knowed nothing about it if you hadn't let on," protested Jim, in too loud a voice as he had stopped to tighten the lace of his boot.

"Well, what did I tell ye, then?"

"Nuthin'. What's the thing?"

"That's it, just nuthin'! That's what I told ye that I told ye!" replied Bill, convincingly.

"What ye yapping 'bout?" suddenly demanded the head man. "You 'ought to be down there by now!" Isaiah pointed at the river with the stub of a finger; what was left of it from his accident with an axe. Well, that was the way he told it.

The men turned to avoid his glare and sort out their peavies that were leaning up against the boats.

"Hmf!" sniffed Isaiah, "men ain't no good nowadays, little undersized whippersnapps. When I was a driver, other than Jack Mann, rivermen made an ox look small."

"Who are you complaining about being undersized, Isaiah?" demanded Lonz. He seemed to answer the description of the modern driver Isaiah was mentioning about as nearly as anyone.

The challenge was obvious, but Isaiah merely looked upon him with disfavor and continued along the men. He eyed them, calculating who he'd send first to pick the jam.

"I've got it now," murmured one of the men.

"Got what?"

"That place in proverbs we was talking about at luncheon. Want to bet?"

"No use in betting on a sure thing; what was it?"

"*Pride goeth before destruction and an haughty spirit before a fall.*" The quoter smiled at his recollection. "Reads like it meant Isaiah, don't it? Want to bet it don't?"

The man didn't have a chance to say, 'No.' The head man bellowed at the two of them. He scanned the others who were close by.

"Here, lay a holt of that there boat," commanded Isaiah. "We've got to get it down to the foot of this place. Lay holt eight or ten o' ye! If men were like what they used to be 'twouldn't take an army to lug one boat. Them men wouldn't lug neither, they'd run a place like this an not say nothin' of the water. I'd run it myself if I had anyone to go bowman."

There wasn't room for breathing space before Lon Spearen was in front of him. "I'm your man, Isaiah."

Now Isaiah Morey knew the Spearen breed. He had known Lonz from a youngster. On the other side, Lonz also understood several things. One was that Isaiah never had meant to go, he knew the water was too bad to run and was only bluffing. Also, Lonz knew that he would not dare to back out. Lonz, being of the river as long as he had, and his father before him, also knew that unless this or something else happened more men's lives than one would be put in jeopardy that day through the head man's ill-humor.

The two faced each other without a word; the men forebore either to laugh or cheer; they understood that Isaiah's challenge had been merely a bluff. Better still, they understood that Lonz was playing a larger game than merely to humiliate his employer—namely to perhaps save the lives of those who'd be sent out to break those jams.

The silence held for five long seconds before Isaiah blinked. "Hmf!" Help me get her ready then."

Lonz placed paddles in the batteau.

The men stepped back, each of them in a state of disbelief. They looked from the head man and his volunteer bowman, and then to the river where thirty-foot logs were being twisted and stacked, locking together as a great, wooden monster.

Isaiah walked close to Lonz. "Do you know how bad that place is?" he whispered close to Lonz's ear as they both bent over the boat to discard unneeded ropes and poles.

"Don't care a hang how bad it is," was Lonz's challenging response.

Isaiah looked at him as if to say that a fool and his life were soon parted, but thought better of the ramifications, so he sniffed and retreated with a, "Hmf!" He knew he was in for it with no way to back down. The span of his natural life looked to have been shortened considerably that afternoon.

Nevertheless, Isaiah had threw the dare, and he went. Drivers, knowing it was a fool thing to try, helped lift the boat. Isaiah took his place in the stern.

"Stern!" *you the reader exclaim*, and rightly so. "He's head man!" You continue, "surely he'd want the place of honor in the bow."

"Oh, he would, you can bet he'd want the bow," *says your narrator*, appreciating you know the honor assigned the bow in running falls. "But he couldn't. Isaiah was too large of a man, nearly the size of Sabattis Mitchell. In that water, with Lonz— and I've already told you the size of man he was—if Lonz was forced to the stern, and Isaiah took the bow, that boat would be so front-heavy, there'd be no control and death would be certain for both of them."

"So that's why Isaiah called for a bowman?"

"You guessed it. He may have made a dare, a dare he didn't expect anyone to take up, but he surely wouldn't have been fool enough to ask for a sternman."

There is no need to follow them down that sluice to tell how they handled boat together. Like most such events it was soon over. The descent of Avernus[40] is proverbially facile; it is the getting back that is uncertain.

Any man can go down over falls, but even some of the best ones stay at the bottom of them; sometimes a week, two weeks, maybe a month, could be forever. Perhaps, if they come to the top of the water, and if their good luck—the last they have—held by them and they are found, they get decently buried.

But surely Isaiah and Lonz tasted life while the run lasted, all its richness of perilous pleasure, all its joy of the full moment. It was strong and keen. And then it became a trifle too keen. Isaiah, looking ahead, saw where the jam made up, at the foot of the run, it had choked the river. The current crowned awfully at that spot and dragged round the corner of the jam with a sucking that would wreck any boat. As a head man, he saw with clarity through that pileup of logs that the boat was *his* and he could not afford to lose it. Likewise the realization hit him, he had but one life of his own to throw away. So it was then, Isaiah lost his head.

"Jump, Lonz, Jump and snub her!" he cried. Oh, if he was in his right mind, Isaiah would have known that a man weighing a hundred and fifteen pounds (wet with his clothes and calk boots on) can't snub a boat weighing half a ton when she is flying down

---

[40] Avernus, in the Aeneid of Virgil, was believed to be the entrance to the underworld.

a sluice like a race-horse.[41] Heck, at his own weight of over two-hundred-fifty, Isaiah couldn't do it in that water.

But Lonz was made of the right stuff. He was Penobscot made. He never faltered.

As they flew past the point of one jam, Lonz made a leap with the painter in his hand and hauled.

You'd might think, at this point, your narrator would tell you all ended well. But she cannot do that.

The old boat never knew Lonz was there. She kept going and flipped him. He went completely over her, like the snapper of a whip indeed. Flipped into the air, he was thrown into the boiling stream as if he had been a trout-fly. After that, Lonz was not obliged to obey any further orders, he couldn't had he wanted to. The boat went on ahead and Lonz could not keep hold of the painter, which probably saved his life. For had he held the rope, he would have been bounced off the bottom and against boulders for another half a mile.

Through the pitch and down the falls he was pushed until he was spun into an eddy, and then finally, a pool he could swim. He crawled ashore after the falls were done with him. Barreled over, he blew the water out of nose and mouth. All in all, he told me later, to himself he seemed quite calm after the ordeal. In his mind he had a clear conscience for he had obeyed the maritime maxim about "orders" and "owners" to the letter of Isaiah's last command.

Isaiah, meantime, had gone on with the boat until she struck, as he had foreseen she must, and was smashed to kindling. But

---

[41] To snub the batteau would mean to jump overboard and with the anchor rope hold the craft fast.

Isaiah was not born to be drowned, none of his kind seem to be.[42] Below the falls, he stumbled ashore down where the water was not quite strong enough to float a brick, or a head man. He, too, blew out the surplus of water which he had taken in. With his bear-size hand, he streaked back his wet hair out of his eyes so that he could see. He wrung out the wrists of his shirt-sleeves to keep them from dripping too big of a stream. Then he began his hike back to the luncheon place where the embers of the cook's fire still smoldered.

As he came upon the remnants of the fire, a cloud had come over the sun. The wind drew chill on a man wet to the skin as he was. Besides the fire seemed the right and proper place to wait 'till he learned how Lonz fared.

The cook put a pot on to boil tea. Men of the crew kept their distance. If Isaiah was out of humor earlier, they didn't want to know how his temper was now.

As he stood over the brands, Lonz came up and joined him. The men with courage clustered around, too, half-way sympathetic, half-way curious to hear what Isaiah had to say about the mischance. He wasn't apt to ever say very much, for he was a man of few words, but they all waited for something.

After a time, he looked at Lonz. Men stepped back for they recognized the look on his face. He was near to remark, *"If it hadn't been for you I never would have got into this scrape and lost my best boat!"*

Then Isaiah put behind him any thought of private squaring of accounts. It was all his own fault anyway, and he knew it.

---

[42] Here, Eckstorm had typed, then crossed-through, 'none of the Moreys seem to be.' Isaiah Morey is a name that appears in more than one story and place in her journal.

Forthwith he made a very handsome acknowledgement—for Isaiah anyway.

"Hmf!" he sniffed. "Didn't know the river was *so* bad as that!"

Lonz sipped his tea. Internally he cackled with the fool of it all and the gratefulness to have come through it alive. "Guess you had it worse in the boat."

"Hmf!"

The black-eyed fellow, under his breath remarked something about nearly all the good men being dead now anyway. As he turned away, under his breath, Bill Smith suggested, "We ought to pass the hat to get enough to buy Isaiah another heel calk."

The fellow best versed in the Proverbs of Solomon quoted very aptly, "I also will laugh at your calamity, I will mock when your fear cometh."

Isaiah had smashed his own boat anyway, and that is a pretty good joke to get off on a head man. Moreover, they all knew that there would be nobody drowned on those falls that day, because for the next twenty-four hours, Isaiah was going to be as amenable to a hint as a pig with a ring in its nose. It isn't every day that you can be sure of making the head of the drive think your way.

"But what did Bill Smith know about Isaiah that he wouldn't say?" *you ask.*

"Ah, well, with all the excitement, nobody was much interested in that anymore. Besides, Bill figured he'd store it up for another day—like water behind a cribworks."

"But you know?"

"Assuredly." I smiled. "Maybe if Isaiah had put more than one calk in his boot, Bill wouldn't have had the embarrassing item on him."

## Editor Comment:

The reader may ask, why did Isaiah dare anyone to run the falls with him in the first place? The men were expecting the boss to tell them to pick the jam. They'd have to get in the boats in order to get to the jam, one or two would hold the boat there at the edge of the logs, while others prodded the logs free. The moment the logs let loose, the boatmen would have to hold steady in order to get those men back in the boats when the jam broke, and then all of them would have to 'put the ash to it' in order to get back to the riverbank before the boat was smashed.

It was ugly water and the river was clogged with logs. Their expertise told them someone would be drowned in such exploits. Isaiah knew their apprehension and made the dare because of it. Had Lonz not taken him up on the dare, Isaiah may have, or he may not have, sent a crew out. We will never know.

## Eckstorm's additional notes:

A Rev. Chapin of Holden says he once saw Isaiah Morey buy four bottles of Jamaica Ginger, knock the necks off the bottles and drink four straight.

Isaiah Morey died Bangor, May 18, 1890.

# A RIVER TALE FROM DAN GOLDEN

## How Dan Golden mutinied and John Ross rose to the Occasion.

**It** is quite impossible to tell this story and not to mention by name Mr. Daniel H. Golden; for he particularly requested, and I as particularly promised, that the next time I wrote anything about him I would give his name in full.

I once gave him a copy of a certain book for singing woods songs.[43]

"And am I in it?" he demanded.

"You are. On the twenty-sixth page."

I found the place for him. I watched as he ran a blunt forefinger down the page, as if feeling for a spot to rest it at. Not finding any, he demanded, "And is my name there?"

---

[43] The discussion between Eckstorm and Golden noted here was about 1904. In her later book, "*Minstrelsy of Maine: Folk-songs and Ballads of the Woods and the Coast,*" (1926) Eckstorm included several times the name Dan Golden. The first under the notes for "*Katahdin Green*" (page 76) and a section titled, "*How Dan Golden Made Up A New Song.*" Before singing for her, he prefaced his song with a bit of personal history and stated, "My name is Daniel H. Golden when you write anything about me again, you will put in my name, won't you?" And she held her word. This note shows Eckstorm, as early as 1904, had researched and published a volume of woods songs; that being a full twenty-two years prior to the book noted above. Mr. Golden, by way of Paisley Scotland, would be pickled to know, he was cast as a character and even sings his ballad, in *I Am Penobscot*, by Tommy Carbone (*Burnt Jacket Publishing*, 2023).

His name was not there. It was my mistake thinking he would have connected the verse printed on the page with his name, but I had erred in not identifying him with the lyrics as the person who had given me the ballad. I explained that I did not know him well enough to be sure he would like to have his name there.

He paused, looking critically at the page. "The next time," he remarked absently, "that you write anything about me—you won't forget my name, will you? It is D. H. Golden - - Daniel H. Golden."

After that I fancied that he felt a peculiar interest in my welfare; for when we chanced to meet, his cheerful hail, "And how is the La-a-ady?" conveyed not alone good-will to me, but the information to the loafing public that I was the elect editor of his literary remains.[44]

The present tale does not exploit Mr. Golden's literary work. It is abstracted from the running biographical commentary of head-notes, side-notes, and foot-notes which accompanied the rendering of one of his own songs. He himself thought that, barring some spectacular rescues, when "we did like noble heroes, me an' Boney Davis," this was about the most showy act of his life. It is doubtful if among all the deeds chronicled of Penobscot watermen there is any that stands forth in such naked splendor as this of the way Dan Golden and "Boney" Davis fulfilled their complyment to run all the rapids on the West Branch in the spring of '75 (1875). It is a story of exceeding rashness; for not only did they dare the Grand Falls at a time

---

[44] Crossed out in the typing, but too good not to include as a note, Eckstorm had written, 'It is pure flattery; but still to walk through life addressed as "The Lady" is only one degree less of pomp and pride than to be born a character in one of the "Duchess's" novels.' The Duchess was the pen name of Irish novelist, Margaret Wolfe (Hamilton) Hungerford (1855-1897).

when the water was very bad, but they defied John Ross to his face.

Now John Ross was the Jim Hill of the Maine woods.[45] He was Head of the Drive that year, and what he said went, or the splinters flew. I confess that when Mr. Daniel H. Golden told me this story, I lost a good part of it through suspense as to how he was going to get through what John Ross would have to say at the end of the tale.

"Yes, I was one of Ross's men, you know; worked for him every winter till last winter and was on the West Branch Drive seventeen springs; *got that down?*—from 1867, every winter till last winter, and how many does that make?" (It made nearly forty, I told him.)

"Good. Yes, that's right. Well, me an' Boney Davis,"—(*I wrote him down mechanically as Henry Davis, of Veazie, for I was aware who he meant*)— "we handled boat together. You see I was a waterman, an' a good one; wan't nothin' I couldn't run. An' one year,—yes, that was the spring of '75, me an' Boney made a comply-ment to run everything there was. For says I, 'We are goin' to run everythin' there is on this river and get us a repitation.'"

The heart of the head man flutters, even of the seasoned head man like John Ross, when he finds a man is getting a '*reputation*,' for he knows that neither men nor boats will be spared in the process, and that he must furnish both and stand the losses.

---

[45] Possible reference to James (Jim) Jerome Hill (1838-1916). Known as the *Empire Builder* he was the visionary and executive officer of numerous railroad lines from the Upper Midwest to the Pacific Northwest.

"An' we run everything," went on Danny (*as his friends called him, and he counting me as one*), meaning of course, everything that ever had been run by anyone; for there are places on the West Branch that no mortal man ever ran a boat over and lived to rejoice in his exploit. What that river is, from Ripogenus to Nicatou Island, in mid-summer drought compared to what it is during the rush of the spring freshet when the logs went down—in the days when there were logs to drive and little storage to control the water—are pictures too unlike for the summer tourist to understand.[46]

"An' we run it on paddles," went on Danny. (His meaning, he knew I understood, that being the riskiest way. For with poles you can snub and hold and consider the rocks and eddys. On paddles you must let her, the river, drive as she will.)

"We run drivin' boats an' wangan." (wangan being the mess— —food and clothing and supplies—all the outfit boats) "An' we never swamped a boat."[47]

One might suppose to hear Danny Golden tell the story, that he and "Boney" Davis were the only men on the drive that year who handled a boat (*'handled boat' is the boatman's grammar*). Yet, what a list he did rattle off—each man's boat, and every man in the boat, and every man's place in the boat, bow, stern,

---

[46] Eckstorm means the years before the concrete Ripogenus Dam, which wasn't completed until 1916, controlled the flow.

[47] Meaning boats used for the drive and to clear jams and the supply boats. The head man would enforce prudence, and in the roughest spots, the boats would have to be lifted from the water and carried, upside down, on the shoulders of ten or so men per boat, over a stump-rutted tote road if there were one, or a narrow boulder-strewn carry path. And then, they'd have to return up the path to get the supplies they took out of the boat. So you see, leaving the supplies, 'the wangan' as it was called, in the boat and keeping the boat in the water to run the falls would seem to make sense; until you've seen Ripogenus Gorge or Grand Falls or any number of other places where boats were swamped and men died on the West Branch.

and 'midships—he had all their names memorized—Inmans and Spencers and Hathorns, Smiths, Davises and Doughties, Prouties and Johnsons and Thompsons, Bulger, Gilmore, Burke, Sawyer, White, Murphy, Sutherland, Carsons; and all the Indians, Sauls and Solomons, Mitchells and Francises, Neptunes and Orsons, Sebatisses and Soccalexeses and Sockabasins; and finally one sweet crew which must have specially recommended itself to Saint Patrick, if they ever had occasion to knock at his door— "Slim" McCann, "Mickey" Gallegher, "Bold Jack" Donough, and "Medford" McAloon. I suspected that, with Dan himself and "Boney" Davis, these six names made up one boat's crew; and, if they did, that must have been one of the selectest crews that ever was gathered on the old West Branch Drive.

But who were the midshipmen in his boat matters not; for Dan and Boney were the heroes while the story lasted.

So Dan Golden ran over the roster of the rapids of the West Branch and what they did on each pitch until he got down to the very end of the good things; to Island Falls and the Grand Falls, where Millinocket is now. And as he progressed the attention of all this cloud of witnesses, experts and rivals—Inmans, Spencers, Hathorns and all the rest, became more and more centered upon himself.

"An' when we got down to Rhines's Pitch, I just slid off at luncheon time an' stole the boat, an' I run over all alone and down amongst the whole of 'em.[48]

---

[48] As mentioned at the start of the tale, Golden remembered the year being 1875. Five years prior it was at Rhine's Pitch when Penobscot nation Governor and then river-driver, Joe Attean would be drowned running that stretch of water. The annotated story is in *The Penobscot Man - Life and Death on a Maine River*.

"An' when we got down a little farther,"–(your documentarian be the blame, if I am mixing up different years here, for Danny, in his excitement of reliving the drive, became too eloquent to follow understandingly, and yet, for fear of meeting some sturdy sceptic who would take the bloom off the narration which follows, I have not dared consult Agamemnon and those other leaders of the Greeks, who knew the matter.[49])

"An' when we got down a little farther––it is there where there is a leaning ash-tree on the right side of the river on Island Falls; you will know the place by the ash-tree; and there was four men on a jam there an' the Injun crews had tried, but they couldn't get 'em off, they ain't got the courage of a white man"–(*and there spoke the Irish-man![50] for Indians and Irish never love each other, but I've left it as Dan had said it, but I won't give my opinion on that here, you've read enough of what I have said on the men to know my high esteem of them*)–"an' they all give it up, an' then says I to Boney, 'Me an' you, we'll try that now.'"

Danny nodded to me, and looked at my paper, to be sure I got that down.

"Then we put our midshipmen ashore an' just took the boat ourselves, an' there was four men on that jam waitin' to be saved or drowned, an' they didn't know which; an' we run her down on paddles close past that jam, not stoppin', for we couldn't stop anyhows. An' we yells out to 'em to jump quick, for we was all goin' into the hands of God quick, an' they all made the boat, an'

---

[49] Agamemnon – the mythical King of Mycenae in Greek legends. Meaning Eckstorm did not consult John Ross as she did with the Attean and Prouty story, which was a storyline she revised based on Ross's comments for the 1904 *The Penobscot Man*; but more was said in the later edition (see annotated book already noted).

[50] The editor wonders if Dan Golden, of Paisely, Scotland, near Glasgow in the Lowlands, would make a correction there.

we went tearin' down over the falls, an' the men on the shore we heard 'em a cheerin' an' I see 'em wavin' their hats, an'---"

Here, Danny sprang to his feet and began to gesture and declaim. His white hair almost on edge from his electric excitement. Not a word could I make out until the last, "And so I done like a noble hero, me an' Boney Davis."

But I understood that in this form he must many times have rehearsed the tale to men in saloons and camps, who waited breathlessly as he harangued and then they burst out into tumultuous applause at his close.

"An' so me an' Boney we had come down the West Branch, runnin' everything. An' we had got down to the very last thing on it, the *Grand Falls*, —ever been there? Know where that is?–(*He didn't let me answer; he knew I knew it; and besides he could have been near curtain close of his act on Exchange Street, standing on a stool, telling the story at that point to strangers, and they might not have known; had they shook their heads he'd have likely given them a much grander description than follows*)—"The Grand Pitch of the Grand Falls they can't never run that, no one, that's straight up an' down; but the two miles above that they run when the water ain't too bad. It's two miles down the Grand Falls, and sometimes the water is very bad. It was then, says I to Boney, 'It's the real thing this time.' But you see we had to go because our complyment was to run everything and this was the last thing there was.

"Says Boney, 'We'll have to kick out them–ah, them–er–midshipmen again. Can't have any loose cargo round under foot this trip.' An' the men was a little mad perhaps, but not so much so's if the water hadn't been so bad. Me an' Boney looked at it, an' we seen it was best to be all ready for what was comin' to us. An' we looked at each other an' we begun to strip, an' we didn't stop till we stood just in our boots."–(Those spike-soled boots are the river-driver's salvation; be it sink or swim, he must have his calks on till the time comes.)

Realizing for a moment he was speaking to a widow woman, he whispered, "You understand why, so you'll excuse the imagery."

I nodded, holding back a smile.

"Well, we got all ready to go, an' there we was by our boat with our paddles in hand all ready to shove off, standin' there as I says, mother-naked both of us, but the boots, an' up comes John Ross---"[51]

"John Ross himself? What did he say?"

"Ah, well, he raised a row, that's what," remarked Danny, a trifle contumacious, even after near thirty years. He took his seat again to regain his composure.

"What did he row about?"

"In a lot less words, he said he wouldn't have us a-stealin' his boat to run no–aw, no--no–one of them falls.

"An' we said we was a-goin'.

"An' he said we wan't a-goin'.

"An' we said we was a-goin'.

"An' we went."

Danny made no effort to report dramatically. The triangular duel of words was no doubt fought out under as sulphureous a canopy of profanity as ever overhung the West Branch valley. The substance of the report was that John Ross objected to having his boat smashed for a fool show-off performance, which would appear to have been well within his rights. But Dan and "Boney" insisted that a *complyment* like theirs was a matter of

---

[51] Ross, the head man of all head men, may not have been along the river where the drivers had been running *his* boats prior to Grand Falls, for the Drive is spread out for tens of miles. He could have been at the head or the rear, but here he appeared, assuredly informed by his superintendents what the proceedings of Danny and Boney had been as they came down the river.

honor and that if they were willing to risk their lives, he ought to
be glad to risk his old boat. Besides that, they didn't intend to to
get drowned anyway; they never had been yet, and they hadn't
lost any boat yet, and it would be time enough for him to fuss
when they had lost one.

There was a certain comicality in John Ross, head of all the
Drive, having to argue with two naked day-laborers of his, about
the possession of his own boat, and then having them turn and
shove off with it in spite of him–their bare-backs to him. He may
have gnawed his mustache; but what was he to do about it? Many
a big bully had he fought and beaten, many a mutineer had he
cowed by his imperious will; but how was he to deal with these
men should they come through flushed with victory, heroes in
the eyes of all their mates? John Ross had more at stake from
their *complyment* than just his boat.

When Dan and "Boney" pushed out in their sharp-snouted,
high-bowed driving batteau, standing up in it statuesquely posed,
they did their best to show off, no doubt. Circus acrobats
swinging on aerial trapeses, tight-rope walkers balancing above
a seething crowd, men who habitually perform deeds of hazard
in the public gaze and live upon public plaudits, believing in their
own lucky star, can understand the composure and elation of the
river-driver making a showy exhibition of his skill.

Only a moment they had for posing with their paddles as they
slowly glided out from the shore and the current began to gather
them into its grip. The eyes of everyone along the river-bank are
on them, and they, about to die, take dramatic leave. What a
picture the man in the bow, a figure-head in marble, high up in
that pointed, raking prow, as lightly poised as a Grecian
Mercury! What a contrast the marble fellow in the stern,
crouched like the Discobolus to the long paddle held across his
knee, as, holding it submerged, he gently steers out into the

current, coaxes her head down-stream, and, without visible effort, drives her into the fluted gore of rushing water between two sunken rocks. That was well done and deserved the 'Bravo!' that resounded from the circus spectators.

But now the battle is on. The man in the bow suddenly springs into life, a nude warrior, the type of mankind contending with the elements. Perilously overhanging the great waves, he smites them with his paddle, prodding down upon them like some later George contending with a more devastating dragon. From him the man in the stern now takes direction, promptly obedient, responding to gesture or by instinct, because words come too slow. Without a glimmer of hesitation—to waver would be fatal—he swings the stern in or out as a flutter of the bowman's hand or the balance of his body indicates a rock to be avoided and the side on which to pass it. Spray; foam; the giddy rush of water; the onset of black rocks tearing along upstream through the crowning current; ridgy waves, sharp-spined along the top; round waves, rolling off into white curls; puffy boils, crowning sunken rocks; hiss, roar, tumult, the tumult of a caldron.

What quickness it all requires! What exertions! What a strain of attention! It is the maddest of all mad games, a man's game every part of it. There is no reckoning it out ahead. Where you passed safe yesterday, you are wrecked today. Where you would have been drowned a minute since, you come out unscathed. The great pulses of the River have ebbed or throbbed, and an inch of difference in the water over a rock was life or death.

White, against the green of the branches of the trees across the river, shine the bodies of the boatmen, gleaming in the spray of the falls, dripping like figures in a fountain when a cross-sea strikes and boards them.

"Ho! but Danny caught it good that time!" cries an on-looker, as a big boil soused Dan in the bow from head to boots while he crouched, prying hard to fetch her round.

"Close! Lord, wan't that a shave!?" exlaims another.

But the rock was passed before the question could be answered and the boat thrashes on.

"Good for Boney! Ain't he the strong man on a paddle!"

"Holy smoke! She more'n grazed that time; see her quiver?"

With such commentary as that, did those on shore accompany events. The man in the bow and the man in the stern were thinking, too–odd detached thoughts that drifted through their minds.

"Nasty big boil that one! Looks like a toadstool turned upside down," thinks Dan in the bow.

"*Just like a cushion, soft enough to sit on,*" comments Boney to himself, as it rushed by him.

"And my birthday comes the twenty-second, If I live till then, I'll like to go to Chemo again." thinks Danny in the bow.

"*And I ain't a-goin' to buy no more tobacco at wangan prices. I'll wait till I git out to the Forks,*" resolves Boney. Though, if he gets through this, every man's plug will be his to bite from, if he wishes, for a week to come.

"She hit that time," thinks Danny. "I wonder what John Ross will say when he sees her pitch scarred."

"*Wish I could swim like them thole-pins,*" thinks Boney.

Some loose thole-pins, which the driving-boats use instead of row-locks, have held his attention more than anything else.[52] They have become almost demoniacally alive, moving with the boat, at first rattling around over her dirty bottom-boards, then swashing in the streaked scum upon the first water she took in. Now, with more water on the floorboards, they were swimming free from end to end of the boat as she lifted and fell. Boney never looks in the direction of the bowman, where it is his

---

[52] Thole-pins are the fulcrum for the oars, attached to the gunwale. In those years, they'd have been made of wood.

business to keep an eye for signals, without seeing the vagrant thole-pins sloshing in the bottom of the boat.

Yet it is great running now–all sorts of water but good. There are crooked channels; loose logs; side-jams; boils, and pitches. Sometimes a splintered ledge rips the water like a circular saw, sending it up in a spirt of spray; sometimes a round rock, lying deeper, throws a turk's-head of boiling water; or, lying deeper yet, is crowned with a glassy roll. The boatmen hate them all, swear at them, revile them, make it a personal quarrel.

"Thought you got me that time? Take that, will ye!" The bowman yells out loud and stabs at a rock viciously. The lunk-headed, hard-hearted, generally reviled rock growls back, as the old boat wallows and thrashes through. Wet! Everything is dripping, and the men are as wet with sweat as with water. It is the sweat of exertion and fear that Dan is wiping off his forehead with his elbow.

"*Wish I could swim like them fellers,*" thinks Boney as the thole-pins take a little jaunt toward Dan; it has become almost a refrain with him, but he drops it short. "*Gee-soo! We are on the pitch now! Now for it!*" he warns himself.

That pitch is a bad place. Before the old boat takes it, Boney looks at the sun, and then he sights ahead. To him, crouching in the stern, there appears, just level with the peak of the high bow, an old, black-headed pine; the boat points just at the top-spray of it, and then, as she swoops down the steep incline, the sharp nose drops like an index finger, drawing the whole figure of the tree, while the thole-pins run forward and frolic between Danny's boots. It takes the breath away; one feels it in the stomach-pit, like riding a high swing.

Her nose is pointed straight for the big boil below and Boney, now overlooking his partners head, can see the stem of the pine tree, while the water runs in roily foam far up into the trough of the bow.

Smart work for Dan now, if she is ever to rise it! But she mounts, though it breaks over her.

"*By jingo! but I'll get my feet wet sure!*" thinks Boney, stepping back as the water runs aft. She mounts with her snout, her head, her belly out, the whole fore-part of her upreared like Leviathan rising from the ocean bed. The water drips from her edges in beady strings. Almost she seems to take a look ahead of herself. Danny's paddle falls short, he has been carried up so high, and on Boney in the stern falls the whole labor of holding her to her stride.

The men down river are now the new spectators of this leg of the *complyment* they've all heard about.

"Good for Boney!"

"Ain't he the strong boy on the paddle!"

Boney feels the shoulder of a big wave lifting, lifting beneath him, raising him upward; he sees the water inside wavering to a level, then setting down on Danny's slope. He feels the buckling of the bottom-board as his own end leaves the water, and he watches the snout of her decline and waver along the bright line of the shore.

Boney thinks, "Ain't Danny pink! an' how his boots shine!" He doesn't realize that he himself is roseate; that it's sweat, not water, which is dripping from him; that his eyes glitter and the strained smile on his face, caused from his digging to set his paddle where needed, is set so hard that his jaws will ache the next day and he not know the reason.

But they are getting through. Slower now; for they are running out of the bad water. Slower, because Boney is holding back a little with his setting-pole. Slower, because she is heavy with water and does not ride so lightly. Slower, too on purpose, perhaps in order to give the men who are running along the banks time to gather at the landing and give them a triumphal welcome.

There is a black crowd of them there already when Boney lays the old boat in very delicately, as if she were a china cup, which might break upon the pebbles. Then they step out, two pink figures, elegantly clad in boots. They are self-possessed but a trifle shy, very shame-faced yet wholly unabashed.

They grin, but they do not speak.

A dozen men had laid hold of the big Maynard boat and roused her up on the beach. The main of the crowd holds back and buzzes. Steps forward and then draws back again. They part to give way.

Danny can see John Ross striding down the carry path, his large frame filling the narrow trail.

The crowd is not quite sure how John Ross is going to take this; it leaves him to speak first. But the culprits, standing each side of the bow of the big boat, right arm and left resting on her nose between them as the high bow snuggles beneath their elbows. On their other sides, a left arm and a right hold out their long paddles upright, as if they stood as the supporters of a shield. They wait, grinning.

"A hell of a blowing up coming maybe," whispers one to the other. "But I don't care now. That show was worth all the heck about to break loose."

"And what did John Ross say?" (I was as anxious as the men on the riverbank.)

Dan sat in meditation.

I supposed he was reviewing some private mortification, or seeking some polite and orthodox way of conveying the substance of John Ross's displeasure; for what else could Ross do but make it hot for mutineers like these?

But it seemed that Dan had thoughts that made him smile just then. He was thinking how he and Boney had fulfilled their complyment to the letter and had won applause from a full house, and finally how they had had the *summam laudem*[53] set upon their work. For John Ross did not play the great man, but *was* it. It was this which Dan had remembered after all those thirty years. For at length he spoke.

"An' when John Ross got there, he come right forward 'mongst the whole of 'em, an' he clapped me on the shoulder, an' he says, 'Dan, you done great!' An' then they all bust out a-cheerin'.

Dan gazed across the room. "Then the Old Man added, 'But,' says Ross looking from me to Boney, the two of us naked behind our paddles, Ross he says, 'I was afraid one spell watching, I was a-goin' to lose...to lose two' "—Danny swallowed, a river-driver among river-drivers, he was a gentleman among ladies, he considered the words—" 'to lose two' " —and then he swallowed again and broke it off differently, —" 'two good men,' says Ross."

Dan rubbed his chin. "And it might be so!" he added sagely.

* * *

### Editor Note

The interview that took place with Golden may have been for material intended for Eckstorm's 1904 issue of, *The Penobscot Man*. However, the story was not included in that book.

It certainly reads like a river-driver tall-tale. As Eckstorm interviewed Ross for her book and she revised the chapter, "Death of Thoreau's Guide" on Ross's *river-driver amongst*

---

[53] Summam laudem - high praise.

*river-driver* assessment of Charles Prouty,[54] it is possible she asked Ross about this Dan Golden story. But then again, she was a lady amongst gentlemen *and* river-drivers, and just as likely, she let Golden have the last word on it as per her mention on not asking Agamemnon about it. Either way, it is a good story for what Eckstorm made of it. So, I will borrow the words of Ross on Eckstorm's re-write of the Attean story and say, *'That reads very good now. That is very inter-est-ing.'*

_____

[54] In the 1926 edition of *The Penobscot Man*, Eckstorm added an appendix to clarify certain points. By that year all the characters had passed away and she felt free to add additional background. She wrote, "*the story of Joe Attien's death was <u>re- written and wholly recast</u> to satisfy John Ross,*" indicating it wasn't as she originally wrote it from her research. The annotated edition, *The Penobscot Man - Life and Death on a Maine River* (2022) by Tommy Carbone, provides additional story details and Eckstorm's journal notes with her further research into that matter - interesting indeed!

# A RIVER TALE – LIFE GULLIVER

**How Life Gulliver laughed when Crazy Bill Harris met a misadventure.[55]**

**It** is first principles among river-drivers that the man who says nothing when a boat is smashed is a good man to work for. They have to refer back to the axiom frequently, because boats do get smashed and there are subsequent reckonings with the head man. That is, there used to be; this is a true tale of an era now departed.

"Smashing" is the correct word. When a batteau goes to pieces she is not merely sprung in the seams a trifle. The whole bottom is ripped off like the sole of an old shoe; she may be laid open from end to end like a split codfish; she may be ground into splinters too small for souvenirs. The tremendous force of the river rends her joint from joint; nothing is left to be mended.

## Bad Place for a Carry

"Babb had the West Branch Drive that year," said the old river-driver, "and I was in Waldo Davis's boat - good careful man Waldo was. We were down on the head of

---

[55] The character, Life, was Eliphalet Gulliver, a head man of the drive. The pronunciation of his name is: E-life-a-let; and thus *Life* was used for short.

Ambajemackomas[56] and were trying to make the carry;—you know how close that carry lies to the head of the falls; never could see how the Lord ever happened to think of putting a carry in any such place, for when the eddy above gets chocked with logs it's all any man can do to work in to that landing without being carried down over Gulliver Pitch.[57]

"We were poking in through the logs pretty well, when something above crowded them and began to sweep the eddy. Nothing for it but for us to jump out and caper for the shore. The old boat had to go down over the falls with the logs and was smashed to kindlings.

"Babb was on the drivers' path and Waldo hunted him up and says, *'I just lost a boat for you.'* That's no good news to a head man.

Babb asks, 'Did ye? Anyone hurt? Boys all right?'

'Boy's all right,' says Waldo.

'Well, it's all right then,' says Babb.

That's about as cool as one could take it. Not a word about the boat. It ain't every head man who'll react as that."

"Did you ever hear of a man who laughed to see his own boat stove?" I asked.

---

[56] Hubbard in, *Guide to Moosehead Lake and Northern Maine (annotated edition),* noted Ambajemackomas was the original Native name of Elbow Lake, which is between North Twin Lake and the dam below it (before Quakish Lake), but improperly applied to renaming of the falls at Gulliver Pitch, on the West Branch below Ripogenus Carry. Originally the pitch was named for Lem Gulliver, who was drowned there; brother of Elifealet Gulliver.

[57] Gulliver Pitch doesn't get noted on many current-day maps, but it's the stretch of white water after the Ripogenus Gorge and before reaching the Horserace Pitch. Even the river-driver telling Eckstorm the story was using the newer applied name of Ambajemackomas by that date, but still calling the pitch, Gulliver Pitch.

He shook his head incredulously. "Couldn't say I ever did. They ain't common that kind, not on this river."

"But, Lewey Ketchum told me about one such himself."[58]

"Well," he admitted cautiously, "guess Lewey'd ought to know."

"It was about Life Gulliver, the same who was with his brother Lem, way back in the forties (the 1840s), when Lem was drowned on Gulliver Pitch and the place got its name."

He nodded. "I've heard 'bout that. I knew Life Gulliver. But I don't see yet what Life found to laugh at about getting a boat stove."

So it fell to me to tell the old river-driver something he had never heard before, a slight and childish tale but rather a merry one.

### Back in the 1840s - Near Chesuncook Lake

The man who can handle a boat is like the man who can handle a horse well—he likes to see what he can make it do. There are tricks too trifling to be worth trying—like making a horse mount a billiard table—unless they can be done with ease

---

[58] Lewey (Louis, Lewis) Ketchum was friends with the Hardy family. In the woods and on the rivers, he was known as a terribly-able guide, so much so, Manly Hardy (per his own journal notes) hired Lewey several times in the 1860s. They traveled the Penobscot to the Allagash and St. John rivers; around Castine and Bagaduce and up the Penobscot to Brewer; and also the Machias and Passadumkeag Rivers. Ketchum was a respected man on the river-drives. The bosses trusted him to head crews of men. The story, *Working Nights* (in, *The Penobscot Man - Life and Death on a Maine River*) features Lewey being in charge of booming logs with a capstan raft on a northern Maine lake. A distinguished picture of Lewey is included in the appendix of that book. He died in 1922.

and certainty; not everyone can be sure of doing the trifle with distinction. So it was here—a brook-drive, a tiny fall, a negligible risk, glory lacking, spectators also lacking—nothing in the world to tempt a real waterman to display; but then—no one but a real waterman could do it; and no one but a very good man or a very poor man would even try to do it. Even then the Evil One must have helped Lewey to think of it, for never since the world began had it entered any other man's head to run that place.

## Hardly Know It in Spring

Lewey was working for Eliphalet Gulliver that spring, and Life, as he was always called, had been lumbering up Mud Brook, which comes out of Mud Pond, which inlets about half way down the east side of Chesuncook.[59] Mud Brook is about a mile long, the outlet of one small pond, nothing more. In summer it will not float a canoe,—(but I am speaking of the old days before the great Ripogenus Dam flowage created the whole Country)[60]—but in the spring the freshet gives it water enough to take down a brook drive; it flows fairly well then and for a few weeks one would hardly know it. The lower end of the stream

---

[59] This is just south of the location on Suncook Lake where the Cuxabexis Drive of Joel Saul came in. See story and map in chapter, *The Ultimate Jewel*.

[60] Eckstorm is making this point to date the geography of the maps of the 1840s. The first built Ripogenus Dam, the one of small early construction and the small dam between Chesuncook and Ripogenus, did not have an impact on the water levels and created thoroughfares as seen today. The interested reader should compare the below map to a current-day shoreline depiction.

was flowed back from the lake, but it has one little pitch on it just as it leaves the pond.

This the drivers had improved by putting in a low dam which they had aproned out into a roll, so that it made a smooth slide with a nice little boil at the end as it dipped into the pool below. This was a great round pool where the current fanned out as it passed through, most of the water rushing straight out at the lefthand corner, but a part, when the spring freshet raised its banks over, wandered off into the alders at the right and rippled through them to regain and join the main stream below. Except for *one thing* the place would not have tempted the rising ambition of a ten-year-old; but that *one thing* made it interesting to Lewey.

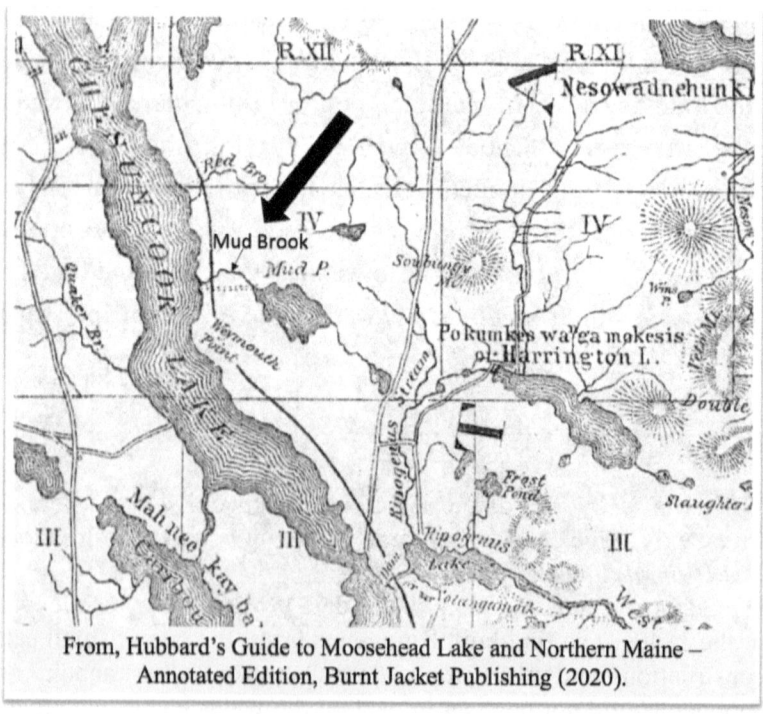

From, Hubbard's Guide to Moosehead Lake and Northern Maine –
Annotated Edition, Burnt Jacket Publishing (2020).

### Unhandy Rock

The *one thing* Lewey noted with attention was a great bald-faced rock which rose from the farther side of the pool dead in front of the little dam. It was as high as a room and square-set to the current. Every log that came over the dam ran bunt against that rock and staggered back as if dizzy from the impact, then turned on its heel and fled swiftly down the current as if glad to get away from the place. That big rock stood square in the shot of the current, bound to pick up anything that came over the dam, about as unhandy a rock as could have been put there. As it was but a step to take the boats out above the dam and lug them down to the flowage of Suncook, no one, until Lewey came along, had ever thought of running the dam.

But Lewey, bound up the pond under explicit orders, stopped to look at the place and Satan found him reasonable. Life Gulliver had sent Lewey in charge of his own boat and another boat to strip the camp at the head of the pond. *'And when you've done that,'* directed Life, *'take out the boats above the dam and I will send up men to lug them down to the flowage.'*

Nothing at all was left to Lewey's discretion. But Lewey stopped and looked at the rock. He looked too long.

It was a bright April afternoon, no leaves out, snow in the woods in deep grey drifts, but the catkins were swelling and the chickadees were whistling their spring song in the low birches. The brook was plopping along gayly, a swift, shoal stream, brown with the overflow and capped by little white-maned ripples that mimicked the big surges of the great river rapids, but were such humorous little waves, six inches, eight inches high perhaps, just right for pea-pod canoes and shingle batteaus, with June-bugs for midshipmen and grasshoppers at the paddles; and some of them went smack at the face of the rock and scooted off downstream in the undertow, while some that struck out to the right lapped the alder stems, and raced around behind the rock to meet their fellows below.

A song sparrow, invisible against his background of streaky alder catkins, was making a racket where the gnarly old willow thrust out branches beaded with silvery buds.

A red squirrel, traveling by the overhead route, leaped on the crest of the rock and sat there chirring. A gay-winged "question-sign" butterfly settled to the sap running from a maple sprout scored by some passing load and flapped his red wings till, raising them suddenly, he eclipsed their splendors by the curtain of their under-darkness and vanished from sight without departing.

## Spring in His Blood

The spring got into Lewey's blood—it seemed to stay there perpetually in those days, for no man went before him when Lewey Ketchum was present. Then something whispered, *'Think you could do it, Lewey?'* And he said to John Reed, of Bradley, who was with him, a good man, *'We could run that place by smart work, John.'*

And John, in proof that he was a good man fell in with the suggestion. *'All right, anything you say, Lewey.'*

The business of the day being decided upon, they went up to the camp along with Crazy Bill Harris and his boat and looked after all as was directed. It was a winter lumber-camp to be stripped for desertion, and every scrap was to be removed. Life Gulliver knew that he was sending a good man when he sent Lewey to strip-down the camp.

So Lewey and the men brought out and folded all the great camp spreads used by the men in their bunks, and he took the bags and Kennebeckers[61] in which the men kept their clothing, and what was left of a barrel of pork that it might not sour in the pickle, and the molasses in the keg to keep the bears from getting it, and the cook's bread-board and what salt and flour there was and all the odds and ends of the better sort. But to Bill Harris and his Frenchman partner fell all the junk about the camp. They made a great heap of it down on the shore—old harnesses, binding chains, pieces of snub-warp, drags, and old sled-shoe, the iron bean-pot, the tug-chains, a spare whiffle-tree,[62] old halters and halter-rope, the irons of a sled-pole, some battered axes and all the old horse-shoes (every scrap of iron being valuable up there), but chiefly the cook's outfit of tin and iron-ware, battered by seven months of hard service. It was a nondescript pile, enough to fill Bill Harris's old boat pretty well to the brim.

## Like A Gypsy Camp

"Hey!" cried Crazy Bill, who of course was not crazy but only rattle-brained, "looks like a Gypsy camp in flush times. I've got the stuff"—and he threw in a broken-handled pitch-fork atop the heap—"to spread the whole West Branch with junk and raise a

---

[61] Kennebeckers - a type of suitcase.
[62] A whippletree, or whiffletree, is used to distribute force evenly through linkages of draught animals in harnesses. The animals used at this time (1840s) were most likely oxen and housed for the winters at the farms scattered throughout the north woods, such as Chamblerlain Farm, Pittston Farm, and Grant Farm. Eckstorm noted horses weren't used on the West Branch Drive at Ripogenus Carry until around 1890.

jim-dandy crop of tinware. Just fork it out on both banks." With a grunt, he threw aboard a litter of old harness. "And my eye little Moses! won't you begin to see things grow—two-quart pails on all the rozb'ry bushes an' pint-cups on all the blueb'ry bushes an old horseshoes turnin' up their prongs for luck at the upper end of ev'ry carry!"

Then he attempted to dance a jig on a pile of log chains, playing the tune on the cook's dishpan. "I'm goin' into the business of raisin' junk for a livin' while Lewey there lays on them counterpanes in the sun and dreams himself away into a state of heavenly blisteredness," he said, kicking up the heel of his spiked-sole boot.

"There!" said he, running down to the water with a big, bailed coffee-pot, and lightly giving it a kick which sent it circling high in the air whence it descended with a splash into the water, "jus' see what I can do distributin' tinware when I try! Here, French, give me seven of them tin plates and let's show 'em what a first-class circus performer Mr. Barnum lost when I went out of the business! Now this is what I call lettin' go of your domain."

Probably the word he steered for was "legerdemain," but he had improved upon it, for none of his domain ever came back to him. He stood, the energetic center of a fountain of tinware which rose circling and descended on all sides of him but never within reach.

"There," explained he, fishing for some of it which had not fallen too far out from the shore, "there's lots of ways of loadin' a boat with this sort o' a cargo."

"If you unload anything like you load up, Bill, you'll cover an acre with your dunnage," said John Reed.

"Oh, 'twill be worth the price of admission to see me unload. I'm goin' to stick the pitchfork right up atop so'st it will be handy."

## The Journey Starts

When Bill was tired of his fun, the two boats paddled down the pond in company toward the dam at the outlet where Lewey had been told to take out and wait for help. But Lewey had not gone into any explanations of his own plans with Bill. He thought it enough, that when he got down well before the dam, he had turned and waved his hand toward the shore and shouted, "Set her ashore in there, Bill. Go in and wait."

Having given his orders, Lewey himself steered straight for the rolling dam. It was a jolly little leap for the batteau to make, and it felt good to feel her buckle to it and take it like a horse. Into the boil she plunged flat-breasted and rose and shook herself and the next instant would have run whang into the big rock; but Lewey worked the bow for all he was worth and John Reed swung the stern around until she turned almost as if on a pivot and shot just clear of the rock and so down the current to the taking-out place.

## Enjoyed It All

Now, Life Gulliver was there waiting as Lewey pulled in. He had been sitting there smoking his pipe and enjoying the day, watching a red squirrel. A chickadee came up and said, "Phoebe, phoebe!" as they do in spring, and a great fire-topped logcock[63] had swept over him in its billowy flight toward the tall hemlock that rose behind the alders where the ground was higher. Life was glad to see all this and to watch the alder fringes swinging

---

[63] Logcock was the lumberman's term for the pileated woodpecker; the 'cock of the woods.'

and to hear the pleasant sweep of the current they whistled as the brook rushed by. He was in a sunny mood.

So, when he saw Lewey and John Reed fetch their boat clear of that big rock he couldn't help but feel approval of their skill. It came to him that he and his brother Lem had always been good in a boat together; that was before Lem got drowned on Ambajemackomas. The thought crossed like a little cloud athwart the sun, the memory of that day when Gulliver Pitch acquired its name forever because his brother Lem had died there. And then the little cloud grew bigger and darker and he cried out, pointing up the river. "You oughtn't to let those boys do that, Lewey!" Life knew Bill Harris was good at a paddle, but he was no Lewey. The head man shook a finger at his foreman to get his attention, all the while wondering why Lewey had given such instruction to Bill.

Lewey, closer to the shore bending over the boat beside him, straightened up and looked back to where Life had his finger aimed. Above the roll of the dam Lewey saw it—the black snout of Crazy Bill's boat poking out by the bushes as she took the fall. (When he told me the story, some fifty plus years after it occurred, he laughed before he told the rest of the story.)

Crazy Bill never stopped to think, never was known to; where Lewey led he followed, hoping heaven would have mercy on him if he needed it. Which was needed very much just then. Over the pitch he bounced, urging the boat ahead. When he struck the boil he whooped and then she slammed straight into the side of that big, bold-faced rock which towered high above his head.

### Spray of Tinware

There's some momentum in a bog boat loaded with scrap-iron, when it is going an eight-mile gait or better. When the nose of that boat hit that rock, it didn't rest there quietly cosseted in a lady's hand. There was a smash and the flying of chips. The boat was shivered from end to end, and then it began on the tin-ware and what Crazy Bill could do with seven tin plates wasn't a circumstance to what that rock could do with a boat-load. The air was full of scrap-iron. It was tossed up in intricate patterns— woven in with binding chains and old hawser, plus bean-kettles and hames and tugs[64] and halter-ropes—mixed in with old horse-shoes for luck and tea kettles and tin-plates and the dishpan—the whole stirred up with the broken pitch-fork as if the invisible Spirit of Evil was making hay of all his old junk. The men, too, went up in the melee and they all rained down on the pool together.

The Frenchman managed to pull himself ashore among the alders behind the big rock; but Crazy Bill went down with the current and never stopped till he reached the eddy, and even then, he wondered at bringing up short of the flowage of Chesuncook. All the junk went to the bottom where most of it probably lies to this day.

When Life Gulliver saw all those pots and kettles and pans and bits of harness flying through the air he sat down and laughed and laughed and laughed. It seemed as if he couldn't stop. All that day long by spells he would burst out into jets of laughter that sometimes grew into great eruptions of mirth. He shook like a jelly just to think of what he had seen. Even the mention of tinware after that day brought on an explosion. But there was something he didn't say; not one word about it.

"And he never said a word about the boat; he was a good man to work for," said Lewey.

---

[64] Parts of the horse's harness outfit; used for draft horses.

At the Maine Boomhouse museum at Chesuncook Lake many artifacts are on display. Several of the exhibited items are noted to have been found in the lakes and river. We may now know a story for some of them. In this display there are axe heads, horseshoes, spikes, and other rusted metal parts from the river-driving and lumbering era.

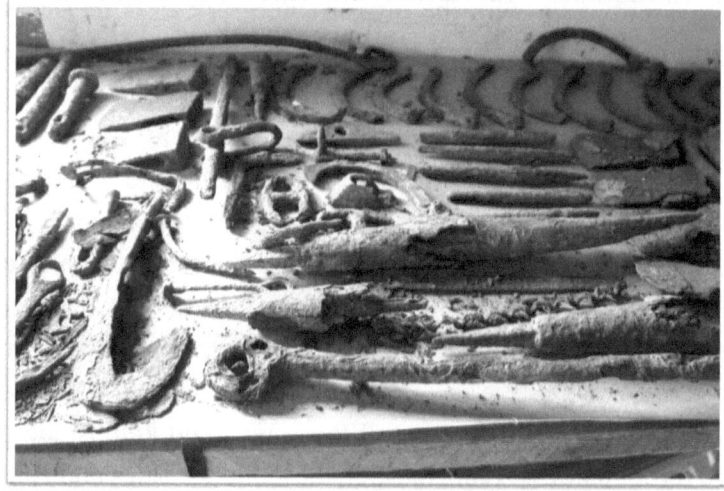

*Editor's Photo*

*Courtesy of the West Branch Historical Preservation Committee*

# THE BROAD-AXE MAN

## Editor Note

There are several connections between Fannie Hardy Eckstorm and her friend David Stone Libbey. Those instances are explored in the books, *The Penobscot Man - Life and Death on the Maine River* and *David Stone Libbey - He Was Penobscot*.

In this essay, the connection comes through David's brother-in-law, James White.

Eckstorm added this note in her journal:

"The following was taken down in 1916 from James H. White, of Newport, Maine, brother-in-law of David Stone Libbey. A version of it was printed in the magazine section of the *Lewiston Journal*, but I never saw a copy of it; published during the war, probably 1918. They paid $4.50 for it, but it was a good sketch."

On September 24, 1916, Eckstorm visited Newport, Maine. She spent time with James White, his wife, Lydia (sister to David Libbey); their son, Dr. Louis White, his wife Gertrude; and Abba Libbey Young, David's youngest sister, and her daughter, Maude. Gertrude White was Gertrude Young White, daughter of Abba and Charles Young. Eckstorm wrote of this, "It was a closely related family."

From her superb knowledge of woodcraft, Eckstorm hewed and broadened this story from the conversation had that evening with James White.

## The Broad-Ax Man

**The** owners and the Master Builder had locked horns. Commerce, represented by the prospective owners of the *Mary Ann Smith*--(her real name now forgotten)–called for a schooner of large tonnage and light draught to enter shallow harbors closed to vessels of the usual type. Goods were waiting there, goods were wanted there, but other vessels were too deep when they had the capacity, too small when they had the draught. So the owners ordered the Master Builder to design a vessel for them after their own ideas.

"The dammed Jerseyman," muttered the Master Builder, hating his commission. When he turned out a vessel, he wanted her to be a beauty, not a cargo-hog.

"See here!" said he; "if you build her that way, you'll have to have a drop centerboard. That means mortising through the keel. It's a blame shame to cut up her back-bone that way. To make her stiff enough you'll have to get a whale of a keel for her, and the Lord Only knows where you'll find it. The tree never grew in Maine that would dress out that size; if it did, I never heard of it. Will you hunt your own timber or will you send to Oregon for it?"

Now, the owners were not sailor men. If they had been they would have felt just as the Master Builder did. But those rich cargoes beckoned to them, and the profits were sure and large, and a vessel of that type would wipe out competing owners, at least until they got other craft like this one. The jibe of "Jerseyman" did not sting them at all. But inasmuch as they were timber experts and knew the stuff that makes a vessel, the last thrust of the Master Builder went home.[65] Hardwood for keels! (is what they were thinking). Douglas fir, sure, it is big stuff, but it was not their idea of keel timber. Perhaps they suspected that the Master Builder had called for a keel-piece needlessly large, one that he knew could not exist, in order to make them give up their chosen model of the *Mary Ann Smith* that was to be. So they called in the timber explorer, who was a Master Broad-Axe Man, who told the tale to me.[66]

"White," said the owner, "you know the woods if any man does. Can you get me a big stick for a keel, a whopping big stick an old lounder of a keel?"

"As big as grows?" asked White. "What does the mould call for?"

"You wouldn't believe me if I told you," said the owner. "The original dimensions." He handed White the drawing. "Look at 'em over."

The Master Builder had called for a hard-wood timber to dress out 24 by 28 inches, and 46 feet long! To this were to be joined two end timber, 14 and 16 feet long–a 76-foot keel overall. The length was nothing; but the size of that center stick was appalling. The tree that made it would have to be three feet

---

[65] James White had mentioned the builder said he'd have to go to Oregon for the timber. The implication was to obtain Douglas Fir, an evergreen conifer that is native to western North America. In those days, there were still large specimens of the trees available in the western part of the United States; some had been claimed to be over 350 feet in height.

[66] James White, with his brother-in-law David Stone Libbey, was a river-driver, lumberman, and supplier of ship knee timber. The two were experts in not only timber surveys and harvesting of quality timber, but also in dressing ship timber by use of a broad-axe to builder specifications.

through at nearly fifty feet from the ground. It must be yellow birch or rock maple, possibly beech, all of them trees inclined to branch low down.

The owner watched as James White surveyed the drawing and the figures with his eyes. "White, can you do it?" Did you ever see the tree that could become such a keel? Can you find that keel for me?" The owner, doubting a tree could be found in Maine, went on, "Or, must we go to Oregon?"

White knew the implication of the last question. Going to Oregon meant putting a softwood timber where every tradition of the trade called for hardwood. Even the owners hated the thought of it. But they dared not ask the Master Builder to pare down his specifications when they had fathered a nondescript like the *Mary Ann Smith* on him. They must win or be jeered at.

White, still holding the paper, dropped his arm to his side. "Think you can find it, White?" the owners asked, anxiously.

"If it is standing in the State of Maine, I can," replied White, confidently. Yet, when he did find it, it proved to be not in the State of Maine, but just across the line in New Hampshire.

It was the great rock maple that grew on Mt. Kearsarge, cut in 1871 by James White of Newport, for Simonton and Holyoke of Portland, Maine. It is the record keel timber of all the Maine shipyards and the pity of it is that it had to go into a freak like the *Mary Ann Smith*, or whatever her name was. But commerce is supreme and sometime master builders created *Red Jackets* and *Dreadnoughts*,[67] and sometimes they made merely *Mary Ann Smiths*.

Then began the search for the timber. James White knew all the woods in Maine and far over into New Brunswick; he knew

---

[67] Red Jacket a clipper built in 1853 in Rockland, Maine. The Dreadnought, of the same year, from Newburyport, MA.

all the lumbermen and timber explorers; all the deer hunters and trappers; all the woodsmen of all types. He had only to ask his friends if they had ever seen or heard of such a tree to eliminate from his search most of the northeastern woods. It seemed as if all the big trees, like the good Indians,[68] were gone long before.

From town to tote road, White heard:

"Fifty years ago, I saw, or heard tell, of such a tree."

"My grandfather used to tell of a tree——."

"When my great grandfather first came to Maine, there was a tree——."

The tales were of the past. The winter was getting along. He must have the timber out before the sledding broke up, and as yet there was no trace of the big keel.

White drifted westward, crossed the Maine line and was hunting for the tree up along the hills of the Saco Valley, in a country so wild and broken that it still held valleys unravished by the explorer. It was one of those bitterly cold winters of the early seventies; when the snow came early and piled up deep, and the frost was severe. Every day White put on his snowshoes and went up among the hills hunting. Then, at last, one day under the side of the hither Kearsarge (for there are two mountains in New Hampshire called Kearsarge) he found a great yellow birch which he hoped might do.[69]

Then he took stock of where he was. The snow was lying five feet to five feet and a half deep. The magnificent tree was well up on the mountain side. He'd need a road, two miles long,

---

[68] Eckstorm here is not making the good vs. bad comparison; but a comparison of the stock of trees, like people, to what they once were. Original, strong, built of quality character from the north woods.

[69] Mt. Kearsarge midway between North Conway, NH and North Fryeburg, Maine.

shoveled out of all that snow to sled the trunk out of the woods. Even if, after proving the wood was found sound and fit, it would be a hard and expensive undertaking to get the timber out.

Still, better contented than he had been any night before, he started down from the mountain, leaving the sunset at his back and snowshoed toward Chatham, where he expected to pass the night. He was trudging along wearily toward food and fire, when off to one side he heard an axe. If there was a camp near, he would beg shelter and save some miles of travel.

He found a farmer chopping cordwood. The farmer asked him some questions.

"You don't look familiar to me. Are you not from around here?" asked the farmer.

"Yes, I'm a stranger, I suppose. From across the border, in Maine."

The farmer offered White a slice of cranberry bread. "My wife always sends me off with enough for days, not merely a few hours."

"Much obliged!" James broke off a chunk.

"Are you here hunting?"

"In a way. More exploring, really. Scouting for timber."

The farmer eyed him. "Any luck?" he asked.

"Fairish," was White's reserved reply. He told how he had found a yellow birch up on the mountain side.

"Whereabouts?" The farmer held back a grin.

"Where a brook made its way down. A couple of miles from the tote road." White wondered if the farmer would know the tree. Anyone who'd ever happened upon it, would never have forgotten the sight of it. He went on. "It might do for the shipbuilder's need. Certainly she seems to be good." White wiped his face with a rag. He hadn't realized he was walking at a crisp pace to find shelter and had started to perspire. "Sure would be a job to get it down out of there."

The native listened with attention. He asked a few questions as to the need. When he spoke, his words were like apples of gold in pictures of silver to White.

"Say, stranger, you don't know it, but you're headed right now for the biggest tree in all this part of the country." The farmer tied on his snowshoes.

As the two walked along over the powder of snow, the farmer made acquaintance with James White. He had read articles by the man's brother-in-law, David Libbey. The two talked of hunting and lumbering. By the time they reached the tree, White had an invitation to lodge at the farmer's home.

"There she is." The farmer proudly pointed.

White's mouth opened. It was, as the farmer promised, a towering rock maple, a wonder for size, straightness and beauty. It held its girth up, up, and up before it tapered or branched out.

"Sir, I thank you for bringing me here. I've been searching for this tree for months." White put a hand along the bark. "Who owns it? Do you know?"

"Sure, I know him." The farmer replied, reservedly.

"Do you think he will sell it?"

The farmer could have cut that tree for the past twenty winters; but he hadn't. He couldn't ever see it going to cordwood, no never. He had thought maybe someone would eventually come looking for quality board-wood. It had always struck him how the tree had never been scouted before. Now he knew.

"For your purpose, yes, I will," was the farmer's reply.

White nodded. He walked around the tree. "If I cut it down and prove it and it proves false, how much have I got to pay for it?"

"One dollar." The farmer figured, being no lumberman himself, that to take down the tree he couldn't ever do it himself. If the tree did not prove to be what White needed, then he'd at least have a felled tree to sell for board-wood with plenty of cordwood left over.

And that is, for a dollar damage, White might cut the tree and leave it where it fell, if it did not suit him. That is what is meant when they say, "Simonton's great keel was bought for a dollar, standing."

The dollar changed hands, and back the next day, with a man to help him, came James White. The snow was lying packed six feet deep at that place, but they dared not fell the tree without bedding it well by cutting small trees for it to fall on, lest it break itself or bury itself too deep for loading. They had to shovel out around the butt; to study its plumb, the wind, how to get the cattle to it, and how to put in the scarf. It took fine calculation to fall such a tree.

Then they laid on with their axes, with the alternating, rhythmic swing of perfect axemen, their blades biting deep and smoothly at every clip. Such a stump as that must be cut like a piece of cabinet work. Besides, it was the axeman's pride to leave a smooth stump, many of the old pine stumps were almost as smooth as if they had been sawed.

At last, under the blows of the axemen, the great tree quivered, cracked, stood, swayed, leaned a bit, then began to sweep evenly downward without haste, until finally, gathering speed it rushed to its fall. The crash made the snow fly as it buried its head, and falling on the springy bed prepared, threw its huge butt high in the air, like a breaching whale, before it lay prone. The great rock maple of Kearsage was down! It was sound as a nut. And the head axeman made sure that it "would square a proud edge" for forty-eight feet, with twenty more near enough to put into the same stick if desired.

Off to Fryeburg rushed James White to telegraph the owners that he had such a tree for a keel as never was seen. And by the next morning's train, up rushed Simonton to see the tree that was such a marvel.

"God! it would make a mast for a thousand-ton gunship!" Simonton exclaimed when he saw the stick. And because he was a broad-axe man himself nothing else would do but that he must mount it and begin "scoring in and beating off." None but himself might be first to make his mark on it. He was not sailor enough not to want to build a nondescript vessel, not to be willing to put in her a timber too big for her, mortised for an ugly drop-centerboard, not to do things which a sailor could not bear to do. But he **was** a timber expert; first and last a broad-axe man, and one of the big pictures of the old Maine woods (even if it happened over the state border) is this old-time merchant vessel-owner, coat and hat off in the stinging cold, standing bent over on the great maple and slicing at its sides beneath his feet with the great broad-axe, swinging it incessantly below him like the bob of a giant pendulum, plumbing by his spittle as they used to, and dressing out the face of the timber, true-edge and to the line, like any wage earner.

It is an art to use a broad-axe. The man who could do it was proud of his skill with that great, flare-bitted axe, turned out a trifle at the corners that it might not bite in, twisted sidewise in the handle that it might swing out enough, left-handed or right-handed as required. The ship-carpenters "tom-jerry" had only a six-inch bit, the axe for cutting knees was eight inches in the bit; but these huge timber-axes deserved their name of broad-axes, for they were ten inches across the blade.

As Simonton swung his axe, like a great hoe, motion just the opposite of the common axe, and as his breath rose and fell on the winter air, and his shoulders heaved and his back and arms felt a welcome ache in muscles long unused but responding willingly to the call for service they knew well, he Simonton, stood there at once an expert and a dreamer, one of the wide-awake dreamers who bring their own dreams to pass. He had dreamed a vessel such as he wanted; he was dressing out the keel which was her guarantee of living; he was creating what he had seen before it existed. He was not the slayer of a tree, he was a poet in wood, and the builder of a ship, the most ideal of man's creations. You don't know how men brought up to timber, love to be near good wood.

The next year after the men had shoveled twenty-five rods to the logging road, they managed the great stick on a sled for four oxen to drag it out to the road. After that, with two sleds beneath it, they had it drawn six miles to Chatham, New Hampshire, then hauled to Fryeburg. Once there, they laded it upon two flat cars, because it was so big.

After the keel had been built into a ship and was afloat on the ocean, the man whose name was spoken in those winter woods between the Maine timber scout and the farmer walked the trail that had been cut for the tree. David Stone Libbey, a master broad-axe man himself, walked six and two miles from the station just to look at the stump that bore it. That, was the way the broad-axe man showed his love of good wood. It comes down by inheritance and it calls their sons and sons' sons, though they do not know what it is that is calling them, since the wooden ship went out of favor.

A wooden ship is a creature born of love. She is the love of the sailor called by the deep, who tells what the winds and waters have taught him about the art of sailing, and the love of the shipwright for the wood that goes into her, who makes the sailor's dream come true. She may be destined to carry coal or codfish, or stinking hides; she may be just an ice-chest afloat, or a limer, doomed to go up in smoke if she springs a leak; she may be any one of the dirty drudges of the seven seas, as ugly, squat and utilitarian as the *Mary Ann Smith*. And yet, in the building of her the broad-axe man and the Master Builder worked because they dreamed her; and sometimes, even into a *Mary Ann Smith*, they put some bit of romance like this of Simonton and Holyoke's great keel.

In these days even more, when the clumsiest tub afloat, the meanest cargo-carrier, the worst old hooker that can be kept from foundering has a value both in money and in patriotic service, when new ships are needed, many and soon, the call of the broad-axe man should be heard by his sons and sons' sons and they should answer and rally and when they shoulder arms, take up not a rifle but this mightiest of weapons in winning this war, the shipwright's axe.

### Editor Note

Eckstorm included a hand-sketch of a broad-axe; she often sketched in her journals. She wrote: 'Broad-axes were made right-and left-handed, the handle having a curve sidewise to make it swing out and not bite into the log; also the corners turned out a little to prevent cutting in. The bit  was ten inches broad. Broad-axes for siding knees were eight inches in the bit. Carpenters' "tom-jerrys" were six inches. The users never carried a plumb; they plumbed by spittle. David Libbey was one of the best broad-axe men. It was work that lamed the arms, but David was double-jointed.

# LETTER FROM DAVID S. LIBBEY

In 1898, Fannie Hardy Eckstorm had written to David Libbey for a favor of information. The topic had to do with Maine woodsmen Eckstorm was trying to locate in order she might interview them for stories. This was in all likelihood related to research for her book, *The Penobscot Man.*

Notice Libbey addresses the letter to 'Friend Hardy.' While Fannie by this time had been married, David was closer in age to her father and he addressed the letter using her family name.

\* \* \*

Newport – ME. Feb. 13th 1898

Friend Hardy:

Your favor came duly to hand, and I was very glad to hear from you. The old timers who used to sell you venison before the war are growing less every year.[70] Alex McClain, Silas McPheters, Josi and Walt Edgerley, J. M. White and myself are about all there are left.[71] Alex and James are older than I. Alex,

---

[70] Prior to the Civil War, for which Libbey served from the autumn of 1864 until the summer of 1865, Libbey was a market hunter as one of his professions. No doubt, although Manly Hardy was a fine hunter, the Hardy family likely supplemented their meat requirements through purchases.

[71] Libbey mentions several of these same names in an article he wrote in 1901. Josiah Edgerley was a cousin of his. James White married David's sister, Lydia. *Deer Do Not Starve, and Partridges Do Not Become Imbedded Under the Crust. Calf Moose Tries*

indeed must be past 80. I have not seen him since the first Sportsman's Conventions (in Bangor) but my nephew, Dr. White of Lincoln, says he is quite feeble.[72] Silas has been at death's door several times with hemorrhage of the lungs; but he was down here this winter, his vitality is wonderful.

Darling was a year younger than I, and had vitality enough to have lasted him 20 yrs. longer if he had had no organic disease.[73]

I suppose that Eaton wrote that article in the Sun. As long as he confines his romancing to tame bears and "sick," I don't mind, but I was obliged to call him down last fall on a yarn that he wrote to the Lewiston Journal about a famous hunter who lived on the Allegash, and killed "the first white deer ever shot in the States, 300 yards with his trusty Marlin"![74]

The Marlin came on the market in 81 (1881),[75] and I killed a snow-white buck in 51 (1851) and had seen two or three killed by others before that, and had seen (mounts from) hunters who had killed them before I was born.

The guides stuff him with all kinds of lies, as John Greenleaf did (in) the Commercial[76] last fall about the trout in Sourdnahunk

---

*Walking on Snowshoes*, reprinted in, *David Stone Libbey – He Was Penobscot*, (Burnt Jacket Publishing, 2022).

[72] Dr. White is the son, Louis, of Lydia Libbey and James White.

[73] Jock Darling. See other sections of this book in the Game Laws chapters and also, *Exploring the Maine Woods – The Hardy Family Expedition to the Machias Lakes* (Burnt Jacket Publishing, 2021.)

[74] A reference to a comment Eckstorm made in her letter to him. Libbey, like Eckstorm, was not shy when it came to responding in the papers about incorrect facts, or items at odds with nature.

[75] The Marlin line of rifles began in 1881 with their first centerfire rifle. The Model 1891 was the company's first rimfire. The Marlin website notes that "Annie Oakley trusted the Model 1891 above all others to demonstrate her legendary marksmanship."

[76] Bangor Commercial, the newspaper.

Lake[77] jumping out on to the ice through holes! I can imagine just how he laughed after he got them to swallow that yarn. I know him well; took charge of the carpenter work on the Franklin Company building at Farmington for him.

White and I are going to Lincoln next week to see Lou and try for trout in Cold Stream Pond and we will try and come over to see you.[78]

Yours Very Truly,
D. S. Libbey

Letter Source: *Libbey, D. S. Letter. Newport, Me. Concerns the passing of the Maine woodsmen, reminiscences, 1898. Box 7, Folder 57, courtesy of The University of Maine, Fogler Library, Special Collections.*

### DAVID STONE LIBBEY
August 22, 1828 - December 6, 1904

David's portrait was taken before 1882 and was included in the book –

*The Libby Family in America 1602 – 1881,*

by Charles T. Libby, 1882.

---

[77] Nesowadnehunk Lake.

[78] Cold Stream Pond, south of Lincoln, near Enfield. James White and Lydia lived in Newport, Maine, near to David and his wife Mary. Lou, is James's son, Dr. Louis White.

# David Stone Libbey

"David Libbey was one of Maine's thoroughbred woodsman and waterman, one of the most notable of our hunters. He traveled to San Francisco and the deserts of Nevada, where he set up mining machinery and met western bad men. Some complimented his writing, saying he wrote as descriptively as Charles Dickens. His knowledge of Maine wildlife was second to none."

Fannie Hardy Eckstorm, 1904

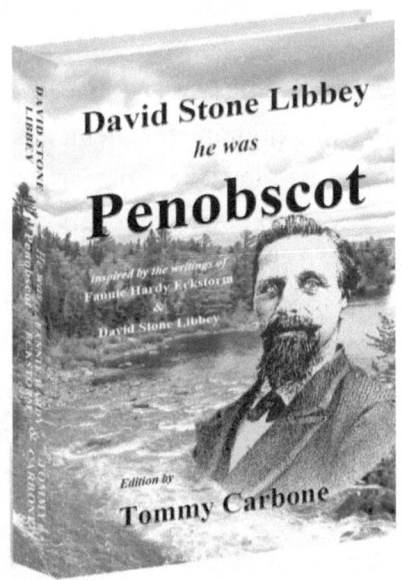

This edited and annotated volume of Eckstorm's initial release of Libbey's journals now includes never before published letters from David Libbey as well as several of his descriptive essays on the Maine outdoors and wildlife.

# IN THE MAINE WOODS

### Editor Note

Eckstorm included this handwritten note in the margin:

"This contains an account of coming out from Ripogenus Gorge to Grant Farm. Probably printed in *Bird Lore* (magazine), but I do not know." F.H.E.

Eckstorm wrote the following account based on her June of 1891 trip to the woods. Fannie went with her father, Manly Hardy, that year to document the West Branch Drive. Included as part of the note is her mentioning that her notes are duplicated. The notes here were written in story form for the magazine, and by her reference to the Seton book she mentions in the text, this story was compiled post 1899.

Her additional notes from the journal of the Ripogenus trip included more on their day-to-day travels and include a mention of Jack Russell. The visit to the Ripogenus Gorge from those notes is told in her story, *Clump of Posies,* in *The Penobscot Man.* However, she did not tell all in that original writing. The annotated version, *The Penobscot Man - Life and Death on a Maine River,* includes never before published information from her journal notes about that trip and the death threat she received from the renegade poacher, Jack Russell. The threat stemmed from her essays of Part II of this book and her information on Russell's activity in the woods north of Moosehead Lake.

This story picks up on the day after the men of the Drive kept on with the logs down the river. The Hardys, along with their guide Wilbur Webster, departed the next morning and were taking a different route back to the train at Greenville. They didn't make their return by the easy water route by which they arrived. The suspected reasons why, and the route, are covered in the mentioned annotated book. In these passages, Eckstorm returns (mostly) to her observations on birds and nature.

## In The Maine Woods

**Of** bird-study in the Maine wilderness, it may be premised that as an end in itself it does not pay expenses. Except for the specialist, content to study a few boreal forms, the results will not come up to one's anticipations; for birds are scarce in the deep woods and but few species are at their ease there. For myself, I never went into the woods to study birds; what ornithological notes I have picked up there have only the value of byproduct. It would be a great mistake to miss seeing the woods themselves while hunting what few birds are in them. Storm or calm, wet or shine, cold or heat, under all conditions the Maine woods are inexpressibly fascinating, and what dead lumber of scientific notes would not one give in exchange for the recollection of such summer sunrises, such calm on lake and land, such fathomless skies and heavenly expanse of water, such a feeling of myriad warm and growing things as still spells for us the days of our week with the river-drivers at Ripogenus?

That Sunday night, the eighth of June, 1891, we encamped alone on Ripogenus Carry. The night before two hundred men had been there or near at hand. But the last of the logs were sluiced, the boats had been dragged across to the *Putting in Place*, the wangan, that is, the commissary of the drive, had been wearily transported on men's shoulders three miles to the Big Eddy at the end of the carry, and the whole drive was well on its way down the Penobscot. In six weeks more, with good luck, the logs would arrive at the boom. And we, not wishing to follow a river packed for miles and miles with logs, must go back up stream, some eighty miles to a railroad,[79] if we went as we came, by water all the way; or about fifty if we left our canoe at Caribou Lake and travelled out through the woods.

In the early morning, when the frost was still on the ground– (though it was June, it had made ice as thick as window-glass one night while we were at Ripogenus) —we struck our tent. How early we were up that morning may be judged by this: After we had breakfasted, taken down our tent and packed all our goods, crossed Ripogenus Lake two miles, and lugged half a mile on Chesuncook Carry, we came upon some Chesuncook bear-hunters just eating breakfast, and these are men who are wont to be up betimes.

On leaving our old camp-ground, our last care was to say good-by to the little hermit thrush that nested almost within our tent door-yard. There she sat, bright-eyed and unafraid, under her quaint little roof of a broken cherry-sprout thatched tent-wise with the dry brakes lodged upon it by last year's snow. I have wondered since if she did not miss her human associates and feel more fear of the prowling skunk and fox that came to sniff the relics of the drivers' camp, than she did of the scores of busy men who for two weeks had been tramping back and forth.

Her nest was built well within the limits of the drivers' campground and less than two rods from the carry road; but she

---

[79] Meaning, back up the West Branch, to Northeast Carry, across Moosehead Lake (by steamer), to the railroad at Greenville Junction.

never seemed at all disturbed by the thunder of the logs going over the falls, the discharges of dynamite used in breaking the log jams, the multitudinous tramp of men, the grit and creak of the unshod sleds that dragged the heavy boats up hill and over to the *Putting-in-Place*. We told the men about the nest for fear someone might crush it by accident; there was no danger of their hurting her intentionally. Not one of them, rough men as they were, ever startled her purposely, that I know, though I sometimes saw them stand and gaze at her little tent. I myself do not know how many eggs she had; I never saw them though I could see her on the nest from our tent door.

This morning we did not see the crossbills at the end of Chesuncook Carry, as on previous years. It was no great loss, for apart from their nests and their curiously irregular breeding instincts, they are birds of little interest, tame, pretty, sparrow-like, more domestic than most of the woods' birds, good for company but rather characterless. Perhaps the most noteworthy point likely to be casually noticed is their fondness for saline food and the way they forage among the slops thrown out from camps for the salty or fatty portions.

Our course took us about four miles up Chesuncook, which is about eighteen miles long and two wide, and across the lake to the inlet from Caribou. It was a calm, delightful morning and as we approached the farther shore, we heard a familiar pounding and saw a patch of scarlet bobbing about a fallen tree. It was our old friend the pileated woodpecker, or as we always call him here, the log-cock. I like the homely name. It confers a well-merited distinction, for he is a masterly fellow, easily cock of the woods or cock of the walk in his own line of work. As the guide puts it, *"an awfully able bird."* '*To be able*' is about the highest praise a guide can give; it implies skill, energy, strength, and initiative. (The best boatmen or river-drivers are known as 'terribly-able.')

This fellow was getting his breakfast in a sightly spot whence he could command a glorious view of Katahdin. He seemed, however, to be paying little attention to the scenery, and even our approach caused no alarm. Perhaps as we paddled up quietly, he missed the noise which is so closely associated with an enemy's approach that he commonly disregarded the warning of sight alone. He is a keen-eyed bird but his hearing is even better ordinarily,

*Pileated Woodpecker*
*Editor's Photo*

unless called, as can be done by the few knowing ones, he is very hard to approach near enough to study without a glass. But on this occasion three of us without cover or concealment, lay and watched him with the naked eye as long as we wished. (I have never carried a glass in the woods. An opera-glass is too weak, my field-glass too heavy, and, going as we always have done by forced marches and with a full stock of provisions for several weeks, one learns to draw a very straight line between luxuries and necessities.)[80]

---

[80] Manly Hardy, in his younger years, went to the deep Maine woods to spend the winters trapping. By the time he was taking Fannie along, his packing must have seemed extravagant. Yet, compared to the camp outfits described by Hubbard (*Woods and Lakes of*

Our bird was scrambling about busily, sometimes on the top of his tree trunk, sometimes hanging beneath it; but as he did nothing worthy of protracted observation and as watching even a notable feed gets at last to be monotonous, we paddled off and left him still whacking his tree.

From Chesuncook we turned up the thoroughfare to Caribou. The water, still held in reserve at the Chesuncook dam, backed up this sluggish stream and filled it more than banks-full, flowing back into the alder-ground till there was on either hand an impassible swamp, quite devoid of life at that time of the day. In past years, too, this back-water had flowed and killed the trees along the lower levels of Caribou and they still stood, gaunt and bare, sufficient evidence that the white man had been there with his improvements. This ghastly ruin of the forest, killed by water, is his mark. But it is not the lumberman who does it; he is but a man sent by the consumer. The building of your house was what made these lake shores unsightly.

As we went up the two miles of thoroughfare, nothing either seen or heard, suddenly a loon thrust up her head and swam the stream, a head without a body, leaving neither wake nor ripple. There is always something a bit eerie about the sight of a head navigating without bodily assistance.

Anyone who understands a loon will admit that it is a most un-bird-like creature and that it is just as spooky on a bright June morning as when backed by all the accessories of wind and darkness. It might be the familiar of the old lake-dwellers,

---

*Maine*) or Steele (*Thomas S. Steele's Maine Adventures*), even in these later years, the Hardy outfit was the bare essentials. Eckstorm's descriptions of the gear and the 'forced marches' are marvelously described in *Exploring the Maine Woods - The Hardy Family Expedition to the Machias Lake*s.

remote, mysterious. The loon and the moose talk to me as the survivors of a pre-historic time; out of place are they, lost, lost, and continually calling back to the remembered past. What else does that long, doleful, echoing shout of the loon convey? What else does one feel when the cow moose gives her plaintive, passionate, homesick call? Aliens, both aliens, and doomed to a tardier extinction than their congeners. If this be fancy without fact, it is at least the innate feeling of those who are truly woods-born.

*Loon - Mostly Submerged*
*Editor's Photo*

We took the sight of the loon as a sign that the lake was near and soon it opened up, a fine expanse of water, perhaps seven miles long, with good shores and a few rocky islets. At the right was the farm clearing where Joe Morris's shanty once stood, and at the left the meadow opening beyond Ragged Stream where we were to leave our canoe and take the road to Roach River. Our guide was to help us with the packs and later come back for the canoe.

I believe the distance to Roach River is called about fourteen miles. And a miser in miles must have measured them, for the measure has been stretched more than ordinary. Whoever hopes a Maine woods mile of the old tenor will not hold out to one and a half or even two, or in exceptional instances rising three of the standard mile, has "never entered here." Those who have, abandoned all such vain hopes long since. It used to be said that the way some of these miles were measured was to start a fast hound running in the grey of dawn and to let him go till he dropped of hunger and fatigue, when they calculated that he had run "pretty near a mile."

The legend will not seem incredible to anyone who has ever tried to follow the old nine-mile-carry from Caucomgomoc to Baker Lake.[81] Even we, who were in a region of miles far more civilized, walked four hours to get to the Grant Farm, taking an easy pace, and were six hours the next morning at a three-mile gait or better, with less than an hour of stops, in getting out to Roach River–ten hours to go fourteen miles!

On the way up the lake there had been a spirited discussion with the guide as to the nesting habits of the mergansers, or sheldrakes, and he anxious to prove a point, had volunteered, if we would veer out of our course enough to land on some of the islets in Caribou, to find some nests for us. The first little island showed no sign of habitation; the next was a paradise of birds. It was a low ledge, at that stage of water some four rods wide by six long, though doubtless larger when the water had been drawn off. It had no trees but a fair number of sapling birches and spruce bushes. There seemed to be only room enough for our three selves and the birds' nests, of which we found twelve, of four different species.

The last of my camera plates had been expended upon our friends the river-drivers and their works, but in memory I can see the stately retreat of the great herring gull, the sharp-winged terns rising in clamorous alarm, the quick flight of the brooding sheldrake startled from her nest, the loud peetOweet of the

---

[81] Eckstorm will again mention this nine-mile-carry in Part II, essay XII when she speaks of Maine's really prime hunting grounds in those days. Manly Hardy had a trapper's cabin at Round Pond, near Caucomgomoc Lake, and most certainly told Fannie about his hikes across that carry. Even today, Baker Lake is considered a prime fishing ground and the area in that region a woodsman's paradise.

frightened sandpiper, just skimming the water as she flew; and on all sides the nests. Along the rocky, mossy margins were seven tern's nests, each one built rather neatly of small twigs and each containing two or three eggs—brown dappled with darker color.

The spotted sandpiper's nest was still nearer the water and had four eggs, something like the terns' in color but characteristically pear-shaped. On the height of the island the herring gull had her dwelling and left two great blotched eggs open to view.

Of the red-breasted sheldrake[82] we found three nests, all rather near together and one of them but eight feet from the herring gull.

One contained three eggs, one seven, and one had no less than sixteen. A pretty nest it was, not neatly made but well located, half hid under the side of a low spruce bush, and rich in its abounding treasure of smooth green eggs, as large as hens' eggs and pearly smooth of surface, whereas the gulls and terns were rough.

*Common Female Merganser*
*(The distinct white chin patch is one way to tell it is not a red-breasted.)*
*Editor's Photo*

The eggs in this nest were partially covered with down, a sign that the complement was full and the bird was

---

[82] While, the red-breasted merganser, on the eastern side of the United States breeds mostly north in Canada, there is a swath of a region in Maine, right in the area of the north woods Eckstorm is describing, where current bird maps show the bird's breed zone.

ready to brood. But though this was well into June, the eggs were not at all incubated. We knew—well, we ate of them. Three hungry people who have been up since summer dawn and are still nearly forty miles from market shouldn't be choosers as to what they eat. If they can't get anything better than sheldrakes eggs, they can support life on those. And there is a proverb against putting all ones' eggs in one nest which might be profitably studied by sheldrakes having sixteen to lay.

So we took as many as we wanted and retired to an adjacent island rather larger and more rocky, without the little bushes that had diversified the other, but softly carpeted with moss and with one or two fire-killed stubs still standing to tell that it had once been wooded. In one of these, was a woodpecker's hole, no longer tenanted by its builder, for in the mouth of it sat a blue-backed swallow interested, but not alarmed at our advent. There we found the empty nests of two herring gulls, and I believe, another sheldrake's nest, also empty. The gulls' nests were neatly built of reindeer moss piled in a circle about two inches high. The covering of the ledge formed as soft a bottom as was needed. We noticed, too, about the rim of one, some herd's-grass hay. It was an interesting matter to determine how a gull nesting in the middle of a large lake, five miles perhaps from the Grant Farm and almost as far from the old Morris clearing, could get English grass for a nesting material. And yet the explanation was not so far to seek. In the winter the lake becomes a road, and the hay for the lumbermens' horses has to be hauled across it. Many spears trail from the load or are blown out by the wind and lie upon the ice until it breaks up when they are floated shorewards. Of such flotsam of the farm came this hay in the sea gulls' nest.

We built a fire on the island and fried our sheldrakes eggs—with a more liberal allowance of pork fat than seems hygienically required with the thermometer up in the eighties—and we sat in the sun, which ungallantly blistered our noses, and tried to call the breakfast a feast. "One might fare worse," was the general verdict. There is always a good deal of philosophy and often some experience involved in that decision. On a cold, bleak day, when the leeward side of your fire is impossible for smoke and the windward side is uncomfortable for cold, no doubt sheldrakes' eggs are delectable; but on a glorious June day of untempered fervency (albeit the morning had been uncomfortably chill), we could appreciate the story the guide told us of old Con Doherny, a man of those woods, who ate seventeen sheldrakes' eggs at one meal—(mind you, they are as large as hens' eggs and more hearty)—and then remarked that "some folks might call 'em good but he thought they alwers tasted kinder fishy." The story may seem to some to have the same flavor, but the guide who told it was ever a most truthful man.[83]

While we were on this island the great herring gulls had taken up their station in the dead trees on the lake shore and kept up a doleful lamentation for their eggs. It seemed odd to see these sea-birds, apparently at home in the tree-tops, but it is a not uncommon adaptation of theirs. A lumberman told me that at Millinockett Lake they had taken to nesting in tall trees. This was ten years since, and most likely since that wonder of the woods, the town of Millinockett, sprung into being full-armed, they have gone elsewhere. But I have heard the same of the gulls at Spednic Lake and it has been reported by Mr. Brewster in Newfoundland.

While we were on the island two Chesuncook bear-hunters, seeing our smoke, paddled up to find out who we were. They

---

[83] The guide the Hardys went with on that trip was Wilbur Webster, a terribly-able guide. More about Webster and what Eckstorm wrote about him is in, *The Penobscot Man–Life and Death on a Maine River.*

said they were the ones who had taken the gulls' eggs on their trip down. It is quite the ordinary thing for the bear-hunters to get some part of their living from the eggs on the ledges. Nor is there any but a sentimental objection to be made either to this practice or to their profession. Cruel as the trapping of bears in steel traps necessarily is, it is the only practicable means of keeping down their numbers. And our Maine bears are not like 'Wahbs'[84] they do not "want to be good;" they are very bad little bears and do a deal of mischief, and they are perfectly capable of taking care of their pretty black hides. It would be a great mistake, for any sentimental reason, to prohibit the bear-hunters from following their trade, and a wholly useless effort, be it said, to try to keep them from getting what they need to eat while doing it.

Along the sea-coast gulls, terns, and sea-fowl may and should be protected, for their persecution is chiefly wanton, but up in the big, grim woods the problem of the hunter is a different one, and as a rule he will not abuse his liberties. Indeed if we could only enact laws that would preserve this hardy race of hunters with their heroic and generous instincts, we should have a breed of game worthy of perpetuation!

In the afternoon we made up our packs and took to the road. I carried eight boxes of camera plates, not wishing to trust them to even the most cautious guide, and this may explain my lack of zeal about not adding a heavy field-glass in a sole-leather case to the outfit.

---

[84] Likely a reference to the bear in the book, "The Biography of a Grizzly." As the book by Ernest Thompson Seton was published in 1899, this indicated Eckstorm was working on this story from her journal notes at least eight years following the Ripogenus Gorge trip.

That night we had planned to stay at the Grant Farm, a lumberman's supply farm part way through on the road to Roach River. The old house was on the eve of being torn down, and it was no part of its charter to board ladies; but the keeper did all that hospitality could do.[85] He gave up his own room and assigned my father and myself not only to the same room but to the same bed. This somewhat extraordinary politeness was fully explained by the condition of the house outside of that room, which was over-run with individuals much smaller than Macbeth but equally able "to murder sleep." Our guide said he never slept at all. There was a barn full of nice hay, but to permit a lady to sleep in a barn—why, there are some things that would shock the gallantry of a Maine woodsman much more than others.

The next morning at four we were afoot again. What time we rose I do not remember, but "Not to be abed before midnight is to be up betimes," as Shakespeare puts it, and conversely to get up too early is about the same as not going to bed at all. So we took the road with the sun, he being red-eyed and sleepy that morning from the smoke of forest fires; and we travelled ten miles, so-called, over a road too deeply gullied by the spring rains to be practicable to any conveyance known in Maine, and topped off with six or seven more, largely of fresh corduroy, on a Maine buckboard of the springless variety, which was like being tossed in a blanket for an hour. Thus we came to Lily Bay on the Lake.

In Maine there is one lake by acclamation: "The Lake" and that is Moosehead. There we found that the steamers were not running regular trips so early and we might have to wait a day or two.

---

[85] The structure at Grant Farm was torn down that year and a much larger building took its place.

Toward night a steamer came in unexpectedly. But it was a special boat; had only come in for the night so as to be on hand bright and early to tow logs; couldn't think of going back to Greenville. Now it is of very little use to attempt to buy a Maine woodsman; if he will not work for love he wont for money; and when he says no he means it until he thinks better of it.

And so it happened, as it is ever likely to do with one of these men if he knew your grandfather, or a man you had been with, if he had heard of you favorably, or even if he took a fancy to your poor self (and they can read the difference between vir and homo out of all rifle range)—why it happened that Capt. Louis Gill without any talk of doing favors, changed all his plans just because he knew my father and he saw a storm coming on, and ordered her about and down to Greenville. No bargain was struck, and one does not expect to charter a steamboat for nothing; but when given a good-sized bill, he passed back note after note, saying that for two of us he thought a dollar and a half would be "about fair." About fair, for the time of himself and crew, the coal of his steamer, for coming twenty-six miles out of his way (including the return trip), and saving us one or two-days hotel bills in a rain-storm! This sort of fairness, of which I have known a great deal in the Maine woods, looks suspiciously like generosity. But it is what you may expect if you are recognized as belonging to the confraternity of the woods.

After all, the best thing to see in the Maine woods is the woods, unless you are able to go straight to the hearts of the people in them, which is better yet. But the birds are of little enough account, except for a few unusual species, and the bird-lover will do far better to stick to his familiar hedgerows within city limits than to go so far afield and perhaps see nothing. If the record of this one day seem to disprove this, remember that it is far and away the best bird-day I ever had in the woods, and I took it just on that account. It also illustrates the point that there is some hard work to be done whether there are any birds or not any birds.

## Editor Note

Compared to the other short stories in this book related to lumbermen lore, this story covers another of Eckstorm's passions, and that was birds. For the interested reader, a wonderful selection of Eckstorm nature-type essays were published in, *Katahdin, Pamola and Whiskey Jack – Stories and Legends from the Maine Woods*.

Along with Eckstorm's notes is a letter she had written enclosing the story to a Mr. Chapman. From the handwritten notes at the beginning of the story, possibly this was sent to *Bird Lore* magazine. She wrote:

"I send the promised article, a little en retard but it wouldn't "jell" as housewives say. It is not what I wanted to do and perhaps is unsuitable to your purposes. If so, you are free to return it. But as I say, to talk about being in the Maine woods and to leave out all the woods and the people of the woods is to do merely the academic thing, which is quite without insight. Hamlet sans Hamlet is dull stuff, and the woods are better than all the birds.

However, with all my omissions, this is much longer than I had planned. Perhaps it is too long. If so, tell me. At least I have left out none of the birds except some swallows which I once spoke of elsewhere. If I have not told all I know about the sheldrake it is because I am not ready to exploit my notes on that subject.

The truth is there are very few birds in our woods that is, in the great forest; and when one is paying out five to ten dollars a day, as one must to travel here, it is quite a minor matter to count the number of bites a blue-jay takes in eating a (metaphorical) cherry. If one can't see something of more account than chick-a-dee-dees he would better pass along.

But I fear you will be setting me down as an iconoclast among the bird-lovers, willing to smash all the pretty ideals of patient note-taking and elegant tabulation which I confess I admire—from a distance."

Brewer, ME
Nov. 12, 1901

*Photo is from Eckstorm's signed letter.*

# THE SHERIFF OF SHOTTINGHAM

Eckstorm included the following as a typed note over this story.

"This was the opening of a book which never was written. It was to tell of what happened about Passadumkeag and Nicatowis in the eighties. The Sheriff of Nottingham was Game Commissioner Stillwell. Shottingham was Machias, in another county.[86] It planned to tell of Lon Spearen, Jock Darling and others I knew personally and their exploits. Because so far as it goes, it is true—and well written—I have saved it. Probably done about 1900."

Many of the names noted above can be found in her other writings. The interested reader of Eckstorm will recognize how she crafted this story based on real locations, events, and people.

**These** coats are yours. I found them in a cedar swamp under ten years' moss and mold; I hang them here by the carry-path where all passers-by may see the size and fashion of them. Be not vexed that what you threw aside, cast-off and forgotten, is deemed worthy to make a show of; men of such size as you and of such cheerful and heroic temper the world must not forget.

---

[86] Nottingham was Bangor and Shottingham the Downeast Lakes Region near Nicatous Lake in Hancock County. One example for the crooked Sheriff of Shottingham will become apparent in the later essay detailing the charges against Jock Darling.

If Tradition were not dead, some of these deeds of yours had been sung long since and your names had rhymed as well as Will Scarlett's and Little John's and Robin's, the father of the good greenwood life. I wish that there were Tradition now that you might have your dues.

But because the times have bred us away from the lusty, lawless Heroic, from the life you lived and I witnessed with joy when we both were younger, it does not become us to tell these tales as sober fact; instead, I have dressed up these sticks and stumps in your cast-off garments—motley, perhaps, if we have strict regard to ownership—and with infinite pains I have set up against those two old ten-pins—the Sheriffs of Shottingham and of Nottingham—so often bowled over by better men that they balance with difficulty, and here with these marionettes and on greenwood stage, I give the little comedy of a merry wildwood life.[87]

My puppets dance and thrust and feint. I hear you whispering as you watch, *"That was I,"* or *"That deed was mine,"* or too that, *"I was spectator."* Nothing, I assure you could better please the master of these wires than that the puppets should move with such a show of life.

But should you hear a doubter scoff, *"Impossible,"* then say to him for me:

"Are not the carries right?

Do not cranberries still grow in the fork of the fang at the Narrows of Nicatowis?

Are there not blueberries on the barrens of Partridge Brook?

---

[87] Interestingly, Eckstorm used the name Shottingham in her writing from the early 1900s; whereas Nottingham in England in the early 21st century was, by some, given this nickname due to a rise in crime in that city.

And whither for deer tracks but to the rushes on Gassobeeis?
Or for wild ducks but to the moose-ear of Fourth Lake?

And do you remember the old bear-biting tree that once stood—now, indeed, no longer—to the left of the carry that led across from Gassobeeis?"[88]

By these tokens, know that the one who knew the beasts and birds and berries, knew also much more deeply the times and the men. And what could not be put down as History, what Tradition was asleep to, is here revived as the pretty mockery of a pantomime. No one says that it is truth, and no one claims that it is serious. That would mar all.

And yet, old friends, to you, and you, and me, who remember–

**"Home was home then, full of kindly faces,
Home was home then, happy for the child."[89]**

Nottingham lies on the west and Shottingham far to the east. Here are held courts and constables and jails and fetters, high justice, low justice and sheer injustice with the whole weedy crop of the law's delays and quibbles. Each has its sheriff, its bailees, justices and squad of official parasites. At Nottingham formerly abode the lord high master of the king's venery with all his meinie[90] of wardens, which made Nottingham a place of much more dread to the men of the greenwood than was Shottingham. And this although that the sheriff of Shottingham had a rare and curious "pocket justice" which he could, by his black art, cause

---

[88] Eckstorm questions here are from her memoir of the 1890 paddling trip to the Machias lakes, see *Exploring the Maine Woods - The Hardy Family Expedition to the Machias Lakes*, (2021).
[89] Slight adjustment of lines from *Home No More Home To Me, Whither Must I Wander*, a poem by Robert Louis Stevenson.
[90] Meinie - feudal retainers

to shrink till it could crawl into his match-safe and ride there comfortable to the journey's end when it would come out fresh and of full size, as big and black as any bottle-imp,[91] and hold trials outside his own jurisdiction. Though this seem strange and beyond belief, yet, there many men alive who can attest the fact. It was this rare wizardry of a circumambulatory court with its justice always ready to lay a fine, the half payable to the juggling master, the other moiety coming at length to the public pouch, if the law was by any means able to force the law to give up what the law had taken—matter difficult enough at all times and most of all here.[92] It was this laying of fines, as variable as whim could dictate, with no redress for injustice but further costs of courts and lawyers; it was the Law making flesh of one and butcher's meat of another that made the air of Shottingham and also of Nottingham, (which differed, but not to better pleasing) seem over heavy for the men of the greenwood.

Therefore it was that the men of the greenwood were seldom seen in either town. They had no liking, said they, for such, bracelets as were bestowed upon them, and the public palaces where they were entertained sometimes were too securely guarded against robbers. For them, with nothing to steal, what was the need of windows with iron bars and underpinning that ran up to the eaves? Thus simply they spoke together of the entertainment accorded them. And when they could, they avoided Shottingham and also Nottingham. And likewise did the sheriffs of those towns view askance the paths that led to the

---

[91] In the 1891 story *The Bottle Imp* written by Robert Louis Stevenson, a bottle imp grants wishes.

[92] Early in Maine game law history, the wardens collected fines directly. They were often accused of pocketing the money as will be explained in the Part II essays.

greenwood, for they said that there the bees sometimes hummed like bullets, and once one had made a hole in a warden's hat. Thereafter this warden, being stricken with superstition, refused to enter any of the forest paths, for he claimed that ill-luck would follow him and such bees disturbed dreams.

But the men of the greenwood said that they had never been stung by such bees and they deemed them harmless to unoffending men. Nevertheless, they watched the paths that led to the forest and the man who entered upon those roads was marked and known, and the report ran before him that one of such and such appearance had entered the dusky shadows that darkened all the floor of the Great Forest. And wherever that man went, unless he could explain and justify his errand, an unseen eye was upon him, a noiseless foot was following. He thought the woods alone and deserted: the silence and the loneliness oppressed him. But it was not the solitude that made his brain reel; it was the unseen company that dogged him like a shadow. He felt eyes upon him, and looking, he saw no man. Whether he ran or walked, whether he sang or was silent, he was over-much companioned. And after a time he came to hate the forest and to desire green fields where the daisies, though they have eyes (and faces also), there is no lurking gaze transfixing one's back and paralyzing one's blood with fear.

This happened often to men who came into the wood to spy upon the men who abode there; without bodily injury, they yet were overcome. But it happened never to the field-born and to the forest-born who came blithely and found the woods kind to them and who saw there men whose hearts and hands went forth to meet them. To these, the Great Forest was a mother entreating them to come to her outstretched arms, inviting them to lie down on her broad shady lap and crooning to them lullabies. These, coming to a camp, would find a fire burning and there would be venison laid upon the coals and at every lake they would be told where to find a boat to cross it. To these all was invitation and hospitality: to the suspected all was solitude and denial and fear. So the Great Forest dealt with those who came.

It was not the Forest that willed it so; it was the ill-deserving of those Sheriffs of Nottingham and Shottingham towns who practiced cruel injustice upon the forest-born and the Forest protected her own and warned off those who would pursue them. Was there ever such a mother? Bountiful in all her giving she held her clusters high, and taught her children to strive for what was free to all. She provided them with meat and fish, with berries and birch-bark, with pitch and pine, with all the necessities of life and there she harbored them from sheriffs and from constables, as you shall hear.

* * *

### Editor Note

I first discovered this *beginning of a story* about two months following the publication of my novel, *I Am Penobscot*. In that book, David Stone Libbey spars with Game Commissioner Stilwell, he has run-ins with the poacher Jock Darling, the one who Fannie Hardy Eckstorm might label a Maine woods Robin Hood character, and he assists in tracking the hide-hunting Nova Scotian renegade.

Eckstorm is a character in the noted novel—as she had to be! Her work documenting that period of Maine's outdoor history assisted in my research for writing the historical fiction book. So, in the end, maybe some of the story she had in mind had its beginning, for there is more yet to write.

The essays of Part II of this book give us the real people and events from which the epic would be based; for how else could one *make up* such a story?

# PART II – SIX YEARS UNDER MAINE GAME LAWS

## Fannie Pearson Hardy Eckstorm

## 1891

*Editor's Photo*

When timid does put on their coats of blue,
And antlered bucks forsake the thicket cover,
To roam, with listening ears, the forests through,
It is October.

from, *It is October*
by Penobscot (David Stone Libbey)

# PART II - INTRODUCTION

**While** Part II of the book has already been prefaced in the book's introduction, a few further comments are necessary. This series of essays were first published in *Forest and Stream*. Miss Hardy wrote them when she twenty-five years old, a recent college graduate, and prior to her marriage in 1893 to Reverend Eckstorm. In this set of essays, she covered the perceived state of the Maine Game Laws. Her analysis was relevant to the times, as the Maine Game Laws were fairly new, controversial, and often misunderstood, and just as much misapplied by those hunting and fishing, as by the wardens and the courts.

The editor admits that such topical essays may not likely have a large interest one-hundred and twenty years later, especially since the game laws and hunting landscape in Maine have changed so much since that time. (While I may use the word 'hunting' the conversation applies as much to the fish laws as the game laws.)

So why re-publish the essays? These essays are important for history and to document Eckstorm's own views on the subject, in her words. A few modern historians (probably one started it, and others made reference) have written about Eckstorm in a way that misconstrued her words and position. This new release of the essays in this annotated edition provides easy access to Eckstorm's own words.

Fannie Hardy Eckstorm was a woman of conviction in her beliefs on woodcraft, lumbering history, Maine folklore, and local Native Americans. Her writings are straight and to the point. There is not much left for interpretation in her position on subjects, especially when one reads her journals and letters.

However, others have chosen to interpret, and still worse change, Eckstorm's position on several topics presented in these essays. This is unfair to this Maine historian who strived to capture the feelings of the hunter-farmer and backwoods settler. If given the opportunity, and if her history is any indication of her reaction, Eckstorm would have easily torn the writers of those incorrect words apart with her rebuke. If in doubt, readers only have to examine the added chapter *Tis Twenty Years Since* in her book, *The Penobscot Man* (annotated edition subtitled, *Life and Death on a Maine River*) to read her responses to some of the reviewers of the initial publication.

Since Eckstorm cannot defend herself anew, her own original words must. For her part, she wrote about the Penobscot men:

"Men do not perish alone, unknown, forsaken, forgotten. The constitution of the universe forbids. The truth about them must leap out some time, and be written on the skies like the flashes of the midnight Aurora; somewhere it is to be known what they were, where they failed, wherein they made their conquests, their treachery, their faithfulness, their cowardice, their courage, their shamelessness, their honor, but most of all and longest enduring, their better parts."

It is with this in mind, I intend to ensure the history of this amazing Maine woman's views can be found in her own words. When historical societies, historians, academics, and authors intend to publish what a person wrote, it's expected they checked their sources. The interpretation of such history through a modern-day lens also needs to be read with caution, and the reader of history will consider the original context. It is not likely this book can counter the easily proliferated webpages where someone can misquote and replicate misunderstood information about Eckstorm with a 'copy and paste.' What I can hope is that the diligent researcher will look beyond the internet to find the true facts. Part II includes footnotes to clarify where others may have taken Eckstorm's writing out of context, or have completely misunderstood her intent, her use of rhetoric, or ignored her own words on her position. Specific references are not included as to the publications with incorrect interpretations, for advertising sources which are incorrect do not further the cause. The editor has made several website owners aware of their misrepresentation.

The researcher is thus advised to check Eckstorm's original writings before requoting or summarizing information found in periodical articles, online videos, and books which may include misinterpretation of her stance on the Maine Game Laws. In those publications, you will find incorrect information where the authors state that Fannie Hardy Eckstorm was against game conservation, came out against the Maine game laws, and supported the ways of the outlaw poachers. Eckstorm's words in these essays are quite clear on her support of the game laws, her outrage for law-breaking, her stance against poachers (even to having her life threatened), and even her support for the law against dogging deer–it was the law, and her stance was it *had to be followed*.

Some of the writing in these essays may seem dry. Eckstorm cites statutes and court cases. Don't let that distract you, even if you are not interested in the topic or the particular case law quoted. Rather, I advise you to consider who was doing the writing, at what period in history, and enjoy her analysis (and some scolding) following her case reviews. For someone not trained in the law, she provides critical commentary on how the authorities misinterpreted the laws, over-stepped their bounds, or ignored precedent rulings. She covers equally well case examples where courts administered rulings contrary to the legal statutes.

Many parts in the series are deliciously fabulous and written in Eckstorm's wonderful, rhetorically-witty style, with references consistent to her other writings referencing characters from Greek mythology and literature.

It should be noted, Eckstorm was not the only person writing of these issues in *Forest and Stream* (and other periodicals) during those years. There were people writing along the same theme as her; as well as those representing the 'sports.' The purpose is NOT to cover the controversy or the development of Maine's Game Laws, but rather is included for the reader to have access to the original words of Eckstorm on this topic.

I have corrected the numbers on the essays as to how they first appeared printed on the pages of *Forest and Stream*, in which two different consecutive essays were labeled originally as number *VI*. In total, there were twelve essays published between March and August of 1891.

Please note that while these essays were written prior to Eckstorm's marriage, and thus appeared under her family name of Hardy, the editor, when notes are added, mostly uses her married name. Therefore, the surname Hardy and Eckstorm are used throughout interchangeably when referring to Fannie Pearson Hardy Eckstorm.

Lasty, some of the incorrect websites and publications have misspelled Eckstorm's first name.
For reference it is spelled, *Fannie*.

# FOREWORD–SIX YEARS UNDER MAINE GAME LAWS

## To the Gentlemen who visit the Maine Woods:
## March 26, 1891

**When** Capt. Drew, the genial "Kennebecker" of the *Boston Journal*, wrote up his cruise to Australia, in order to get as long a start as possible, he went back to his trip to Trout Brook on the Passadumkeag;[93] and so in writing on game matters I have begun by telling of the region round Nicatowis because that is supposed to be as far away as anything can be from a wholesome love of what is lawful.[94] That I have not told you what you expected to hear from that place, may have caused some speculation, and what I shall say will perhaps cause more; but whether you agree or not, hear me out. It is not an easy story to tell, and it is impossible for any one person to present all sides. I speak for the side which never has been told and for the people who cannot speak for themselves. If I make mistakes or misrepresentations, the road is open for both their

---

[93] Drew, John H., 1834-1890 – A sea captain and later correspondent of the Boston Journal. He was born in Chelsea, Maine, which was formerly a part of Hallowell, along the east side of the Kennebec River. Drew wrote essays about his time at sea.

[94] In this sentence, Eckstorm is referencing her earlier set of essays. Her and her father went to a Nicatowis because the thoughts were game wardens were rarely seen there. Some have interpreted that the Hardys went to that region to be *far from the law* in order to poach. Not so. The Hardys were there partly with an objective to research for this set of essays. The story of that trip, in wonderful Eckstorm writing, is told in, *Exploring the Maine Woods – The Hardy Family Expedition to the Machias Lakes*.

criticism and yours.[95] I would request, however, in advance, that critics sign their own names and place of residence, since otherwise discussion will not greatly help the matter which needs mending.

I ask your patience. What I have to say cannot be said so that all will take it kindly, and I must seem at times to speak bitterly, for I speak the thoughts of my people. Nevertheless, I have been at some pains to put these things as mildly as possible. I have written all the sketches previously published that you might be the more willing to take my word for what I shall now say, thus saving the bitter retort to facts, names, and dates. And I have chosen to treat it historically rather than polemically, because unless the statement of the facts is convincing, no amount of argument will be.

Those of you who have been in the country of which I have written, know that I have told the truth; those who have not been there but who know and love the woods, can tell whether my observation is exact, my eye correct, whether I know what I have claimed to know. I only ask those who have credited what has been said to believe what will be said. I know this a great deal better—was bred up to it from childhood, have studied it these three years and held my peace, have strengthened my own opinions and observations with those of the best-informed men in the State. Now after all that I have seen and heard and written down, I prefer to let these papers on game rest entirely on my own credibility. I only ask you to remember that I do not always undertake to express my own views; that I am not writing what ought to be, but what is; that though I may sometimes seem to misstate facts, I am only

---

[95] It has been written that the positions taken in these essays were those of Eckstorm. That is a mistake. Eckstorm was attempting to write for a class she felt whose position had been underrepresented in the outdoor articles. In several sections she clarifies her position on support of the laws. Also, she reiterates that she is attempting to write for others. Any misunderstanding on that is the fault of the reader, and not Eckstorm's.

undertaking to tell what is generally believed here, which whether true or false, influences public opinion; and that when our opinions differ, I am talking about matters concerning which I know more than most of you possibly can know.

I shall not undertake to exhaust any subject nor to tell all I might tell, rather to give such facts as appear to me best to represent the subjects treated; but, if I tell something of deer hounding, the cause of the warden-murder, the effects of the Graves case, the Jock Darling case, and other much disputed matters, is it agreed that for the time being all foregone conclusions are set aside, and these subjects are looked at from the standpoint of the people for whom I write. For we are at a crisis in game matters here, so serious that great caution in action and full freedom of discussion are the only means of our delivery. Few dwellers in our cities and larger towns can be aware just how matters stand, and it is harder yet for those outside the State to comprehend them.

I am speaking for the farmers, lumbermen, explorers, guides, hunters, and all others of the section hereafter to be described who may be classed as our rural population. I am addressing those who visit the Maine woods, which includes many of our own citizens with the many from outside the State; but more particularly the gentlemen who visit the Maine woods—a much smaller class, whom it may be hard to separate from the "outsiders" and "sports," so-called, for whom no great regard is professed.[96] If I do not seem to distinguish the two, understand now for all that the present company is always excepted, and that you and I are the people who never broke a game law;—at least I am sure I never did,[97] and if you

---

[96] Eckstorm is making it clear that she is not placing blame to all honest hunters, or even all 'sports,' but the few who were wasting game or hunting for sport or in the closed seasons; or were hide hunters who wasted much of the game.
[97] To the historians and authors who have written that Fannie Hardy Eckstorm opposed conservation of game and was against the Maine

have done so at any time to meet your necessities for food we will not quarrel over that, knowing that as we say, you did it "reasonably." I have the honor to extend you a hearty welcome, irrespective of the money you have spent on the guides you have hired here. If you have come and paddled your own canoe, as some of you have, so much the better. If you have not hesitated to help the guides with the camp work and on the carries, it is to your credit. Your welcome here *never* is gauged by the money you leave, for the people whom I represent above all other things judge and prize a man for what he is.

Fannie Pearson Hardy

---

Game Laws, you ought to reread the start of this sentence, and pay close attention to the essays that follow. As for the second part of that sentence, such a stand does not say Eckstorm opposed the game laws or was against conservation.

# I. WHO OWNS THE DEER?

## THE FARMER SPEAKS TO SOCRATES

Socrates had just come from his easy conquest over Euthydemus, when Agelæus, one of the rabble, came up to him.

"I would like to ask you some questions, Socrates," said he.

"It would be more to your advantage if I questioned you, Agelæus," returned Socrates, seating himself on a curbstone. "However, if they are profitable questions, I will answer them."

"Indeed, they are profitable; they concern my moral duty to my neighbor and that of other men to me. I ask to be instructed. I am a farmer, Socrates, and the other day my goat broke her corral, so to speak, and put for neighbor Æpolus's garden, where she ate up all the winter cabbages which he was intending to sell at the Prytaneum at once and a half the market price—supplying government, you know; cabbages are cabbages this year, and the archons[98] have all they can do to get enough to keep the visitors from Sparta in Spartan broth. It is about as cheap as anything after all, and seems palatable to them."

"It does not become such as you, Agelæus, to talk politics," remarked Socrates. "What is your point?"

"I want to know must I pay for those cabbages?"

"Certainly."

"But I shut her up all right, and the old idiot broke out without my connivance or cognizance, all on her own hook. Am I to blame for that?"

"Yes."

"Then a man must pay for damage caused by his own property?"

"Certainly."

---

[98] Archons – chief magistrate or magistrates in ancient Greece.

"That's just what I wanted to find out. Æpolus, you see, keeps sheep and lets them run loose. It was only yesterday that they got in among my choice tomatoes and trampled them up so I must sell out the whole thing to the canning factory for ketchup at a big loss. Mustn't he pay *me*?"

"Certainly."

"But he won't."

"He can be made to; the laws see that all such injuries are redressed. It is the part of the good citizen."

"It is your part to answer, Socrates; you've had your play, now ante. If the laws shouldn't touch this case, would I be justified in killing them until he took care of them?"

"No: for the law provides that the owner must pay such damages, as I have already told you, and it will make him care for his animals."

"That's just what I want to know, Socrates, for we haven't got to the end of things yet. There is a herd of deer which come every night and trample down my beans and buckwheat. Unless that is stopped I am a ruined man, I shall have to come on the town. Will the State stop that, Socrates?"

"It cannot. These are wild creatures."

"But the State owns them?"

"Certainly."

"And they have come into my field and trampled down my crops—my beans, too; I had both white and black. This new ballot system, you know, requiring a fresh bean at every ballot to prevent fraud was going to make a big call for beans. I know of three or four election rings formed already to get around it, with all sorts of devices for making an over-count. I was expecting to make large sales. Now, will the State pay me for those beans, I want to know?"

"Of course not."

"Weren't they destroyed by the deer? and doesn't the State own them?"

"Very likely, but the State will not pay."

"Mustn't the State pay for damages caused by its property?"

"O, Agelæus, you are a clown and a rustic, and for aught I know a fool also not to understand that the State has peculiar privileges, peculiar rights—"

"Ha, the State! I have heard you talk about the State before, Socrates, you have queer notions about the State; but it seems to me that the State, which is so rich and powerful, ought to be at least as honest as the private citizen, and else pay damages or keep her deer fenced in. I want to know what I can do about these deer spoiling my field of beans."

"If you wait till October, Agelæus, the State will allow you to shoot them, three of them if you know where to go and whom to go with. This should be ample payment."

"It seems to me I have heard something before now about a bird in the bag being worth two on the snag, and meantime my crops are spoiling. That kind of business won't keep a man in sandalia not to speak of chitons."[99]

"But the State is wise and understands—"

"It's a poor kind of a State in my opinion, Socrates, that doesn't pay any attention to us farmers. I pay my taxes and I own a share in those deer if any part of the State is me. Are they all to be saved for the guests from Sparta so that the tavern keepers of Athens may have geese to pluck? But while we are talking of these matters, I would like to know whether other States than Attica own the game in their countries?"

"Indeed, they do, Agelæus - Boeotia and Argolis, Phocis and Arcadia, the whole of them in fact."

"How is it, then, if our deer go into Boeotia? Or if their deer come here? Or, indeed, as sometimes happens, if the whole tribe migrates from one State to another? Can they kill our deer because they have strayed across the boundary? You would not let me do that to my neighbor's sheep. You said that he was responsible for them. Do we pay the Boeotians damages? And how is it if theirs

---

[99] Chiton – a tunic that fastens at the shoulder worn in ancient Greece and Rome.

come here? Are they subject to our laws or do they still obey their own? I would like to know these things, Socrates."

"O, Agelæus, I am puzzled. I am floored. You are a dolt I know, but you do ask hard questions."

"There is one point more. If this game belongs to the State and the State prescribes certain days on which it may be sacrificed, as it were, I suppose that the State does it impartially, so that all the citizens may have an equal chance. It belongs to the State wherever it is, and at these stated seasons is free to all."

"Certainly. The State strives above all things to be impartial."

"Then is it not permitted for one man to capture and hold alive any game animal that he may keep it for his own pleasure or sport, and deprive the other citizens of their shot at it? Indeed, I know it is not; for Penes, a neighbor of mine, who is a poor man, caught one a week ago intending to make a pet of it, but Thersites informed of him and the officers made him release it, saying that it was not legally captured."

"I heard of that. Ageleeus."

"But Plutus and Croesus, who live near the Academe, have a whole park full of them—it is what I think they call a preserve—and what is more, they have special laws passed prohibiting any but themselves and their friends from killing the creatures, so that they are no better than licensed butchers in spite of their aristocracy. But I would like to know whether they really own these or whether the State does, and by what rights they obtained the privilege. Did they pay the State for them, or are the deer sold with the land like a kind of prize package business, in which they run their risks of something or nothing, a prize or a blank? But if it was by the beans, why should not I who am a bean grower—"

"Keep thyself from the traders in votes and from things above thy understanding," interrupted Socrates. "As for these, Dolus is their lawyer and craft is in him. I confess that I do not understand these matters. But it seems to me more the part of the good citizen to cry up the majesty of the State and the infallible justice of her laws than it is to dabble in dirty broils about dumb animals. For myself, I will return to my work of asking questions and training the youth to answer me with sense and fitness."

"Go your own way, old Soc," replied Agelæus. "If the laws won't adjust my grievance and don't undertake to be consistent, I rather think I can settle the matter myself. I pay my taxes, I vote, I serve in the militia, I do my duty as a citizen. If the State won't either shut up her deer or else pay for the damage they do, I'll take my pay in venison whenever I can get any. That's all today, Soc."


Fannie Pearson Hardy


## Editor Note


The moral, so eloquently written by Eckstorm in this piece, is the question from the farmer who wants to know why some are allowed to get around the laws, or at least appear to do so. This seems unfair and he appeals to the great philosopher for answers. The farmer, frustrated with the State and the laws, decides to do what he can on his own to make matters seem fair.

To the historians and authors who read this piece of rhetoric and stated these were Eckstorm's opinions as she was writing for the farmer, that is incorrect analysis. As stated in the *Foreword*, Eckstorm clearly stated she was writing for the class of citizens whose arguments were not being heard, not that their opinions were right, or wrong, or that any of it was her own opinions. Read on, she will make this clearer in the following essays.

# II. WHY THE FARMER COMPLAINS AND WHO HE IS

## APRIL 2, 1891

**The** Greek farmer, neither in character nor ability, represents the class of men who live on our hill sides and forest clearings, but what he says is just what I have heard, and in much the same temper, from many of our farmers and back settlers.

That they should hold such views is natural, even unavoidable, under present conditions. Farmers, who are not guides nor hunters part of the year, are not very well acquainted with the game laws; many of them never saw the printed statutes and have no other means of judging the import of the law than by what they see done in its name. They have heard it said that the game laws were passed for the benefit of all; but what they have seen of the execution of these laws leads them to believe rather that the claim is a blind, and that the real object is preserving game for privileged classes who can pay for it, and keeping it from them, the poorer classes. If the suspicion at first sight seems absurd, consider whether any other view would be more likely to prevail among men who have had contrasts like the following thrust upon their notice.

A farmer on the Penobscot captures a caribou in close season[100] intending to keep him alive, and an officer is straightway sent by orders from Bangor to force him to release the creature, under threat of prosecution. Prosecution, for having the animal in possession? No, for putting on snowshoes in order to catch the creature, because

---

[100] The "close season" are the dates defined in the game laws for which game may not be taken. The "open season," are the weeks open to specific game.

putting on snowshoes is *prima facie* evidence of an intent to hunt, whether one has a gun or not, and under the law the attempt is punishable. But while such wire drawn logic is used against the farmer, two full-grown deer, which must have been taken in close season, are kept by the month and the year at the Bangor House, within a quarter of a mile of Mr. Stilwell's office.[101] The immediate inference is that the rich and the poor are differently regarded by the laws. Again, a farmer who tries to sell eight or nine partridges in close time is fined, although he proves the birds were killed legally in December; but togue and trout are openly sold in close time in city markets. The poor man has no chance, they say; the rich man can do what he pleases.

Again, two farmers each killed a caribou a little before the open season began; neither was a hunter, neither knew what kind of a creature he was killing or that it was illegal; both were fined. But men from our own cities and others yearly violate the laws, knowing well what they are doing, and no wardens are sent into the country where they are known to have gone for this purpose. This injustice in the execution of the law is mistakenly, but naturally, laid to a partiality in the law itself. The law favors sportsmen, it is said, and is against our own people.

But the farmers see this difference between rich and poor made not only in capturing alive, in killing and in selling game, but even in transporting it. A hunter buys a ticket to Boston and checks his deer as personal baggage, just as sportsmen do daily, but he does not go on the same train with them. The deer are seized at Bangor on the ground that the owner must accompany them personally. The State law about non-transportation does not say this, by the way, but it is the interpretation at Bangor.

The query comes, what is there wrong in it?

---

[101] In the prior essay, Eckstorm had Agelæus ask about Plutus and Croesus, who lived near the Academe, holding a park of wild game. The Academe being a reference to The Bangor House. E.M. Stilwell served as Maine's second fishery commissioner from 1879 until about 1892.

Were not the railroad requirements met in having the deer checked as personal baggage and the ticket punched with the baggage check, so that nothing else could be afterward sent on that ticket? A sportsman's deer would not have been seized if the owner were detained by sickness or accident from going with them, is the comment, and the suspicion of unfairness is strengthened when this case is compared with another a few years back, when the non-transportation law was at its strictest. Then the orders issued at Bangor forbade any conveyance, public or private—railroad, stage or private team—to handle or convey more than one moose, two caribou or three deer under penalty of seizure of the whole load of game. The Maine Central R. R. issued the strictest orders on this point and refused to carry any game; seizures were frequent. But, nevertheless, this railroad at one time forwarded a load of deer—nine, it is said, including one white one tagged to a prominent railroad official, and all or a part of them killed with dogs by outside sportsmen. The load passed through Bangor, the officers there knew it, and yet no seizure was made. Comparing this with the foregoing, what inference could well be drawn except that the laws had not been fairly executed? It is only a step to the assertion that the laws themselves are unjust, and the step is taken by those who know less of the law, than of what is done by the officers of the law.

The cases given above are not fictitious. The information regarding the farmer who caught the live caribou, was given personally by Warden Eben F. Morse, of Eddington, who was sent to release the animal, and the ground for prosecution, absurd as it seems, is as he gave it. Warden A. J. Darling, of Enfield, gave the information regarding the farmer fined for having partridges in possession, and said that he tried to get the fine remitted because the man was too poor to pay it and the violation was unintentional.[102] If the farmer had been able to go to law about it, he could have won

---

[102] Warden A.J. Darling appears on the *Commissioners of Inland Fisheries and Game* report into the 1900s. In 1904, for example, he received $452.70 for *'services at Enfield Hatchery, and repairs.'* Not to be confused with Warden Jock Darling.

the case, as Benjamin Young of North Milford won his case on deer. Warden Alec McClain, of Mattawamkeag, said that he fined one of the farmers who killed a caribou, but should not have done so if the man had known enough not to sell the horns in close time to the station master at Mattawamkeag.[103] The other, Milo Merriam, of Sherman (I believe), personally told my father of his case, and said that the caribou came out among his sheep at Benedicta, and he killed it not knowing what it was. The last case is the Walter McPheters case, soon to be tried in court.

Of the instances cited on the other side, the first is too well known to need comment, the second will be referred to later, the third is notorious, and the last is based on information from various sources and the admission of the highest authorities here. These are not a tithe of the contrasts which might be cited; but these are enough to show how the present feeling could arise. I must not be understood to say that the laws are invariably or even half the time executed after this fashion: but to bring them into disrepute does not need that the majority of the grand total of indictments should have been of this sort; but only that the people, whose individual judgments make up the public opinion which I represent, should have seen three prosecutions of every five that have come to their notice conducted contrary to their ideas of fairness and justice, or if strictly legal in form, enforced against one class of law-breakers, while another class seems to have been scarcely noticed.

In what I say now, however, and in what I shall say, I am not speaking of the State at large, but only of the section included in Penobscot, Hancock, Aroostook, Piscataquis and the upper half of Somerset counties. Washington county might perhaps be added, but I do not know enough of the popular feeling there to speak with any certainty. Waldo, Knox and Lincoln, by their situation on the

---

[103] Eckstorm issued this correction under a future dated essay. Erratum. —I notice that by a mistake in copying my last paper I wrote that the caribou horns were sold to the station master at Mattawamkeag, when I should have said at Kingman, which is the next town above. —F. P. Hardy.

seaboard, have less interest in game than the other counties; and of the region west of the Kennebec I know nothing, though I judge a much better state of feeling prevails there than here, I speak of and for the country rained by the Penobscot, Union, and St. John rivers and their tributaries, and the territory about Moosehead Lake, which is always treated here as if it belonged to Penobscot instead of to Kennebec waters because most of the travel to and from it comes this way. These four counties and a half cover more area than the other eleven and a half—considerably more than the States of Massachusetts, Connecticut and Rhode Island combined. The population of these three States taken together, by the census of 1880 (the last not being at hand), was 200 to the square mile; that of Maine, 21. The proportion of native to foreign population in the three States was less than 70 percent; that of Maine, more than 90 per cent. But in the region of which I am writing the contrast is much greater. With half the area we have little more than one-fourth the population—not more than 12 to the square mile, by the census of 1880, and the ratio of native to foreign born must have been more than 95 percent. In these four counties and a half there were only a dozen places of more than 2,000 inhabitants, and five of these—Bangor, Brewer, Hampden, Orono and Oldtown—lie almost adjoining each other. The significance of these facts in relation to what I propose to say is this: The absence of large towns shows that manufactures[104] can occupy comparatively few of the inhabitants; the great preponderance of native over foreign born shows that under similar conditions they will be sure to think nearly alike; the scattered population shows that agriculture, under which lumbering may properly be included, must be almost exclusively followed. Since the population is practically homogeneous both in race and in occupation, I must either entirely misrepresent them or else represent what is known politically as an overwhelming majority.

Now this section contains by far the greater portion of the forest land of the State, including all the best of the deer country and nearly all the moose and caribou country in the State. The

---

[104] Fabricated stories.

inhabitants of this section as a whole must therefore know more and care more about game matters than those of any other section. For another reason also they are better informed.

Bangor lies in this section and Bangor is the great lumbering and sporting center of the State. Whatever is done in the woods, in the course of time drifts down the river to Bangor, and there is caught by those who stand waiting for it. Things that the doers supposed were buried in the wilderness—what was done, what was seen, what was said, even, come to be talked over publicly on Bangor streets. As it is the center also of all the railroads leading to the great game country, most of the sportsmen who come to hunt must pass through it, while game seized in transportation is more often taken here than anywhere else. Then, one of the game commissioners lives here, so that it is headquarters for official news. Besides, Bangor and Ellsworth are the two principal county seats of the region described, so that most of the game cases that pass into the higher courts are tried in either one or the other of these places. While many of the people may not be able to tell a deer from a caribou, there is, nevertheless, no other place in the State, or out of it, where Maine game matters are so well understood and so much discussed as in Bangor; and a knowledge of what is said and done there is indispensable if one would speak on game matters.

This knowledge I may claim to have from having lived so near as to be almost in the city and from peculiarly good facilities for obtaining information. Other circumstances have given me a considerable acquaintance with woodsmen, guides, and hunters, both white and Indian, and opportunities of knowing about many more whom I never have seen, therefore I know definitely for whom I am speaking and what are their views. In addition, I have been through the game regions of which I speak in close time, [105] for the express purpose of seeing what was done and hearing what was said before the better class of visitors had arrived, so that I can speak from my own knowledge on some points where I speak most

---

[105] As noted in the earlier footnote on a stated purpose of the Nicatowis trip, and also the trips north of Moosehead Lake.

strongly. The information obtained from these sources, the fact also that the people of this section, for the reasons given above, must be practically of one mind upon game questions, and that I am heart and hand, by birth and education,[106] one of them—lead me to suppose that I can represent their views. Do not misunderstand me as doing more than presenting these, explaining their origin and to what they will lead; as I have purposely shown you in the preceding series, I am too prejudiced to be able to sit in judgment on the laws, and I shall not attempt it. But by reason of this very prejudice, I am able to get at facts which you could not, and I can reflect public opinion in a way that your critical and judicial power, which fits you for discussing what I am debarred from, could not arrive at. It will be done solely for the sake of producing a better understanding between you and those for whom I am speaking. When you reflect that the people here are the natural game wardens of this great forest region and that the very existence of the game depends on their good pleasure, the importance of your knowing how they think, feel, and talk about these matters will be self-evident—a sufficient reason for my saying what I have to tell you, a sufficient excuse for giving some good advice, which must be heeded if sportsmen would like to come here and enjoy the privileges they have had heretofore.

I have already told something about the commonest claim here— that the game laws are enforced so as to favor sportsmen—and that many say the laws themselves warrant this. On the former of these two points, I have given some evidence, the other I will illustrate briefly in my next paper, with some other claims of a similar nature. It should be stated that the latter of these two opinions is more prevalent among farmers and those less likely to be well-informed on the subject, that the former is held by guides, hunters and others who have had better opportunities for studying the printed statutes. And here let me state unequivocally that whatever the individual opinions quoted hereafter may seem to claim, to my best knowledge and belief the people as a whole do not ask to have the game

---

[106] Education in relation to the ways of the woods and the people of them.

commission abolished, do not ask to have visitors excluded from the State, nor more rights given to residents than to non-residents, nor to have the laws changed.[107] Some localities would like to have one change made and some another, but they are not agreed upon any unless it is the law regarding winter fishing. The laws, they say, are good enough; let them be enforced. Or, we have plenty of law on the statute books, we would like to see some of it in the woods. Or, give us good officers and we will see that the law is respected, for the law is good.[108]

Fannie Pearson Hardy
Brewer, Maine

## Editor Note

The appendix includes several letters, including an exchange involving Manly Hardy, which provide additional context on the game law debate and opinions.

---

[107] To those who have misinterpreted Eckstorm's stance, here she is, writing as she says to present the views of the Maine hunter, that these same Maine hunters are not asking to do away with the game commission, nor to have the laws changed. Are not these statements alone enough evidence to say that she was not representing the poacher or those who opposed the game laws? But read on.
[108] Does this in any way indicate Eckstorm was against the game laws?

# III. THIS, THAT AND THE OTHER CHARGE

### April 9, 1891

Most do not profess to believe that the laws as now on the statute favor any class, resident, or non-resident; but those who hold the opposite opinion claim to have some show of reason on their side. The following extract from a newspaper article by an old Aroostook trapper deserves careful attention as illustrating not only the way in which this conclusion is reached, but the plainness in speech and strength of feeling with which game matters are discussed here. There is no doubt in the writer's mind about the animus of the law—no hesitation in declaring that "the shifting of the game from rural to aristocratic hands is the final and main object." I hold the original of the article of which this is an exact copy. It was also published in the *Bangor Daily News*, Feb. 12, 1891, over the writer's own signature, with the title of his own choosing.[109]

### THE ARISTOCRATIC WAY
### * * * Start of Letter * * *

Now, then, let us decide how the penalties for breaking the game laws compare with the penalties for breaking other laws. It would be out of all reason to punish a game law breaker as severely as a horse thief, and yet he Is punished far more severely—$100 for killing a $10 moose, and the same for attempting to do so by unsuccessfully hunting him; and as earning a thing favors (in a moral sense) ownership, then the moose is his unless prior

---

[109] Eckstorm did not include the name of the writer.

ownership can positively be proved and thus the law sustains its moral right.

If the State should weave the principle of punishing the attempt to commit crime, as she does the committing of crime, into her other penal laws, the game law breakers could not complain of the inequality of her tyranny. If she claims that that peculiar feature of law-making is necessary to check such a heinous crime as seeking one's own food in the forest in the teeth of the doubt regarding the right of the State to make the law at all—and having severely earned it, too—then I would beg leave to remark that it might likewise be a fine thing to weave a similar principle into the punishment of other milder crimes, such as murder in the first degree, arson, burglary, larceny, etc., etc., etc.

And while a horse thief is not materially punished for simply keeping the fixings for running off horses, we are fined $20 to $100 for keeping the fixings (dogs) to run wild hoofs. Why does the State thus make an exception of the game law breakers? I will try to show further on. But, again, I shoot a partridge in close time, worth from 5 to 10 cents [that is, in the place where he lives], and am fined from $5 to $10, one hundred-fold the value of the bird. Apply the principle to one who steals a $100 horse, and a $10,000 fine is his fate. Why this severity on a breaker of the game law? I will show further on. But again, you send your horse, worth $100, up to Massachusetts on the train. I send my bird killed in open time (my lawful property) on the same train, under the sanction of the Constitution of the United States, and while the State defends you, it punishes me one hundred-fold right in the teeth of the United States charter which says, "Commerce between the States shall not be restricted," which, if applied to you, would cost you $10,000. Why such terrific, outlawed tyranny? I will show further on. Again, the fish law places a fine of $20 for an attempt to break the law and $1 apiece if the fisher is successful. What is the proportion here? Well, suppose he catches 50 cents worth per fishing trip, then the fine is at least forty-fold. Why this severity on this class of law breakers? I will tell further on. But again a fine of $10 is placed for killing certain fur animals from the first of May to the middle of October. Now muskrat are prime through May and are worth about

20 cents, and I happen to know as a hunter that May is as good as any month or the year to hunt them, and 100 of these being a fair month's work, it follows that the hunter is fined $1,000 for a meritorious month's work.

If this principle was applied to everybody, then everybody would rebel, and nothing, or rather nobody, to rebel against; and this law might well be called a duplicate of the Devil's Statute Book. But if plead that this was an inadvertence, I answer, "If ignorance of the law excuses no one, then ignorance of law-making excuses no State," more especially such an unparalleled abomination, and besides one which has been on the statute books some twenty years.

But why all this severity and even recklessness, even to the violation of the Constitution of the United States, and the undermining of the underlying principles of equity and decency? I have promised to tell why and I will do it.

The whole thing is got up by commercial men under the assumed object of protection; and in part this is true. Still my best opinion, after looking the field all over, is that the shifting of the game from rural to aristocratic hands is the final and main object. Where is the evidence? Why, everywhere a sportsman and a backwoodsman kill a moose unlawfully on the same day. The rich sport pays his $100 and keeps right on; the other hunts inside four walls; and the city chap has entire possession of the hunting grounds. Thus, though the fines are equal, the effects are quite opposite, and the desired effect is consummated.

### * * * End of Letter * * *

This is as nearly independent as any opinion can be; for the one who writes is by his tastes, habits, and location, little likely to hear these matters much discussed, and he says in addition in a personal letter: "About all I know is what I have dug out alone while hunting. I have nothing personal in the matter, never having been troubled by any agent of the State. My main objection is that the sporting organizations mean mischief, and that the underlying principles of the whole code tend to destroy our Americanism."

But although he reaches this conclusion independently, he is not alone in holding it. By an odd coincidence, the same issue of the paper which printed the above contained another article, by a gentle man not known to me, though he writes over his own name and from the same county and town as the other, which shows that this feeling is far from being uncommon in this section. He writes (and the character of his article is ample evidence for the correctness of his statements): "The game laws have not received the hearty endorsement of many of our good citizens, because in their judgment the law favored the sportsman more than the citizen and settler. Whether this be true or otherwise it matters not, so long as the people put this construction upon it. If any were in doubt, we have only to make September an open month and all doubts will be removed, and suspicion will resolve itself into absolute certainty. Then all sympathy and aid will be withdrawn and each settler will become a party to the general massacre, fully persuaded that he will have his share of the spoils. Such talk is already being indulged In and it means more than the language implies."

It is not necessary to dwell longer on this point since no good would come from it even if the fact of such a partiality existing in the laws could be established, while the claim that it exists there is too common to need formal proof and is as well illustrated by this one example as by the thousand which might he cited. But it is a fact, and a fact to be regretted by all, that game matters and game legislation are coming more and more to be regarded as a contest between rich and poor, non-resident and resident, sportsman and farmer, the game being only the *casus belli*—the excuse for the war. To strangers to our customs and ways of thinking, "the transfer of game from rural to aristocratic hands," must seem the very shadow of a grievance. But it is real and weighty here where equality is the air we breathe and every man is known by his first name, where social distinctions are scarcely recognized and even to talk of "privileged classes" gives offense. Very little respect is shown for money, though the ability to acquire is recognized; for an outdoor life, among physical hardships and dangers has caused personal prowess to be generally regarded as a better endowment than a fortune; money won't buy everything here, is a common sentiment, and many a man will do as a favor what he could not be hired to do for large pay. But the influx of a large number of visitors, competing with each other, has produced an impression that 'outsiders' think money will do everything. These outsiders are the "aristocracy" referred to, and the point feared is not so much that a class with leisure at command shall be able to spend more time and so have more opportunity for hunting than a laboring class, as that what always has been shared by all shall become the monopoly of those "who think they can buy the air of a free country." The feeling is deeper than a stranger can easily comprehend. The time will not soon come here when the typical farmer or woodsman will prefer five dollars or thrice five for showing a sportsman a deer, to the right to take his own chances at the deer if he prefers. He cannot understand how natural rights can be bargained for money, and be looks with suspicion on whoever tries to buy him out.

It is this—and it is useless to evade the matter in trying to give an account of the dissatisfaction here—which has given rise to the charge that the game Commissioners wish to save the game for sportsmen. They have spoken so much of the amount of money which sportsmen leave here—where money never has been the popular standard in game matters, but the equal rights of all to fish and hunt—that their statements, however true they may be, because they run counter to the feelings of the people, have helped in arousing opposition to sportsmen. All the classes of residents whom I have heard speak on the subject agree in this; they have no game to sell—do not know anyone who has any; sportsmen may come as much as they please and take their chances with other folks, but no game will be saved for them; game is free here and will be as long as it lasts. It is the Commissioners, not the people, who have talked of the amount of money sportsmen leave; no one else sees millions in it; and if there were a thousand dollars for every head of game killed that would not satisfy us that any man has a right to kill game animals wantonly and waste them. "Sport" is a term not understood here. The condemnation of waste is universal, and the chief reason why sportsmen as a class are not welcomed with more than toleration is the inexcusable waste of game, of which they have been guilty these many years. "A mink, an otter, and a sport," the saying runs, "are the only creatures in the woods that will kill more than they can eat."

For the lack of cordiality shown toward sportsmen as a class, they themselves are responsible; for as a class they have broken our laws, transgressed our customs, interfered with our lawmaking, tried to raise class distinctions both by urging special privileges for non-residents and by their bearing and words while here. These are true charges; and yet, so far as I am aware, they have not produced any other influence adverse to sportsmen than a failure to respect them as a class. There has been a marked change within a few years in the way sportsmen are spoken of by the guides, who know most about them. Formerly it was "the gentlemen I was with," or "the man I was guiding for:" but now it is, "two sports I had last fall," or "a city dude that was here," or at the utmost stretch of civility, except when some always-welcome guest is spoken of, "the man that was *with me*." These phrases indicate exactly the popular feeling which verges on contempt if it does not pass the line of it— for the majority or those who come here to hunt—not of the tourists and anglers, for I am not speaking of them. This is the figure at which sportsmen by their own actions have placed their valuation; it expresses toleration rather than regard or ill will. The bad feeling felt toward sportsmen is caused by something of which I cannot but think them ignorant, though their actions here do not tend to disarm suspicion on this point. It is impossible that they should know what we know about the management of game matters as conducted in this State, or that the laws are not enforced against non-residents in the same way that they are against residents. We have known it so long that we forget that everyone does not see the same, and sometimes suppose that non-residents who come here in summer have an interest in continuing the present state of affairs. That this is unjust both to visitors and Commissioners, does not make it less harmful to them; for "there is no mistake about the fact of partiality in the administration of the laws, and the only way in which this can be accounted for by those who know only one side of matters is that the Commissioners know it, the visitors wish it, and the object is to save the game for those who pay cash for it, "transferring it from rural to aristocratic bands." This arouses the bitterest feeling against sportsmen, and it certainly is as much for their interests as for ours to know the facts and to be able to show that they do not desire any such thing. Just where the error lies, I will show later, but as to the justice of the ground on which the complaint is based, did anyone, on thinking the matter over, ever see a warden in the woods anywhere over the whole Moosehead, East Branch, West Branch and Allagash country—the greatest hunting ground in the State— before the first of October? It would be strange if anyone did, for not only have we never heard of it, but on the 31st of March of this year, when my father asked Mr. Stilwell personally if he ever had sent a warden into the woods during the summer months, Mr. Stilwell did not mention a single case. And yet this is the time and this is the region, when and where the majority of visitors from outside the State go to hunt, and it is well known that they kill large quantities of game illegally and waste the most of it—that they have come for this purpose. But wardens are active in winter, and the same visitors who broke laws in summer with utter disregard, are urging them to exterminate the race of "crust-hunters." Is it strange that this having been the case year after year, the people here should declare that all the visitors wish is to be allowed to do as they please, and that they hire the wardens to let them alone?

I can show another way of explaining the matter without necessity of claiming that this ugly charge is correct; but it will be very much for the advantage of sportsmen who come here to disprove it themselves by demanding that good and trusty wardens be placed in the woods next summer. If they do not do this before next July, very few in this State will disbelieve the charge. If I seem to neglect the fact that people from outside the State have been fined before now, it is not because I have forgotten it; this is a broader matter. For the half of the year when non-residents are here and the laws are constantly violated, no attempt is made to enforce them, as we know and the Commissioner admits; for the half of the year when few except residents are in the State, they are at least partially enforced. The people here demanded that the laws should be uniformly and justly executed, and yet matters have grown worse every year. It now remains for the summer visitors to state openly whether they wish them enforced in summer, and to do it over their own names, so that we may know who they are. For everyone who comes here is known by a larger circle than he is aware of. He sees very few of the residents, knows next to nothing about them, and thinks that they know as little of him. On the contrary, no one comes here whose whole cruise is not known by at least twenty residents, sometimes by hundreds. What he has seen, done, and said; what kind of a man he is and all the particulars concerning him, are told from one guide to another; are discussed in a dozen lumber camps during the winter; are told again on the drive in the spring, and then are carried to a score of different towns to be talked over by the inhabitants. Instead of being done in a corner, what he has done is better known than if it had been published in the daily papers. Next fall is to be the decisive time in game matters in this State, and it is necessary that those who speak should speak right and then should live up to their professions.

Of the charge of unconstitutionality of the laws I will not now speak, since as I understand it, it is directed rather against interpretations of the laws than against their explicit meaning as they are printed, and the present discussion is a consideration of matters affecting sportsmen from outside the State rather than local topics.

A subject of much interest to sportsmen, if they could hear it discussed as it is here, is the way game matters are managed in the Legislature. Abundant discontent prevails. It is claimed that petitions sent in by the people are disregarded; that officials are bought up, that log-rolling and wire-pulling are openly practiced, and worse practices are carried on behind slight screens, while the whole is controlled by railroads, hotels, and politics. That these charges are unreasonable and exaggerated **is not** to be denied; that they are baseless is another matter. We have only too good reason to fear a substantial truth at the bottom of some of them; for, speaking plain heartedly, non-residents have too openly declared an interest in our game legislation for us not to take them at their word. Mr. J. F. Sprague, of Monson, Maine, writing in *Forest and Stream* in October, 1883, says of the sportsmen who came here at that time:

'Instead of these laws failing to secure the approval of this class, they have ever been their truest and most staunch and reliable friends, and in more than one instance these "professional men" from other States have inspired or originated the acts which are now the very laws so despised by "Olibo."'[110]

In the *Forest and Stream* for Oct. 30, 1884, "Special" writes:
'The request to change the beginning of the open season there [In Maine] to Sept. 1, will come from some of the leading sportsmen and friends of game protection in Massachusetts, Rhode Island and Connecticut. * * * The request for change will come from sportsmen who desire to add shooting to the fall fishing.'

Rev. Newman Smythe in Scribner's Magazine for October, 1890, says:
'Efforts have been repeatedly made by the Kineo Club to have the laws so modified that, while the wholesale slaughter of deer and moose may be prevented when they are helplessly yarded in the deep snows, some opportunity for legal shooting may be granted somewhat earlier than October; and a bill which was introduced into the last Legislature of Maine for this purpose, passed one branch of that body but was defeated In the other by some influence adverse to sportsmen. Gentlemen who take to the woods in summer generally denounce, and are quite ready to help expose indiscriminate and wasteful killing of fish or game; but as in the course of the season they bring considerable money into the State, they naturally think that some liberty might be granted them of feeding.'

It is the same old story of crust-hunting, and the amount of money left; and we notice that the gentlemen neither wait for the law to be changed nor for open season to begin, so we fail to see what difference it makes.

Then we hear the other side from our representatives, how they were approached, how the lobby was too strong for them when

---

[110] Letters from 'Olibo' are included in the. Appendix.

some popular measure came up; of the bills that failed to pass, and the people who were there to get them through. One bill I remember, as reported by our own representative as long ago as there were pigeons in the State, tried to make it a State prison offense to fire a gun within 200 yards of a pigeon bed owned by a certain game club from out of the State. We have heard the boast of the man who declared that people outside the State could pass "any reasonable laws" in Maine. We have heard Mr. Stilwell say, when he was opposing an open September some years ago, that "the men and the means" were there to put the bill through. On the whole, we are "ower canny" to disbelieve those who say that our game laws are fearfully and wonderfully made.[111]

We do not deny that many of the bills introduced and advocated by those outside the State, make good laws—better perhaps than we should have made for ourselves; but the fact that they did not originate here arouses suspicion of their import, and, to our minds, makes the moral obligation less. Even if it were all good and disinterested, we have had too much of it. If for ten years Maine people had besieged the New York Legislature with bills proposing this and that means of purifying the municipal affairs of New York City, and had concerned themselves in season and out of season in telling New York people what to do about it, much the same state of feeling would exist there toward us that exists here today toward those who have made our game laws for us; and however good the measures proposed might have been, they would hardly be called popular measures, nor the reform a popular reform.

How much has been done by those outside the State we cannot say; but if our present trout law was a native production, it is the oddest bit of legislation with the oddest history of anything ever produced here. One thing I do know, for I was a child at the time and frequently saw the man most active in it, heard him talk on the

---

[111] 'Ower canny,' a Scottish reference. 'Fearfully and wonderfully made' based on Psalm 139. On one hand, the laws were good, but they were not considered 'fearfully and wonderfully made;' as if written by a creator.

subject and remember the particulars. The law forbidding the killing of moose for five years was proposed, drafted, and principally carried through by a Massachusetts man, Mr. John M. Way, who published the first tourists' map of Moosehead Lake.[112] It was a good law and was very well supported, but was hardly a popular measure, and was not primarily intended to benefit the people, but to increase the number of moose available for sportsmen. Mr. Way saw the need of this. The previous winter he had stayed six weeks at Haymock Lake in the camp of Mr. Gardiner G. Grinnell, of New York, and Capt. Samuel Cole, of Greenville, trying to kill a moose illegally. To illustrate how the law was passed let me quote from a private letter written by a prominent game club man to Mr. Way, who showed it to my father: "Don't get up petitions, for that will stir up the opposition of the country members. Get the right men at Augusta fixed and rush it through, for it is hard to unmake a thing after it gets to be a law."

This is not the kind of legislation that does much good here, and friends of game protection will be doing a favor to themselves and us if they try to discourage it.[113]

Fannie Pearson Hardy.

---

[112] John Way, Jr., in 1874, issued one of the earliest guide books to northern Maine. Thomas S. Steele wrote, "John Way was one of the best map makers the region had ever known." See, "*Thomas S. Steele's Maine Adventures*," a two-book annotated edition by Tommy Carbone (Burnt Jacket Publishing, 2021).
[113] For any who may miss the point here and say Eckstorm was against conserving game, Eckstorm was not concluding that the proposed legislation for a five-season moose moratorium was bad; in fact, she stated the proposed law was a good one. Her critique was over the backroom deals and the process used to enact such legislation. Maine would eventually outlaw the moose hunt and it would not return until the animal population reached sustainable levels.

# EDITORIAL – THE MAINE GAME SITUATION

### April 16, 1891

### * * *

*Forest and Stream* issued this editorial on account of the letters they were receiving from readers.

### * * *

The Maine game question is so important that it is well worth our while to try to understand it; to learn all we can about it: to hear all sides.

Two classes are interested, residents and visitors. The chief importance attaching to the papers written by Miss Fannie P. Hardy is found in her claim for them that they give the side of the residents, or at least of those residents most nearly concerned. She professes to speak for this class—a class which is less often heard than the other: and she claims that her peculiar opportunities for gaining information and her long study of the subject enable her to represent the views of these people accurately.

Miss Hardy is a daughter of Mr. Manly Hardy, of Brewer, Maine, engaged for many years in fur trading (a business from which he has only recently retired). Mr. Hardy has had an acquaintance wider perhaps than that of any other man in the State with hunters, trappers, guides, lumbermen, and other dwellers in the woods, upon whose co-operation the preservation of game so largely depends. More than this we understand that Mr. Hardy enjoys the respect of the Game Commissioners, as a citizen who has always obeyed the letter and spirit of the game laws, even when such compliance involved great personal loss to himself.

From all this it would seem that Miss Hardy's claim that she is qualified to speak for these people is well founded; and if it is; and if she can tell us how the Maine residents look at this game question, it is surely desirable that we should hear what she (for them) has to say. Their views may be full of error, their attitude a mistaken one, their logic at fault, their position untenable, their practices indefensible: nevertheless, all these must be accepted, as actually existing conditions, which should be taken into account in the effort to provide the remedy and save the game. For that, unless a change shall be inaugurated, the game is going, appears to us to be beyond dispute.

If what is told by Miss Hardy in today's issue is insufficient evidence as to the doings of so-called sportsmen in Maine, turn back to the *Forest and Stream* of Dec. 11, 1890, and read there what "Special" wrote of the wholesale destruction of Maine deer by jacking and dogging and other modes of hunting in the summer months of 1890, and up to the opening of the season, Oct. 1. According to "Special's" report, this killing out of season and by forbidden methods was done by sportsmen from outside the State, or by guides employed for them. His account and Miss Hardy's amply corroborate each other. Their reports and much other information which has come to us indicate that the illegal destruction of large game in the Maine forests last year was practically unchecked, and exceeded that of any previous season.

The result appears to be this: The people of Maine, or at least that class for whom Miss Hardy speaks, having seen the deer and moose thus wantonly killed and wasted by sportsmen in the summer months, have themselves given over all restraint and in their turn have slaughtered the game in winter and without regard to the laws.

This, we are told, is the actual condition of things. We need not now discuss the moral aspects of the case; we have already said that two wrongs do not make a right: but the situation is one that cannot be touched by an abstruse or argumentative consideration of the points of ethics involved.

We confess that we do not at this moment see where the remedy lies. Perhaps Miss Hardy may have one to suggest: or it may come from elsewhere: but we are not without confidence that it will be found, and that the discussion of the question by Miss Hardy and by those who will doubtless follow her will aid in its discovery.

It surely must be discouraging to every true sportsman (and we know many such), who visits Maine, and by his practice, example and influence there strives to awaken among those with whom he comes in contact a respect for game protection and an observance of the laws, to find that after all he is in a minority; for it appears from what Miss Hardy has written that the Maine people themselves have acquired their notions of "sportsmen" as a class chiefly from the lawless individuals who in the close season commit outrages which are abhorred even less by the native of Maine than by sportsmen of better type themselves.

Editor - Forest and Stream

*Editor's Photo*

# IV. ON THE WASTE OF GAME BY SPORTSMEN

## April 16, 1891

**I think** that in my last paper I brought forward evidence enough to show that sportsmen from outside the State have been influential, if not mainly efficient, in bringing into the code of Maine game laws many of their present features. I asserted that, though equally responsible with us for the proposition and framing of these laws, sportsmen as a class had brought discredit upon themselves by inexcusable violations of the laws, involving the waste of large quantities of game and that, moreover, though this was known, they had not been held to account for their deeds in the same way as residents of the State—two circumstances which have aroused bitter feelings against sportsmen, the first because it is a direct affront to our ideas of economy, the latter because of its unfairness.

That laws have been proposed and partly carried through by outsiders no one will have the temerity to deny in the face of the facts that might be furnished, but it may be claimed that I have not proved either the waste of game by sportsmen or the partiality in the execution of the law. For the latter, since the Commissioner's silence may be taken as presumptive proof of the assertion, it is enough to ask if anyone ever knew a sportsman, visiting in the summer or fall the section of which I write, to be arrested on evidence that the warden gained personally in the woods without the aid of an informant, excepting only that case at Gassobeeis where the three wardens arrested, by mistake, on a warrant sworn for "Jonathan Darling and others," three sportsmen who gave their names as Doe, Roe and Poe, supposing that they were capturing Darling also, who proved not to have been of the party at all. Rarely wardens have gone into the woods in the fall to make seizures of hides, and a few times to Nicatowis to watch for Darling; but none have been stationed at important points to patrol the game country and prevent the illegal destruction of game. Prevention never has been sought, but only the occasional capture of an offender after the harm was done.

On the former of the two points—that sportsmen kill large quantities of game illegally—I can satisfy even the sportsmen themselves. They will hardly challenge the statement that nearly all the game that is *wasted* is killed by non-residents—in summer, sportsmen; in winter, Canadians. But before taking up this point, a word may be necessary to explain why residents of the State seem to put less stress on the illegality of breaking game laws than on the wickedness of wasting game.

In our eyes, however good it may be, a game law is not founded on moral distinctions; to break it is a misdemeanor, but not a crime nor a felony, and no wrong is attached to the violation when it is done to supply necessities. At the most, it is a transgression of a standard put up arbitrarily, whose violation involves no moral wrong doing, except the technical one of acting differently from the tacit agreement made at the time of its enaction. That this is a wrong is not to be denied; but here comes in one of the bad effects of having laws of doubtful origin. With the increase of the conviction that our laws have been tampered with by those outside the State, has spread the denial of the moral authority of those laws, until at present it is frequently asserted that it is not wrong to break a law which was not made by one's representatives. That the laws are good, in the main, does not materially alter the public opinion on this point. The present situation is sometimes compared to that in Boston just before the Revolution, and it has been not unwittily said that the cause of the discontent is the same as then, *taxation without representation*. Be that as it may, there is very little compunction felt here about breaking a game law when anyone wishes to do it— sportsmen and residents are at one in this. But the residents are restrained in one way which does not seem to affect visitors. The people of Maine consider it a sin to waste food. They might break the law with untroubled consciences; but they could not persuade themselves that there is any excuse for wasting what they got, even if they obtained it legally. Sportsmen evidently do not feel so, and here arises a difficulty. To illustrate: We can understand perfectly the temptation to a sportsman who sees a cow moose splashing through the lily pads a few rods away—how the destructive instinct of curiosity, as in a child, almost forces him to shoot unless there is a wholesome certainty of detection and punishment—that is the temptation to an illegal act. But how a man can shoot at a moose when he knows he can use but 50 lbs. of the meat and that he must leave several hundred pounds equally good to spoil, is beyond even our imagination; that is a positive sin, and if the man, is a man he will not do it. We never forgive those who have done it. We never quite trust them afterward. The man who has not sufficient self-control to hold himself from taking life unnecessarily, lacks the poise which makes a man well-balanced and trustworthy, and by a subtle undercurrent of thought is set down as lacking courage also. He is a "sport" (the word is abominable, but it supplies a lack and tells the kind of man meant and the feeling entertained toward him).

The mistake that seems to have been made by many visitors is that they have paid for the game and are at liberty to get as much as they can—as if it were a lottery, the amount of the prize not depending on the value of the ticket but the luck of the drawer. We claim, and we certainly are right, that they have paid nothing at all for the privileges they enjoy, and have no right to any more of the game and fish than they can use or legally carry away. They have paid the railroads a certain sum—for transportation; they have paid the hotels—for board, which they must have paid at their homes if not here; they have paid the guides—but it was for transportation and personal services. If they had been capable and willing to undergo the hardships, they might have walked hither carrying their own packs and eating wayside berries, with theoretically no expense to themselves. Would they have been paying for the game then? Not one cent has anyone paid for the right to fish and hunt; it is a gift from the people of Maine.[114] We say that the sportsman has no more

---

[114] In 1899, Maine implemented the first hunting license program, known as "The September Law," hunters were permitted to kill one

right to kill game on account of what he pays out while he is here, than he has to shoot farmers' sheep and cows when he is on a railroad train on the score that he has paid for his ticket and meals. Whoever owns the game, the man who lives outside the State certainly does not; but he is given the same rights which the probable owners assume for themselves—the right to feed himself economically at a certain season, a limit being set which is supposed to be liberal enough to provide for all his necessities. It is considered here that it is an uncourteous act to take all a man has because he offers all anyone wants; and so, when a sportsman kills a moose where a deer would serve him, or a deer when trout and partridges would suffice, he is doing a wrong act even though the law allows it, and an outrage to hospitality.

This is the ground of objection to waste of game: First, morally wrong; second, ungrateful. That the charge of sportsmen wasting game is not unfounded will be proved. Instead of giving individual instances for each year, I will abbreviate by quoting from the Commissioners' reports and *Forest and Stream*, when I know that the statements agree with facts that have come to my notice.

The Commissioners' Report for 1883 says:

'We have been credibly informed of three moose wantonly shot down in hot August weather by a party of whites (we will not class them) when even the trophies could not be pleaded as a temptation, as but one bore horns. Of other as flagrant cases, committed in the same region, we are in possession. The destruction of this valuable game *is greater by residents of other States than by our own, while arrests and convictions are mostly of our own citizens.*'

---

deer in the month of September for a license cost of $4.00 for residents and $6.00 for non-residents. The license program was wildly unpopular for cost and for the earlier declared open season date of September for the reasons Eckstorm points out in her essays. A revised hunting license program was rolled out in 1917 and was more successful than the first attempt. (maine.gov/ifw/warden-service/history.html, cited February 2023.)

The Commissioners' Report for 1884 says:
'All the severity of remark that the Commissioners felt warranted in uttering last year in relation to the acts of summer visitors, has been more than borne out, more than confirmed by the experiences of the year. * * * We again repeat, the meanness and infamy of the acts seem to be in almost direct ratio to social position, education and profession. * * * *The law has been better observed by our own citizens than visitors from other States.*'

This is supported by what "Special" says in *Forest and Stream*, July 10, 1884:
'Concerning game protection in some sections of Maine, matters are not just what they should be. * * * Just such sportsmen are causing the friends of game protection a great deal of trouble. They demoralize the worst and lowest class of the guides with their money. They care nothing for the future of the game; they are not citizens of the State; their only object is to kill a deer or a moose and come home to be regarded as a great hunter by their friends.'

In *Forest and Stream*, Oct. 30, 1884, "Special" says:
'There has been some hunting of deer with dogs, but *generally by persons living out of the State*, and the law fails to reach a poacher of this class. He kills a deer in close time or with dogs and escapes from the State; his crime is regarded as of too small magnitude to bring him back by requisition, and he steers clear of Maine soil ever after. * * * A few cases are also being worked up by the authorities where deer and caribou have been killed before the season opened. These cases are also generally from out of the State.'

Because the Commissioners and "Special," who has always exactly reflected their opinions, have ceased to speak thus plainly, it may have been supposed that the evil has ceased within a few years. It has not. It has increased proportionately to the increase of the visitors if not faster. Fish, it should be said, are not wasted as formerly, but in the palmiest days of skin hunting the slaughter of moose sometimes was no worse than it has been this year, and fewer deer and caribou were killed then because there were almost no deer and caribou in the State. Leaving the gap between '84 and '88 because it would take too long to give the history of those years, I may come to what I have seen myself in 1888 and 1889. Of course, my own experience is very limited, and would be worthless if not borne out by the testimony of many others.

We were in the woods these two years in the months of August and September, when it is illegal to kill any game animal. We traveled as rapidly as possible along the main routes, not going into the side streams and remote places where sportsmen were going and were at that time staying in numbers, and where they did most of their hunting. We endeavored to ask no impertinent questions of those we met about their business or what they had seen. And yet in 45 days, of which 5 were Sundays, when we did not travel, 3 were spent in travel on railroad and steamboat, and 7 days' time lost by foul weather or other circumstances which kept us within a few rods of the tent, leaving 30 days of actual travel, we knew of fourteen violations of the game laws, which may be tabulated as follows:

Four deer, wholly saved, by residents of the State.

Two deer, at least partly saved, one by resident, one by non-residents.

One deer, probably partly saved, and probably by residents; the names were left, but not where they lived; the size of the party would indicate that most of it was eaten.

One deer, mostly wasted, by sportsmen from New York.

One caribou, all wasted except one hip, by sportsmen from outside the State.

Two deer, without even a pound of meat cut from them, killed by "sports."

Three deer, moose or caribou, not seen but smelled. From the stench, probably the whole, or nearly the whole, was wasted; from the location, off the line of travel of residents and far off from any houses, probably killed by sportsmen.

All but the last five were actually seen, and of the last three we had sufficient olfactory evidence; the two deer wholly wasted were shot between Aug. 22, when we passed down the West Branch, and Aug. 27, when we returned to Chesuncook, where we were informed of the case by one who had examined the deer carefully, and said that they had no mark on them except the bullet holes. We also saw trout and whitefish left to waste–not even thrown into the water where the eels could get them.

This is my own experience. I have compared it with that of others, and will present some extracts from letters giving the opinions of men whose information is probably as great as that of any man in the State.

This comes from an experienced woodsman, not a guide, living at the foot of Moosehead Lake, and so situated that he knows what is done in the woods at all seasons:

> 'I think there is a great deal of large game killed and wasted by summer visitors. What is killed by our own people is made good use of. which is far better than some of the sportsmen do, as they shoot it down and never touch it. I don't think there are many fish wasted by sportsmen: the guides look after this pretty well.'

This is from the head of Moosehead Lake, a point which seventy-five out of every hundred who go into the great game country of the West Branch, Allagash, and East Branch must pass. It contains a good word for sportsmen which I am happy to repeat. The writer's knowledge and veracity cannot be doubted:

> 'It is my opinion that ten times as many moose and deer are killed in the summer months as there is killed in open season and crust-hunting together. There is a growing tendency among the better class of sportsmen to come in the open season. There were more parties left Kineo for the woods after September 25, this year than any two years before.'

One reason for this probably was that the full moon came very late in the month, which made moose calling begin later than usual.

This comes from the neighborhood of Chesuncook:

'Nine-tenths of all moose killed here and near Chesuncook are wasted except skins. I knew of the last season of more than twenty-five moose skins being taken out to sell and only a part of them were brought out to use.'

It may be said that probably most, if not all, these moose hides were taken by one man who stays around Chesuncook. He has killed this year certainly twenty, probably thirty moose, and some reports which investigation has disproved would make the number much higher. This shows who kills the moose? Hardly. As usual the man is not a native of the State, but in this case happens to be a bummer from the Provinces.[115] Our native-born white hunters do not kill game to waste. As the man who wrote the letter quoted from above, says: 'People living here, citizens of the State, do not kill to waste, but Canadian hunters do, and most of the moose hunters are Canadians.'

A guide who has been a great deal on Passadumkeag waters, writes:

'Last summer more than one hundred deer were killed and wounded on the Passadumkeag Stream in the months of July and August, and I saw lots of them rotten on the shore.'

Although not so stated, this must have been done principally by sportsmen. The doggers do not go to work so early, and do not run deer into the streams but into the lakes. The fact of the deer being killed on the stream shows that they were shot while feeding in the water. Settlers would not have left the deer to spoil after killing

---

[115] Around the time of the American Civil War, the term 'bummer' was associated with a loafer, or idle-person; possibly derived from a German word origination. The Province man accused here was Jack Russell. Eckstorm labeled him a 'bummer' because he drifted with no occupation other than killing game for hides in all seasons. He violated the game laws and wasted the meat, leaving it to rot in the woods.

them. I have been told of two sportsmen who went to this region to fish in July, and who killed six deer in spite of all that the guide could do or say against it. When we were in there, we saw no sign of waste, except the forequarters of two deer which had been skinned out and left. Most guides, it may be said, would not call this waste, because the forequarters of a deer are small and light compared with the "saddle," and are not as good meat.

Instead of quoting what I have received from Aroostook, I prefer to repeat what someone who signs himself "Back woodsman" writes in *Shooting and Fishing* for April 2, 1891; the sentiments are the same:

> 'Almost all of the violations of the law in summer are done by tourists and fishermen while going the rounds of our lakes and rivers. They are armed with repeating rifles, and shoot at every living thing they see, whether it be a nursing doe or a chickadee. This is no fancied sketch, but plain, unvarnished facts, and I claim these are the most despicable of poachers; for what they kill is left to rot; while the native crust-hunter usually takes his ill-gotten gains to his family, and in a good many cases is the only meat these poor folks have through the long, cold winter. The latter class are the ones usually caught, as they make more tracks in snow: while those on the water, in a canoe, with a good fat purse to bribe the guide to silence, go unpunished. As a general thing, there has been more poaching the past winter than usual. The law violators attempt to justify themselves by saying if they do not kill the game, the tourist will.'

It certainly is true that more game has been killed this winter in close time than for many years, but it has not been by accident nor entirely because the snow has been deep. It is an avowed retaliation for the enormous waste of game last summer and fall by sportsmen. In November I knew as well that it would be done as I do now that it has been done. Anyone who was in the woods last fall could not fail to predict it if he knew anything about the waste and the feelings of the people. And next winter the same will be repeated unless sportsmen reform very suddenly.

Concerning the waste of game in 1890 by sportsmen, it is enough to say that it has been unparalleled. Without touching at all upon what has been done the length and the breadth of the State, I will give a few facts regarding what has been done in the immediate neighborhood of Chesuncook Lake. And I will quote from only two men, who write only a part of the cases they have known this year. I asked only these two in that vicinity for information because there was danger, if I asked many, of getting the same instances repeated again and again and thus making the case appear worse than it really was; for, of course, no one could tell whether five independent witnesses going to these different ponds and lakes saw the same cases of waste or different cases, without going into a more extended investigation than the importance of this case warrants. Therefore, I call on but two who tell only a part of what they know and confine themselves entirely to cases where the meat was wasted. The first says:

'I went to Duck Pond to get some fresh meat myself and I found three moose dead that had been killed some ten days there, only one hindquarter taken. Mr. Hosford and wife went to Cuxabexis Lake on September 25, they found two large ones there left. I saw one left at Mud Pond and at the foot of this lake, and at Harrington other people saw the remains of six.'

Here is a perfectly trustworthy man who tells of thirteen moose which he has known to be wasted, and twelve of the thirteen killed on four ponds or lakes lying within the limits of three adjoining townships. He makes no mention of deer or caribou, nor of any cases where only one moose was left in a place, except two which he saw himself. This shows that he is telling the smaller part of what he knows about. But it may be said that, since no particulars are given, a large part, if not all these, might have been killed by Jack Russell, the Nova Scotian renegade, who killed so many last year for the skins.[116] As to the absence of names of the offenders, I

---

[116] By naming Jack Russell, Eckstorm, even though she wrote the accusation as, '*might have been killed by Jack Russell,*' became the

particularly stated in asking the information that I wished it for publication and did not want the names; but I think I made it sufficiently clear that I wished to know of cases where *sportsmen* had done the wrong.

We will grant that the above proves only a heartless and inexcusable waste of game; the following shows who was responsible for something similar. This writer knows nothing of what the first had written:

'Last August a party camped at Mud Pond landing two weeks. It is a well-known fact that there is not a trout-fishing ground within five miles, but they were within easy reach of Mud Pond, Quaker Brook and Caribou Thoroughfare, three of the best hunting grounds on Chesuncook.[117] This goes to show that it was hunting and not fishing they were after. In Quaker Brook I saw the body of a large deer with only the horns taken, and after they left, the body of a moose and a caribou were found in Mud Pond. Near September 1, two calf moose were killed at Duck Pond by a party; they lay about two rods apart. The hides and a small piece of the meat were taken. Near the last of September a party of sports killed a bull and a cow moose on Caucomgomoc Stream near Little Scott Brook. They camped till October and then brought the hides and head out openly as killed in October. The meat was left. I made a trip to Loon Lake

---

subject of death threats from the Nova Scotian renegade himself. From her journal notes, she evidently received the information and the name of the offender from Wilbur Webster. The story is told in, *The Penobscot Man - Life and Death on a Maine River.*
[117] The point being, it was August, open season for fish, but closed for large game. When Mrs. Eckstorm's source makes mentions of the lack of '*a trout-fishing ground within five miles,*' he is likely referring to brook trout and not lake trout (togue). While the fish species distribution is different in current years than at the time of the writing (for various reasons, natural and man-induced), the point is, by the source analyzing the location of the camping and time of year, one can surmise the purpose of the intentions.

September 1, and saw a dead caribou at the foot of the lake, and got the smell of tainted meat in a number of places on Loon Lake and Hurd Ponds. This is only a few cases of a great many that have come to my notice.'

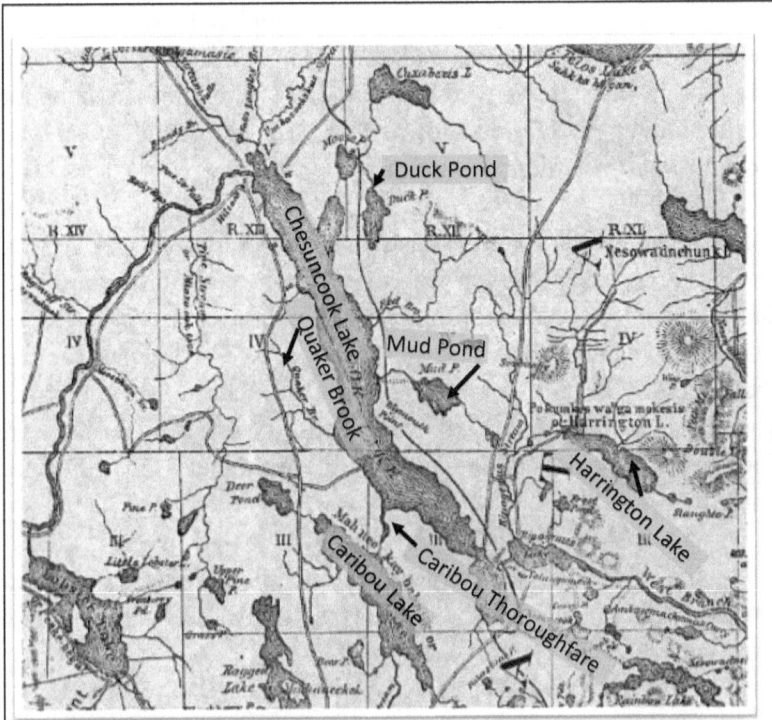

Area near Chesuncook Lake—from Hubbard's 1899 map. The Caribou Thoroughfare no longer exists as shown, as it is now part of the waters between the lakes.

Comment seems superfluous. Here are five moose, two caribou and one deer wasted, Four of the eight were seen by the writer, and all but one are expressly stated to have been killed by sportsmen; for "a party" does not mean Frenchmen, Indians, residents, nor Jack Russell. If they were sportsmen in this case they probably were in the other, for two of the instances referred to by each man are probably inclusive of each other. The three moose which one saw at Duck Pond probably include the two which the other saw a few days earlier. The moose and caribou which one hears of at Mud Pond probably cover the moose which the other saw there. If so, there is no doubt that sportsmen were the murderers. Here are at least eighteen large game animals, principally moose, wasted in the immediate neighborhood of Chesuncook; and if I say that this is one-fifth of the waste on waters that run into Chesuncook last year, I am putting the statement so low that those who know most about it will laugh at the caution shown. This does not include what was honestly eaten whether summer or winter killed.

Besides these thoroughly trustworthy accounts, various reports have come to me from men whom I know to be truthful, but who did not actually see the game. Two different men tell of a moose wasted at Moosehorn Stream on the West Branch above Chesuncook. One of the best guides in the State tells me that his brother saw a cow and a calf sunk in the West Branch between Northeast Carry and Chesuncook, and two others tell the same thing.

Another correspondent writes me concerning what a guide and hunter told him:

'--- was telling me that he saw a Boston man that was guided by one Joe ---, an Indian guide, who shot and killed eight deer in two days and never used only part of one of them, and then he asked his guide if he could not take him where he could find good shooting; and that was last summer. He said that he saw four big moose lying dead just as they were shot by a New York party, and if this kind of work is carried on we know that our game must play out in a short time. There are lots of moose being killed in this section.'

This account is almost startlingly like a story Darling published; although differing in some particulars, there is no disagreement between them. I do not present it as being absolutely correct, for I have not investigated it further, preferring, since I had the matter at a point where it would be easy to find out the real facts, to treat it merely as an example of the way that the news gets around here. That there is truth in it cannot be doubted.

If enough evidence has not been presented to show that the sportsmen who come here "have brought discredit upon themselves by inexcusable violations of the laws, involving the waste of large quantities of game," more definite evidence with names and dates can be furnished.

Fannie Pearson Hardy

**CALLING MOOSE**

from, *Woods and Lakes of Maine - Annotated Edition*

by Lucius L Hubbard,

annotated by Tommy Carbone.

# V. VARIOUS MINOR MATTERS

### Editor Note

In this essay, Eckstorm is addresses the differences in conditions in Piscataquis County. A letter is included from J. F. Sprague, a local resident, who took exception to the characterizations presented of the region.

* * *

### April 30, 1891

The last paper was on an unpleasant topic and needs the relief of the brighter side to prevent misunderstanding, for some will say: "Are there no good sportsmen then?" And those who have come here and left a record of honorable acts will ask in discouragement, "Have all that we have done counted for nothing?"

Far from it! to both. There are such honorable sportsmen—to them these papers are addressed. They have done well and it is remembered for them. We look for some of them every year, and are glad to see that they have returned; when finally they shall cease to come, among those who regret their loss most deeply will be some at this end of their accustomed haunts. A man is prized here for what he is, and is judged by what he does; nor need the one who has lived honorably and spoken truly ever fear the judgments of Maine backwoodsmen, or an uncordial welcome to Maine.

I have a curious matter to present, which I can in no way explain without taking into account the influence of such men as these. In the four counties of which I speak there is one that in some ways is so different from the others that at first it would seem it ought not to be counted with them. In area it is one of the largest in the State; in population the smallest of all. More sportsmen go there than to all the other three; and in proportion to its area more such enormities as were described in the last article are committed than in any of the other counties. And yet the residents of Piscataquis County do not, so far as I have been able to learn, either feel or speak upon game matters in the same way as those of the other eastern counties. I have not so far found that they were greatly disturbed by the present unhappy state of affairs. At first it would seem that this county ought to be classed with the western part of the State; but in all its interests it belongs to Penobscot waters, and so a different explanation must be sought. What? In the first place some of the grievances of the eastern part of the State have scarcely touched this county; but even so, why should it not sympathize? In the supposition by which I have been able to explain the matter I may be wholly or partly wrong, but it is the only one by which I can account for a noticeable difference.

I think that the character of the summer visitors who go there largely explains it. That county includes Moosehead Lake, Katahdin Iron Works and many other resorts more or less known. It is visited by people who go for recreation, for fishing and for hunting. Now, of those who go for the two former purposes, a very large part stay at hotels or near enough the settlements for the residents to know them personally or to know of them, and a better class of visitors than most of these could not be desired. The people there form their opinion from these. Of those who go to hunt most pass beyond the settlements into the deep woods, and they are the ones whose misdeeds are so widely reported. The eastern counties hear of these principally—and much less of those who stay on the borders of civilization. But Piscataquis people know the latter also, and while no less severe in condemnation of such waste and slaughter as I have reported, do not blame the whole class of summer visitors, but the individuals who are responsible. In this way the presence of these well-disposed, honorable men coming to stay for a time and not merely to pass through the country, seems to me to account, in part at least, for this manifest difference in feeling, and so to be its own reward. Lest a mistake should occur, I will say that by "sportsman" as I have used it, and as it is used in this locality, I mean those with whom hunting is the principal object—not fishermen nor tourists, but those who wish to kill large game. In using it I do not intend to include any other class of summer visitors.

Of those who come for this purpose, observation and consultation convince me that the majority come and go in close time and kill what they get illegally; but there are certain honorable exceptions of whom it would be a pleasure to speak if space permitted, but who surely are no more condemned with the majority than are these others of whom we have spoken above by the people of Piscataquis County.

Lest there should be a misunderstanding on another point, I wish to state again that in what I have said so far, I have tried to represent other people's views rather than my own, and to give their reasons for these opinions instead of those which I might hold personally. For my own opinions on most of these matters I conceive to be of little value. That I sympathize fully with the people who say these things is most true, but does not make it necessary for me to believe all these charges correct, even though they may not be baseless. I do not believe that our Legislature is wholly corrupt, nor that the game laws have been unfair, nor that all visitors are lawless and all residents are saints—nor, it may be added, that the people here all think so.[118] What we all hold is that grave wrongs have been done—and I will show some of them in the forthcoming papers—which have greatly disturbed a very large number of people, which have caused loss of property and loss of life, which still endanger both and are fully sufficient to account for all the complaints that have been made and for others yet more radical. I might claim even more and be fully able to sustain it, but this is enough. In the papers which have preceded I have tried to represent the state of public feeling at present, thus preparing by anticipation for those which follow which will tell the causes and deal with facts instead of with theories.

If it should be asked after this part, *Where* is the good sportsman? It will certainly be asked after the second, *Where* is the good warden? He is not very abundant here, but in this immediate vicinity we have one man who deserves special mention. Mr. Eben G. Morse, of Eddington, is a warden whose justice, faithfulness and honesty are believed in by the people here. I have never but once

---

[118] Emphasis by the editor.

heard him accused of doing anything which was not honorable, and that he did not do, although there was reason for the suspicion. I may make this personal mention here, for it is he who has suggested that I should explain more fully some points regarding my article published on April 2, mainly those relating to the holding of game animals alive. This I am the more happy to do, as it may not only bring out some facts clearly, but will illustrate an interpretation of the game law which caused trouble three years since.

Mr. Morse writes: "The law making it subject to fine for hunting and keeping alive is of recent date, and was not in effect nor passed at the time that the deer kept at the Bangor House were caught; and Mr. Beal or any other person, rich or poor, had a lawful right to catch and keep such animals. But later on, and before Davis caught the caribou, the-law was amended so as to prohibit the hunting in close time." Mr. Morse thinks that insufficient information was given on these cases, which was indeed necessary at that time on account of lack of space.

Regarding the Bangor House deer, I may quote the following letter from their owner:

"To the best of my memory I bought my first deer in the spring of '82, buying two at that time. The next winter I bought another, and then raised several. In the spring of '84 I bought an albino buck, the other buck having escaped. I had them every year until I sold them in the fall of '88. My impression is that those which I bought were in captivity but a short time. Trusting that this is the information which you desire, I remain, very respectfully, F. O. Beal."

The point of my reference to these deer was that they were allowed to be kept in Bangor at a time when other people were required to release deer and other animals which they had captured, and that this gave rise to the complaint that one man was favored more than another. The complaint was made. I did not seek to discuss its justice though I tacitly admitted it; nor did I try to give the whole facts. These, as the letter shows, were that one deer was undoubtedly legally held, having been taken before 1883; and that the white one was not legally held as the law was afterward interpreted, though supposed by the owner to be so; that neither was disposed of until after other people had been forced to liberate animals, and that then they were not set free but *sold*. The facts have borne out the statement which I made. It would be interesting to trace their history from this date.

But respecting the change in the law to which Mr. Morse refers, there was no change in the law from 1883 to 1891, but there was a change in the interpretation; which is what Mr. Morse means. This occurred in 1888 or a little earlier, but was not legally established until 1889. Until last month there was no explicit law against holding live game taken in close season, and it very rarely can be taken when there is no snow on the ground. Since our game laws were first originated in 1830 there have been but two passages which could apply to such a case.

Sec. 11, passed in 1878, reads:

"Whoever has in his possession the carcass or hide of any such animal, or any part thereof, between the first days of January and October, shall be deemed to have hunted and destroyed the same contrary to law," etc.

Sec. 9 on moose and 10 on deer and caribou (Both passed in 1883) say:

"And no person shall, between the first days of January and October, in any manner hunt, kill or destroy," etc.

The two are not mutually inclusive. On the one hand it is forbidden to kill large game at a certain season, and also to hunt it. On the other it is forbidden to have in possession dead game taken at that time, but nothing is said about live game captured then. If it is legal to have the game alive in close time, why is it illegal to hunt it then for the purpose of keeping it alive? If it is illegal to hunt it for this purpose, why is it legal to have the game so taken? It is evident that all depends on the definition of hunting if we are to construe the law in the strictest way.

But at first it was not so interpreted. For nearly five years it was admitted that anyone could capture and keep live animals taken in close season. Hence the keeping of the albino deer at the Bangor House. In 1888, or a little earlier, the opposite interpretation was unexpectedly put upon the law. and it was declared illegal to keep any game animal taken in close time. Did this refer merely to those taken after this decree, or after 1883, or after the decision of the court in 1889? It would be hard to say: but there are a number of instances of animals being let loose before the law court gave its decision on the James vs. Wood case.

The grounds of this change in interpretation are interesting. There was no possible reason except what could be reduced from the one word "hunting." The one who held a game animal taken in close season could be prosecuted for hunting it, but not for having it. As Mr. Morse says: "The having it in possession was not taken into account, only to prove the hunting. I admit that the law did not prohibit having live deer, moose, or caribou, if taken in open time or if obtained in any way without hunting it in close time." This sudden change in the meaning of the law caused some trouble. The Davis case occurred about this time, and in the western part of the State there was a famous one which was carried up to the law court—Isaac H. James vs. Thomas P. Wood, a game warden, who, without process, released or caused the plaintiff to release from his own enclosure, a moose and a deer. The moose was captured by Mr. James in March, 1888; the deer bought by him the same month. In the lower court Mr. James was awarded $125 damages. The case was then carried to a higher court, and the opinion of the law court given Dec. 11, 1889, was in favor of the defendant warden.

Mr. James's moose and deer were set at liberty June 6, 1888. As evidence that the interpretation of the law which allowed this to be done was considered very doubtful, I may say that on September 14 of the same year (1888) I saw a full-grown caribou, with fair-sized horns, confined in a pen near the railroad station at Winn in this county. I was told that it was taken in close season. I was also told that a warden had been sent to release it; that the possessor had refused to allow him to do it; and that the warden had yielded. What became of the animal afterward I do not know. The Bangor House deer were kept somewhat later than this, I am very sure. Mr. Morse tells me that he has known several to pay fines for keeping live game "after it became unlawful," which I understand to be previous to Dec. 11, 1889, as I have heard of none since then, though some who had captured deer have let them go.

In support of my definition of hunting, and to show that Mr. Morse did not proceed as too many wardens have done here in pursuance of plans that no court would uphold, even when he released the caribou on the ground that to put on snowshoes to follow it constitutes hunting, I will quote from the James vs. Wood case, Law Reports 82, Maine 179: "The plaintiff followed the moose in the forest until it became snow-bound, and then, by the use of a rope, tied it to a tree, and finally bound it upon a sled and hauled it some fifteen miles to his home, where he confined it until it was released by defendant. Without doubt this conduct resulting in capture was in violation of the statute. The plaintiff did not destroy or kill the animal, but he did hunt and thereby capture it."

This matter which from one side is unimportant, from another has weight. It shows a law changed from a looser to a stricter interpretation. In my next article I will show another which has had just the opposite history during the eight years past.

Mr. Morse calls my attention to an error in one of the cases mentioned. I wrote partridges "legally killed in December" when I should have said November. I am likely to make other similar mistakes, and will correct them when brought to my notice, if not too trivial or having no real bearing upon the point in question.

Since writing the above I notice the following in the Bangor Daily Whig and Courier, April 25:

"A buck caught at Moose River has been brought to Portland and placed in Deering Park as a companion to the fawn presented to the city by Captain Winslow last spring. A yard will soon be built for them."

If true, this is an ample commentary on what has been said. Are there any deer in Deering Park? If so, by what right?

Fannie Pearson Hardy

## Editor Note

In the October 11, 1883 issue of Forest and Stream, J. F. Sprague wrote: "It is useless to deny that they were openly and notoriously making an attempt to violate the game laws of Maine." (Sprague's response to "Olibo," about sportsmen poachers. The full letter is included in the Appendix.)

In the following letter, Sprague criticizes Hardy's opinion, where he claimed she did not speak for how the people of Maine felt for sportsmen, specifically the location of Maine around Moosehead Lake, which was near his home territory of Monson, Maine. In actuality, he was directly supporting her thesis in her critique based on her definitions of woodsmen, hunters, fishermen, tourists, guides, and sportsmen; of which the last of 'sportsmen,' consisted of various classes, the worst in her analysis being those referred to as 'sports,' and of being a very small percentage. Hardy wrote herself that she was speaking for a very distinct group of people, and that was the most rural hunter, farmer, and woodsmen. She was very clear that she was not speaking for all, for herself, or for all of Maine.

\* \* \*

## J. F. SPRAGUE - A LETTER TO THE EDITOR, 1891
### Editor Forest and Stream:

If a perfect history of the travels and transactions of the sportsmen in the entire Moosehead Lake region could be fully brought to light by an impartial investigation, I am satisfied that it would completely demonstrate the fact that the cases cited by Miss Hardy are only exceptional ones. On the other hand, she does not represent the "residents" of Maine as a whole. She is speaking only for a fractional part of the citizens of this State, as I firmly believe. Neither does she voice the sentiment of a majority of those residing near the great wilderness country frequented by sportsmen. I can recall cases which have come under my own observation where several hundred dollars have been paid into the treasury of

Piscataquis County for fines for violation of the game laws by residents of other States.

I know that during the past three years we have suffered by a lax enforcement of these laws. I know further that as bitter complaints on account of this have come from backwoodsmen and guides in the Moosehead section, who are during every summer season largely associated with the sportsmen, and necessarily influenced more or less by them, as from any other source.

Now, if these sportsmen as a class were as destructive of game in intention or in practice as Miss Hardy avers,[119] it goes without saying that they would impress their ideas upon the guides. That they do influence them to a great extent is undeniable, and the fact that they do not, as a general rule, countenance or aid infractions of the laws while guiding, but that many of them are among the staunchest and most sincere supporters of the code, is to my mind positive evidence that the great mass of their employers have done everything in their power to educate them up to this standard.

I hope that as Miss Hardy has opened it, the *Forest and Stream* will give both sides of the question. I do not feel competent to give the other side, but I hope others who are will join me.

I feel, as do many in this section, that we are, as residents, and as real backwoodsmen, being misrepresented by her.

J. F. Sprague – Monson, Me.

## Editor Note

The following was published by the editors of *Forest and Stream* on the waste of game in the north woods and near Moosehead Lake.

## Editorial – Sept. 17, 1891 – Harlow Letter

The Bangor News prints a letter from Edgar E, Harlow, of Greenville, Moosehead Lake, and the News appears to think the statements in the letter worthy of credence. It recounts the following

---

[119] Eckstorm did not class all sportsmen into one class and she was clear to say so.

list of game animals recently discovered by Kineo guides, and says that not a single offender has yet been brought to justice: "One dead cow moose at Thoroughfare Brook, Eagle Lake; one dead moose on Russell Stream; one dead caribou on Russell Stream; one dead deer on Russell Stream; one dead moose at Duck Pond; one dead moose at Eagle Lake campground; one dead moose at Caucomgomoc Lake; one dead caribou at Black Pond; one dead deer at Horse Race, Caucomgomoc Stream; one dead moose at Spencer Pond; three dead deer at Spencer Pond; two dead moose at Soper Brook, Eagle Lake."

We would be glad to learn that this report is an exaggeration, for if the facts are actually as given, they indicate in the Moosehead region a demoralization worse than that already described in the *Forest and Stream* as existing in other sections. It must be remembered that the open season for moose, deer and caribou will not begin before the first of next month.

## Editorial
## Maine's Big Game – Oct. 1, 1891

We referred the other day to a letter written by Mr. E. E. Harlow, of Greenville, Me., in the *Bangor News*, stating that several moose, deer and caribou had been wantonly killed in the vicinity of Moosehead Lake, by persons undetected. The *News* returns to the topic, and says; "From a personal acquaintance with Mr. Harlow, the *News* knows him to be the soul of truthfulness. He has been around Kineo and Greenville for several seasons past, and knows a majority of the guides intimately. Hence, he is not liable to be imposed upon by 'hunter's yarns.' The inference is that he was rightly informed, that the guides saw what they reported, and that Mr. Harlow consequently gave a correct account of actual events. Since printing Mr. Harlow's communication, the *News* has taken pains to ascertain how far the law is violated in the Moosehead region, and while it is not ready to publish all the details learned, enough was found out to show that Harlow's report did not half tell the tale of illegal slaughter that is practiced in that vicinity. Employees of the *Bangor & Piscataquis Railroad* state that deerhounds and foxhounds are constantly going 'up Moosehead way,' and that the owners of these dogs declare openly they are going to dog deer. Names of parties who keep dogs at Greenville for the purpose of chasing moose were also given, and many other valuable pointers to show where the law breakers hide. The same story with variations comes from other parts of eastern Maine. The name of a sporting rendezvous at Chemo, where dogs are kept to run deer, has been given to the *News* with other particulars that would be of value to, and is available for any honest game warden in the State. The *Forest and Stream,* with the instincts of a true sportsman, would be glad to learn that the reports are exaggerated. So would the *News*; and while the *News* is practically convinced that the reports are true, it still waits, hoping to hear of arrests for law breaking, or, what is better still, a cessation of the most unholy practices that now prevail. The State of Maine is a grand old State. It is full of brave, law-abiding men and noble women. It is a shame, the *News* confesses, that there are cowardly lawbreakers who lay claim to citizenship. Yet it is a lasting shame and disgrace to the game commissioners and wardens to allow such deeds to go on from year to year without making a vigorous attempt to bring the offenders to justice. In conclusion, the *News* requests all persons who know of parties who are violating the game laws of this State to send full particulars to this paper. The names of those sending the particulars must accompany every letter, but will not be used if the writers desire to remain unknown. It is time that the pirates of the forest were shown up. They have ruled the State too long."

# VI. ON NON-TRANSPORTATION IN OPEN SEASON

### Editor Note
In this essay Eckstorm quotes statutes and case rulings to explain how non-legal methods had been used to deny the transport of legally killed game and the confiscation of legal game. She brings to light the facts on how some Mainers may have been treated unfairly, and even robbed of their legal possessions. It is clear she also supports the right of out-of-staters to legally transport their game under the law.

\* \* \*

### May 7, 1891

**For** the plain words to our visitors that have preceded, let us even use Robin Hood's own apology:

"Nay, my Lord Bishop," said Robin Hood, "we are rough fellows, but I trust not such ill men as thou thinkest after all. There is not a man here that would harm a hair of thy reverence's head. I know thou art galled by our jesting, but we are all equal here in the greenwood, for there are no bishops, nor barons nor earls among us, but only men, so thou must share our life with us whilst thou dost abide here."

Most sportsmen will remember that we have had a very strict non-transportation law—at least, they will say that their impression is such. Of any twelve men here, who are interested in game matters, the majority will say the same—a very strict non-transportation law, strictly enforced, recently so modified that game legally killed can be shipped to points inside the State but not outside. It will be generally admitted that from 1883 onward we had a law which practically forbade any deer, moose, or caribou to be transported from point to point, except by private conveyance.

Let us hear from "Special" (in letters from several years ago):

— — —

*Forest and Stream*, Nov. 13, 1884: "It is not pleasant to be obliged to say that even under the very strong transportation law of Maine, deer carcasses and even moose antlers do get out of that State and are seen here.[120] * * * A fine pair of deer antlers came through the other day, and worse yet, five carcasses of venison came through last week. The name of the express company is known which forwarded them and the Maine Commissioners have been notified."

*Forest and Stream*, Nov. 27, 1884: "Even ex-Governor Connor could not transport a deer, killed honorably in open season, from Bangor to Augusta last fall. Commissioner Stilwell when applied to said: 'Governor, I can do nothing for you under the law.' * * * This was under the first enforcement of the new transportation law in that State, which few at that time understood."

*Forest and Stream*. Dec. 11, 1884: "As for venison, there came through from Maine the season before the non-transportation law went into effect between 1,800 and 2.000 carcasses. They actually rotted outside the Boston markets. Thanks to the good work of the Commissioners, such barbarous and wicked waste of noble game has been stopped. * * * Not a day passes but what the wardens at the large shipping points in Maine seize partridges, ducks, or saddles of venison, being smuggled through to Boston or New York. The tricks of the poachers are as curious as they are numerous, etc."

*Forest and Stream*, Feb. 26. 1885: "The Legislature was also asked to legalize transportation of game over the railroads, when accompanied by the owner, but no satisfaction to the market hunters or the market men was obtained."

— — —

---

[120] 'Special' was from near the Boston area.

Is this not strong corroboration of the all but universal impression that the transportation of game was forbidden in Maine at all seasons? To be sure, one man is the author of the whole of it; but he asserts what we all know, that the Commissioners declared this was the law; that the wardens executed it as law; that the people believed it to be law, and that they even petitioned the Legislature for a change.

Let us examine the legal history of the subject. Our first non-transportation law was that of 1878, which read as follows: "Sec. 13. Whoever carries or transports from place to place the carcass or hide of any such animal or any part thereof, during the period in which the killing of such animal is prohibited, forfeits forty dollars."

What was the change in 1883 which everyone admits? We quote from the Revised Statutes, Chap. 30, Sec. 13: "Whoever carries or transports from place to place the carcass or hide of any such animal or any part thereof, during the period in which the killing of such animal is prohibited, forfeits forty dollars."

Has there been a change since? Book of the Game Laws, 1890: "Sec. 13. Whoever carries or transports from place to place the carcass or hide of any such animal, or any part thereof, during the period in which the killing of such animals is prohibited, forfeits forty dollars."

**To the self-same tune and words!**

That is all anyone can find anywhere in our laws regarding non-transportation at any season. **There is not the change of a jot, nor title, an iota, nor a comma in it.**[121] For thirteen years now we have had this non-transportation law and no other.

Why is it that the Commissioners can do nothing to help the ex-governor "under the law?"

Why is it that the wardens are all instructed to seize game legally killed?

Why is it that the Legislature is asked to alter a law which never existed?

---

[121] Emphasis is the editor's.

And how could such a delusion gain ground over a whole State, when there was no change at all in the law and had not been for five years?

If not in this law there had been a change in another which seemed to affect this. In 1883 the one moose, two caribou, three deer law was passed. This law, limiting the number to be killed, also made it illegal to have more than the prescribed number in possession—a necessary measure, throwing the burden of proof upon the accused when proof by the accuser might be impossible. Whether it was intended to do more than this is not for the unlearned in the law to say; but that the phrase "to have in possession" was too sweepingly interpreted at first, there can be no doubt. It was officially declared that to handle a deer in any way was to have it in possession. The strictest orders were given that no conveyance, public or private, should carry, haul, or in any manner convey more than one moose, two caribou, three deer for the season. Stage drivers were warned not to do it under penalty of seizure of all deer so carried.

"This new game law," said one of the shrewdest lawyers in Bangor to another, "is a queer kind of a law. Now supposing I have three deer legally killed, and you have three that you have killed legally, and you have a sled while I haven't any. Now if as a favor you tell me to pile my deer on your sled, the whole six can be seized, can't they, by this law?" The other agreed. When I asked one of them a week ago if he remembered the conversation, he said that he did not, but until he looked the matter up, he always supposed that the law would sanction such an action.

But how did this gain general acceptance? More than in any other way, by the refusal of the principal railroad and express companies to transport venison. When large corporations admitted that to convey game from one place to another was to have it in possession and gave up their business with game on account of it, it was natural for private individuals to suppose that they had carefully examined the whole field. Perhaps they did according to their light, but they could not have had the best of legal advice, for we now know that no transportation company can refuse to take what is offered. Neither could our Commissioners have consulted able counsel, or they, too, would have known that common carriers cannot be said to have "in possession" what they are conveying. A little investigation would have convinced them that they had no right to interfere with the transportation of animals legally killed. Apparently this investigation was not given; because for years we have witnessed the curious anomaly of a whole force of special officers, hired and paid to execute the fish and game laws, being detailed to carry out the orders of transportation companies to their own employees—orders which themselves were untenable and illegal; and being instructed to enforce the orders not by punishing the delinquent employees, but by confiscating the goods which they received in disobedience to the commands of the company, but which, once received, the company was in honor bound to deliver safely.

The transportation companies have received goods up river, and the officers at Bangor and elsewhere have seized them and converted them to their own use without even a form of law; yet, it was not contrary to the laws to ship these goods, the transportation companies could not refuse to take them, and the wardens or officers who made the seizure very often transgressed every form of law in doing the same. Complicated and absurd as this state of affairs seems, it has prevailed here for years.

This is ridiculous, but it may not have been intentionally unjust at the first. Let us be charitable enough to grant that the Commissioners, wardens, and railroad companies at the first thought that they were keeping the law to the letter, and that they erred only through over-zeal. Yet in the *Forest and Stream* for April 24, 1884, "Special" says:

"But when early last winter, Payson Tucker, superintendent of the Maine Central Railroad, issued his remarkable order to forward no more moose, caribou, deer, or other unlawfully killed game over his road or its branches, [122] the backbone of Maine market-hunting was broken. He was immediately followed by a similar order from

---

[122] This railroad order was related to illegal winter hunting, but the effect on transport during the legal open season carried over.

the managers of nearly every other express and transportation company with lines leading out of Maine."

This admits that the order was a private one in every case. But before the year is out, as may be seen by the quotations already given, he speaks of "the strong non-transportation law;" calls those who undertake to ship game which was legally killed "poachers;" and quotes Mr. Stilwell as saying that shipping could not be allowed "under the law."

Now there was no such law and had been none. Instead of that (though "Special" may not have known it) more than a month before he wrote this last extract, and fully eight months before those previously quoted, a case had been decided in Bangor, which seems to show that the ex-Governor could have transported his deer and could have done it "under the law."

It was the Allen-Young case, which may be found in the Maine Law Reports, 76 p. 80. The facts are these:

Benjamin L. Young, of Milford, on Feb. 17, 1883, shipped by express for Boston two deer legally killed Dec. 30 and 31, 1882. At Bangor, Thomas F. Allen, a game warden, seized them on the plea that they were shipped contrary to law—which was admitted. But Mr. Young maintained that as they were legally killed, the law prohibiting the shipment (Sec. 13, already quoted) was either defective or subject to a different interpretation. The case was carried before the full bench of judges, and Mr. Young's claim was sustained. The judges' opinion is of great interest, but too long to quote entire. "We fail to see," they say, "any motive for making the mere transportation of the hide or carcass of a deer from one place to another a crime when the deer has been lawfully killed and is lawfully in the possession of the one who transports it [the shipper? or the express company?]. Certainly, one may reasonably doubt whether such could have been the intention of the Legislature; and the act being a penal one, a reasonable doubt is sufficient to make it the duty of the Court to adopt the more lenient interpretation and construe the term 'such animal' as meaning an animal unlawfully killed, as was done in construing a similar statute in Com. v. Hall. Mass., 410."

The trial of this case before the Bangor Municipal Court was in March, 1883. The decision of the judges was given March 4, 1884. The case itself occurred more than six months before the question of non-transportation in the open season came up. The decision was given nearly six months after the transportation managers had refused to receive venison. In giving their decision the judges must have known of this later much-discussed phase of transportation, although they do not refer to it explicitly. In framing an opinion, it is at least probable that they would word it so as to apply to cases likely to come up under the new arrangement if this change could in any way affect the question of transportation. This is their opinion:

"The transportation of the hide or carcass of a deer from place to place in this State is not unlawful at any time if the deer was killed at a time when it was lawful to do so."

Need anything more be said on that point?

It should be noted that what the judges say of transportation "in the State," does not prohibit transportation outside of State limits. Mr. Young's deer were marked to "Boston," yet the case was decided in his favor. The judges had no jurisdiction over inter-State matters, is the meaning. There is nothing in this to support the view of a witness in the McPheters case (see below) that it is illegal to send venison out of the State, though of late this has frequently been declared.

Here, as early as 1884, only a year after the three deer law was passed, six months after transportation in open season was forbidden, is a decision which settles the whole matter so far as the duty of the Commissioners and wardens is concerned. True, it does not say whether a transportation company can carry more than three deer for the season; but it does say that any man who legally owns three deer may carry them where he pleases. If the railroad and transportation companies cannot take these deer for their owner, or think they cannot, that is their business. If they do take them, it is at their own risk, not the owner's; and if anybody is to be arrested it is the plain duty of the wardens to arrest the railroads. It is no longer a question in which the game or the owners of it are concerned.

Did the Commissioners forbid the wardens to seize game in transportation after this decision? The decision was given March 4, 1884. Read (again) what "Special" says under date of Dec. 11, 1884 (*see quotes earlier this essay*). There is no lack of corroborative testimony. Did the Commissioners know of this decision? They did. First, it was their duty to know it, understand it and act in accordance with it. Second, the suit was begun by one of the prominent wardens and he was defeated—which could not fail to be known to the Commissioners. Third, Mr. Stilwell himself was present at the trial before the municipal court and knew the facts. Yet the work of seizing game while in transportation in open season did not fairly begin until the fall of 1884, and was kept up until January, 1889, in spite of this decision.

It is this on the one side that makes people here believe that this interpretation of the law was not accidental.

On the other hand, the action of the transportation companies laid them open to criticism on the same score. If they had refused to take any game because it made them liable to suits for damages, they would of course be liable as long as the law was in force, and that law (Sec. 12) still exists. Nevertheless, the transportation companies repeatedly ran the risks of this penalty. Game *was* put on board the trains, and the employees allowed it. They refused to handle it themselves, but they did not interfere when the owner picked up his own deer and carried it aboard the train, even if he carried it into the passenger car, as my father did once.

A guide writes me: "All parties that I have had, have carried their game home, they would put it aboard themselves and watch it, but most always had a lot of cheap talk with the railroad men and wardens. But when the men hung to their game the wardens did not dare to meddle with it."

In short it was not very long before non-transportation became this: 'No deer can be carried unless the owner is with them to keep the wardens from seizing them.' The railroads, it was discovered, could carry all they pleased; they were not liable for having them in possession. The wardens, however, could seize anything that was carried—at least did seize everything they wished to. The result was that no one was responsible except the owner of the deer, whose right to convey his own property over public lines of travel was neither protected nor recognized. The cases of illegal seizure of game, belonging both to sportsmen outside and to citizens, are too many to admit this statement's being questioned. Non-transportation came to be as I have said: *merely a question of whether the owner was present to prevent himself being robbed.*

At last it became customary for the company to check deer as personal baggage, both for convenience and safety. The railroad employees no longer refused to handle it, the companies were gracious about receiving it and the owner rested easy at Bangor, Still all was not safe, as the McPheters case shows. This case has recently been settled and I have obtained the printed report of evidence, attested by the clerk of courts, from which I quote the following to show what has been done in Bangor in the name of the law:

"Walter F. McPheters, plaintiff, called by his counsel, testified: I shipped these deer at Costigan by rail to Boston, Nov. 5, 1888. Costigan is in the town of Milford, in this county (Penobscot). They were checked; I took checks for them. There was nothing on them to indicate the direction or the person to whom shipped, but the checks. I have the checks now. I bought a ticket for Boston at the same time I shipped the deer. I saw them put on to the cars. * * * The next thing that came to my attention, I heard the deer were taken in Bangor. I went to Bangor to see about them soon afterward. I received no notice from any officer or any court of any seizure. I went to Bangor to see about the deer about the 25th of November."

Cross Examiner—Question. "Did you have any trouble in getting the railroad to take the deer?" Answer. "I did not. There was no conversation to me or in my presence by any of the agents of the company. I had bought my ticket before I asked to ship the deer."

The deer were seized by George W. Harriman, of Bangor, a private detective, warden, and special State liquor constable. He admits taking one whole deer and two saddles which had checks agreeing in every particular with those which Mr. McPheters showed. He testifies: "I took them at the Maine Central depot in this city. We brought them to Mr. Page's market for storage. Mr. Mayville, Mr. Nickerson, and myself were the men that took the deer. We took them directly to Mr. Page's market. I went with them. Mr. Nickerson was on the wagon with me. We left them in Mr. Page's market."

Question. "Did you ever see them or any portion of them again at Page's market?"

Answer. "Yes, sir. We divided them; each one of us took one."

A little further on:

Question. "What did you seize them for; under what claim of right?"

Objection Admitted.

Answer. "We supposed we had a right to, *as it was wrong to ship them out of the State*." (FPH: The italics are mine.)

Question. "You did not then claim to have any right of seizure except upon that ground?"

Answer. "That is what we supposed."

The answer shows how little of the law some of our wardens, who have been longest in the business, know, and the kind of acts in which they will engage. No evidence is brought forward to show that Mr. Harriman used a warrant. By the testimony of himself and the other two it is shown that they divided the deer among themselves without appeal to any of the proper authorities and without notifying the owner what had become of his property. The same thing has been done repeatedly in Bangor. I select this case from many other (examples) merely because the testimony was given under oath and is a matter of court record. The suit itself, though won by McPheters, is wholly indecisive, because it was brought against the marketman who received the deer, instead of against the officer who took them, on account of a technicality.

The case of George W. Bennett against the American Express Company, an action to recover the saddles of three deer, is a test case. The agreed statement of facts published for the court, attested by the clerk of courts, says that on Dec. 5, 1888, George W. Bennett delivered at Newport Station on the M. C. R. R., a box containing the saddles of three deer legally killed, to be shipped by express to Boston; that the express agent was not at the station when Bennett left, but delivered the box to the express company's car, giving no receipt or bill of lading; that said saddles was seized by Thomas F.

Allen, a game and fish warden, on said fifth day of December, and removed by him from said express company's possession at Augusta, Maine, without any search warrant or other legal process, and without objections from the express company or their agents, and have never since been delivered to said express company." It is also agreed that the express company had notified its agents not to receive any venison for transportation, but that they had done so previously, and that in this case no questions were asked as to the contents of the box. Verdict for plaintiff.

The case is so important that it is worthwhile to quote some of the authorities which were cited at its trial, 1890. They settle conclusively the whole non-transportation question, as it was under the laws previous to March, 1891. (FH: Italics my own):

- A delivery is always sufficient if the proper servants of the company accept the goods to carry, whether any bill or entry in the books of the company is made or not. (Redfield on Carriers, Sec. 101, page 82, and the cases cited.)
- Common carriers are insurers of all property intrusted (sic.) to them, except against an act of God or an enemy of the Government. (Plaisted vs. B. & K. Steam Nav. Co., 27 Me., 132 Fillebrown vs. G. T. Railway Co., 55 Me., 462.)
- The American Express Co. did not restrict their liability, as no notice was brought home to the plaintiff, or was assented to by him. (Fillebrown vs. G. T. Railway Co., 55 Me., 462; Bucland vs. Adams Express Co., 97 Mass., 125.)
- Neither can they so restrict as to release them from liability for loss occasioned by their own negligence. (Sager vs. Portsmouth S. & P. & E. Railroad Co., 31 Me., 228, and the cases therein cited: True vs. International Telegraph Co., 60 Me., 13.)
- The American Express Co. surrendered the box of deer saddles to Thomas F. Allen[123] without demanding his authority and

---

[123] FH (original footnote): Thomas F. Allen, of Bangor, formerly a policeman, now a private detective and game warden. The partner of Harriman above named. For some years, Mr. Allen has been the leading game warden of this section.

without objection on their part or by their agents. (Statement of Facts).

- Carriers are compelled to solve claimants' right at their peril. (Redfleld on Carriers. Sec. 244, page 197).
- On service of a legal process he may surrender goods into the custody of the law. (2 Pars. Contr., 207).
- Allen had no right or authority to seize the deer saddles, as he had no warrant or other legal process. (Constitution of Maine. Art. 1, Sec. 5. U. S. Constitution, Art. 14. Sec. 1 [and other cases]).
- The saddles were *not in the possession of the American Express Co. within the "meaning of Sec. 12. Chap. 30, R. S.* As a common carrier has only an insurable interest and a lien for his freight. (Redfield on Carriers, Sec. 308, page 226, and cases cited).
- Also such could not be the fact because it would be in violation of the Inter-State Commerce Law. (U. S. Constitution, Sec. 8 Spec. 3.)
- Common carriers cannot select what they may carry or what they may refuse, but are bound to take all which offer. (Redfield on Carriers, Sec. 100, page 82 [and several cases].)
- When the box of deer saddles were taken by the defendant company for transportation out of the State, and transportation began, they became subjects of commerce, and were governed by the laws of the U. S. (Coe vs. Enol, 116, U. S., 517. 10 Wall, 557-565 18 Fed. Rep. 10.)
- Commerce with foreign countries and among the States strictly considered, consists in intercourse and traffic, including in these terms navigation and transportation and transit of persons and property, as well as the purchase, sale and exchange of commodities. To regulate it, as thus defined, there must be only one style of rules, applicable alike to the whole country, which Congress alone can prescribe. (Various references.)

That is the Bennett case, decided last year—a conclusive demonstration of the colossal humbug of non-transportation in open

season. Strangers, and citizens alike, have given up their property
to those who showed no right to seize it, who had no right, either
legally or morally, and the authorities have never once come out to
tell us what our rights were, nor to stop the depredations. That at
first this was done in ignorance is possible, though no excuse.

That the authorities should have remained ignorant all these
years, requires faith amounting to credulity to believe.

That the railroad and express companies should know so little of
the laws on which their charters were founded as to have done this
ignorantly, is inconceivable.

The fact that such an imposition should have been allowed to go
on year after year does not greatly increase the credit which will be
given to any explanations that can now be made by those who
allowed it, or who first schemed it.

It is said here that it was done to stop market-hunting, so that the
deer might be saved for sportsmen, attracting them hither and
increasing the travel on the railroads. A small object to gain when
obtained by the suppression of both law and right, the toleration of
a scheme of systematic robbery against which private redress was
hard to get, the transformation of a people that were over-trustful
toward those who managed their affairs into a people hard, bitter,
suspicious, accusing.

Anyone who has not lived near enough Bangor to know what has
been done there these last seven years does not know the long story
of fraud and oppression and downright robbery which I could tell in
all its particulars past the possibility of doubting the recital, if I were
to go into the individual cases which I have known. No possible
excuse can be offered by anyone engaged in such actions, but no
good could come of telling more than has been told; it is enough to
know that the wrong has been done and that it will not be soon
forgiven.

We hope now, since the past is past and the future always has
some gleam of brightness, that a better order may begin. We have a
new law this winter which we understand. It is the same law that we
have been drilled on these seven or eight years in advance, which
has been enforced before it was on the statute books and declared
to be, while as yet it was not. It reads:

1.   "Sec. 13. No person or corporation shall carry or transport from place to place any moose, caribou or deer or part thereof in close time, nor in open time unless open to view, tagged and plainly labeled with the name of the owner thereof, and accompanied by him under a penalty of forty dollars; and any person, not the actual owner of such game or part thereof, who, to aid another in such transportation falsely represents himself to be the owner, shall be liable to the penalties aforesaid."

We understand this law. It does not depend upon doubtful interpretations. It will be respected as long as it is fairly executed. If we had had this law eight years ago, or had had the one then existing executed according to its obvious meaning, there would be less reason for explaining how Maine people have come to say hard things of the game laws. On this point of non-transportation in open season, our legal right, we have been so harassed, so often called poachers and law-breakers when we were doing nothing contrary to law, that we are more lenient than we otherwise should be against actual transgressors, and toward those who have done this injustice, are—not boisterous nor vindictive, but very stern.

Fannie Pearson Hardy

# VII. POISONING

May 21, 1891

We have a law regulating the sale and distribution of poisons. It has remained on the statute since 1857 without substantial change and without repeal at any time. The latter part reads:

> "If any person for the purpose of killing wolves, foxes, dogs, or other animals, and not for the destruction of insects or vermin, in a building, leaves or deposits any such poisons within two hundred rods of a highway, pasture, field or other improved land, he shall be punished by a fine not less than twenty nor more than fifty dollars; or by imprisonment not less than thirty nor more than sixty days."

It is my object to show that this law has been recklessly violated; that this violation has been charged to wardens; that the breaking of this law and the suspicion that wardens did it have caused much of the feeling that exists in the eastern part of the State against the game laws and their administration—these three things only; but I shall probably show that the feeling and the suspicion are not altogether unreasonable. If I dwell more on the belief of people here, in this essay in particular, than on an elaborate setting forth of the facts involved, it is because the collective loss which these facts represent is small relatively to the effect it had upon public opinion, because also this is purposely left as a matter of circumstantial evidence; and because my object is not to do more than to explain and account for the state of feeling which should no longer be disregarded. So far as the testimony here given needs any guarantee it may be said that it comes from men believed to be truthful, who do not live near each other. These men belong to different classes and occupations, who cannot have had any means of knowing what has been told me by anyone but themselves. I have received nothing contradictory to what is given here, and I do not publish all that would confirm these statements.

## I. Poison has been laid out contrary to law and domestic animals have been killed by it.

Previous to the Graves murder, in 1886, I heard of a number of cases in which animals were killed by strychnine, and among them some which are quoted below.[124] This shows that these claims are not of recent manufacture. Although, I then had no reason for remembering or noting the incidents given, I recollect that the reports came from a number of different towns, and that Passadumkeag was one of the principal places which suffered. This winter I asked a man whom I remembered as having spoken of the matter, whether he knew definitely what happened there. His reply was substantially as follows:

"Know? Yes, I was there at the time it was done. There was poison left in doughnuts and biscuits—strychnine enough to kill anything, and they left it close to the railroad station and all around town. Yes, it did do damage. I know of some cases. A man at Gould's Ridge had a dog killed, and found a piece of poisoned biscuit in his yard. A Passadumkeag man lost two horses; one was a farm horse and one was a colt worth $200. The horses had been in the dooryard all night, and in the morning they were dead, with a piece of poisoned bread near them. But there was worse than that— had a child die that same day, and they thought it was poisoned. It was a little child, out playing with the dog, and they found a piece of doughnut somewhere. The child brought it into the house and

---

[124] This might be better worded as 'the murder of Maine Game Wardens, Charles Niles and Lyman Hill by Calvin Graves in November of 1886.' The wardens attempted to take (or kill) the dog that Graves had been suspected of using for driving deer. Eckstorm covers the case in detail in a subsequent chapter.

very soon the dog died. The child died that same day. They thought it was poisoned. No, we did not know who did it. but it was laid to the wardens; it is all guess work who did it."

This is almost a literal transcript of notes taken during the narration. Names were given which I have omitted for obvious reasons, and it is possible that there may be some minor errors in taking down the facts; but the veracity of my informant is beyond question and all that is claimed by me is that he believed poison had been laid out in more than one instance. However, a letter subsequent to this shows more. "You wanted to know about Passadumkeag," he wrote. "I was in town when the child was sick but went home before it died that night, and all I know is what they told me; and for the horses I *saw them*."

This proves conclusively that two horses were poisoned and that the same day this was done, a rumor of a more serious nature was started. I wish, however, to disclaim any belief in the latter. I have spent some time in trying to investigate it and have been unable to disprove it, but also unable and certainly not desirous to prove it. It is an odd matter and those who might have denied it have not chosen to do so; had they done so it would not have been mentioned here although it had its influence. It should be said that I have found no proof that any warden laid out poison in Passadumkeag, but a strong and somewhat pointed suspicion to the effect that it was done either by a warden or someone in his employ.

So far we have proof of two horses killed by poison From another source, the poisoning of dogs at Gould's Ridge and in the town is confirmed, with a repetition of the rumor that it was done by wardens. Still another, repeating substantially the same story told by the first about the child, makes the more definite, but perhaps not more correct statement that it was "the same night that [a warden] poisoned all the dogs and cats in town."

Another from a town nearby writes that he never has heard the child's death ascribed to this cause, but knows "that strychnine has been left in our highways by being put into doughnuts, etc., and that one cow was poisoned that was hitched near the house in the field

(— —'s of Olamon[125]). Some four years ago [the warden mentioned by the last correspondent] went through this section and immediately after he passed, dogs and other animals dropped dead."

A man from still another town tells of poisoned biscuit being brought into the house by children, but gives no particulars. He also speaks of a house dog and turkey being poisoned in the dooryard. Another says that his daughter's pet cats died with evident signs of strychnine poisoning,[126] and that he supposed poison had been laid out by a warden—whom he named—for dogs. These are a few instances out of many, but they are definite, not general, statements, and illustrate the variety of the casualties that have occurred here. It is certain that the law prohibiting laying out poison within 200 rods—five-eighths of a mile—has been grossly violated.

As it may explain other matters, I wish to state why I do not undertake to prove more here. I could not well do it without the use of names. Matter of importance has been put into my hands with the understanding that it was to be published if desired, but without any limitation or caution as to its use or the use of names. I have therefore preferred to err on the side of caution and have adhered to my plan to give names only when the point was one of public record or notoriety, or else supposed to be a matter of personal indifference.

---

[125] Olamon is a town between Greenbush and Passadumkeag, Maine. The farmer's name was left out of the essay.
[126] Strychnine is a white, odorless, bitter crystalline powder. Today (2023), strychnine is used primarily as a pesticide, particularly to kill rats. "Dogs are most commonly affected; oral exposures of as little as a few tablespoons of strychnine-laced bait are enough to induce toxicity," by Patricia A. Talcott MS, DVM, PhD, in Small Animal Toxicology (Second Edition), 2006.

## II. This poisoning of domestic animals has been generally charged to wardens.

People living in four different towns on Penobscot waters have given me accounts of what has been done in their own towns, and these and others have told of cases in towns where they were not resident. All seem agreed that persons unknown were guilty, and most are of the opinion that these men were wardens. The names of two wardens are frequently mentioned, but no third except a man, sometimes called a warden and sometimes not, who was known to accompany one of them on a trip and a man believed to be employed by a warden. There is also an entire agreement as to the methods used west of the Narraguagus,[127] and as to the odd fact that bread and other cooked food was frequently the bait employed.

Is there a possibility that any number of the animals that died were killed in some other way? Not the slightest. The signs of strychnine poisoning are unmistakable;[128] besides, the poison was found in a number of places.

Could they not have been killed by malicious people who wished to cast reproach on the wardens? To a very limited degree this might have been done, but not to this extent. The work was carried on for three falls, '84, '85, and '86. and in parts of three different counties, Penobscot, Hancock and Washington. I have reports from Penobscot, Union River, Machias, and St. Croix waters, showing that it was done on all these within three years. It was not done to kill foxes or wild animals. The season of the year was too early, the places and bait both unsuitable. None but domestic animals or men would be likely to find the bait, and few other creatures would be attracted by it. The reports that bread, biscuit, and doughnuts were frequently used show that it was done by the wholesale by some

---

[127] Narraguagus Lake area, in Hancock County, Maine.
[128] During those years (late 1800s) barring toxicology reports, strychnine poisoning was assumed based on the rapid rigor mortis of the affected animal.

person, or persons, who wished to carry bait in bulk and must have a kind easy to procure and convey. Whoever did this work made a business of it.

There were men who were suspected of doing this, as I have said. They were watched and followed, unknown to themselves. One of them was seen repeatedly, and wherever he went poison or dead animals were found. He made two trips with different companions, and both times the same results attended him. There certainly was some reason for suspicion of this man, if not of his companions.

There is a printed statement also, which never having been denied may be taken, in connection with some other matters as authoritative. "Special" made it in the; *Forest and Stream* for Jan. 8, 1885. It shows that elsewhere at this time, wardens were engaged in poisoning. He says:

> "The deer hounders, or rather their poor dogs, have fared hard this year. The Maine game law not only forbids hounding, but provides for the destruction of the dogs. By the game wardens a war to the death has been waged. A great number of poor dogs—or perhaps good dogs with unworthy masters—have been destroyed. If one apothecary would tell his story, pounds of poison would be accounted for. Repeating rifles have also been employed by the wardens."

In support of this statement, I am at liberty to say that about the time this was published Mr. Stilwell asked my father to listen to a letter which he had received from someone residing on Machias territory.[129] He did not read either signature or superscription, but the writer gave a detailed account of a trip taken by some warden, the amount of poison which he had distributed, and the report that he had killed every dog on the route except one belonging to Shaw Brothers, which was kept at a camp where the warden could not get at him. A Bangor man, who was on Machias about this time, reported finding five pieces of poison laid out in the road between

---

[129] E. M. Stilwell and Henry O. Stanley, were Commissioners of Maine Inland Fisheries And Game. Manly Hardy was a supporter of the Game Laws and kept in close contact with the commissioners.

Fourth Lake Machias and Lower Dobsy, a distance of about one and a quarter miles. While it is possible that none of this was put within five-eighths of a mile of Shaw's house at the end of the carry, and that none of the rest which was laid out elsewhere on Machias was distributed within the legal limit, the practice could do no good to the cause. In this district the law about poisoning was not scrupulously regarded, as has been shown; and I have deposited in the editor's hand proof that would justify popular suspicions as to who did the mischief. This, however, I consider too confidential to be published. There is an incident which is strong circumstantial evidence of the same that I am at liberty to give.

A year ago last fall, the man who went as guide for us, told us of a narrow escape his cousin, his uncle and four other men had from being poisoned by wardens a few years ago. This winter I asked one of the men who was of the party—a very well-known and much respected guide—for the facts. He gave them in great detail, every point that was essential, and I wrote down the more important. I understood him to give permission to use his name also, but as there is the possibility of an error here, and as I cannot now send manuscript for his correction, if any is needed, I will not make him responsible. My notes say that on Jan. 27, 1891, he told me that a party of six, including himself, his uncle, another guide and three sportsmen from New Haven, Conn., all of whose names he gave, were camping in a lumber camp at Brandy Pond on the West Branch of Union River. They had with them two dogs—one three-fourths foxhound, which belonged to him; the other, as I understood, not a hound. They were hunting deer, but I do not know whether these dogs were, or could be used to run deer.

While they were there, the warden whose name has been left blank several times, with a companion, who is variously reported as a warden and as not being one, came to the camp and tried to induce them to put the dogs out after deer. They left the camp for two or three days while this warden and his companion were still in the country on, as everyone reported, a poisoning tour. On their return they made a bean soup and were about to thicken it with a piece of bread which one of them saw lying on the table, when it was said by someone that the bread was too dry. Instead of using it for themselves it was given to the dog owned by the narrator, and the dog died on the spot. They could prove only the fact of the poisoning, not who did it When they left the place the warden and his companion had been near; when they returned both were gone. Whoever may have been the guilty man, someone was narrowly delivered from the crime of killing six men who had done him no injury, against whom he could plead neither injustice, personal danger, nor a violent and overmastering provocation.

Comparatively few of the wardens in this State were engaged in this wretched poisoning, but the few were diligent. For their misdeeds some who were innocent were suspected, and under the cover of them, men who were not wardens at all may have used their opportunity to do evil. It was a practice which could do no good; which might do, and did do, much harm; which would disparage the cause in whose service it was carried on, and alienate rather than attract the support of those without whose hearty cooperation game laws must be a failure. Nothing can more certainly react against an object to render it unpopular than the attempt to push its claims by overriding greater ones. In the eyes of the people, it was more important that their property should be safe than that deer should not be dogged. Both were desirable, but the former was the greater. The latter could not be enforced at the expense of the former. If there was reason to suspect that officers of the law in enforcing one statute, broke a law much more important, and in the process, they lost the support which was needed to make their cause good. It does not matter if they did not all engage in it, or if they did not do all of which they were accused. One murder grew out of this, and there is danger yet.

Of the warden who has been principally accused so far, it may be said that the charge does not greatly injure his reputation. He has been guilty of about all the petty sins on the catalogue; he attempted blackmail, illegal seizure, breaking and entering a locked storehouse, is an habitual drunkard—of which the editor holds proof—but he is still a warden.

Fannie Pearson Hardy

# VIII. ON KILLING DOGS

## May 28, 1891

**I Am** going to give the tradition of the origin of the law permitting the slaughter of deer dogs, to show the consequences of the practice, the unwisdom of it, the extra-legal abuse of this doubtful privilege, the trouble certain to come from it and the fact that the Game Commissioners were fully warned of what was sure to happen. We cannot deal with compliments now, and the burden of this whole miserable business of dog-killing, with its dreadful consequences, must be left to rest where it falls.

Deer dogging is not a recent practice in the eastern part of the State. As early as the forties considerable of it was done, although it was by no means general; for the people of the southeastern part of the State were a race of still-hunters. It is hardly necessary to say that at that period there were few if any deer, except stragglers, west of the Penobscot, so that both still-hunting and dogging were necessarily confined to the regions where both have flourished most ever since. Dogging was not illegal at this time, and did not become so at any season of the year previous to 1853, while it was not prohibited until a later date, sometime in the sixties, I believe, though my earliest note of it is 1871.

As has been said, dogging was not at first illegal, and though most preferred still-hunting, it was practiced to some extent, especially in the latter part of the forties and during the fifties. It was then that Rod Park and his pack used to make "such gallant chiding" over the rough granite country that slopes down the Union River. It was noble music say those who heard it. Park was a Veazie lumberman, well known all over the State, an admirable marksman both at game and target, a fine still-hunter for deer, an expert at all outdoor games and employments, the most buoyant, whole-hearted, irrepressible, fun-loving, and laughter-making man that ever drew violin bow and loved his friend's quarrel better than his own. His delight in good company drew him from the solitary life of the hunter; his overflowing energy attracted him to the woods; therefore, he loved his dogs. He always had a pack of favorites, not blooded, perhaps, but well-chosen and remembered long after the limits of their doggish lives. Hunter, and Panther, who were slain, old Jack who fell by a bullet, and old Spot, the most lamented of all, were of them. Two lawyers, Bradbury and Wiggin, were frequent companions of Park's at this time, and they hunted together in the Union River country, sometimes from canoes, but most frequently on the runways, which Park liked best. "A cry more tuneable was never holla'd to," but it was not music to the still-hunters.

There were wolves in the country then and the deer being in constant alarm from these, were more frightened of the dogs than they now are, so that a pack of hounds was a serious disturbance to still-hunting. But Park was a favorite and the hunters did not wish to trouble him or his dogs, although they complained loudly of his companions. Park was a poor man like themselves, they said, but that rich men's sport should destroy their occupation was a serious grievance, and on account of it Park lost some dogs. Yet there was in this nothing that would cause recourse to law making. There was, however, another trouble to which Park always attributed the origin of the first law permitting dogs to be killed.

Park had his enemies as well as his friends. Those who have driven from Bar Harbor to Bangor on the Tally-Ho which ran eight years ago,[130] before the railroad was put through, may remember just half way between Ellsworth and Bangor, on the top of a long hill, two old, blackened houses, the only ones for some miles, which stood on opposite sides of the road not far apart. They were the half-way taverns on the stage road, Johnson's on the right and Mike Mann's on the left. The hill is still known as Mike Mann's Hill. This hill lies midway between Fitts's Pond (now Phillips's Lake) and Reed's Pond (now Green Lake)—two places at which Park and his dogs used to run deer. The tavern keepers on the hill had the bitterest enmity to each other, which Mann at least, who was small in spirit as he was large in stature, extended to all who patronized his rival.

---

[130] A Tally-Ho stagecoach could carry up to twenty or more persons.

And Park always stopped at Johnson's. Whether there was any other cause for this ill will is not known, but on account of it Park was subjected to much annoyance by Mann when he was in Mann's vicinity. At one time the road leading down to Reed's Pond was filled full of big hemlocks at a certain narrow place between ledges. Again, Parks had some birch canoes left near there maliciously destroyed. These and other troubles occurred about 1851, but the feud was continued.

In 1853, by the margin of the R. S. of 1857, a new and very remarkable game law was passed:

"No person shall hunt or kill on any land not his own in this State any moose from the fifteenth day of March to the first day of October, or any deer from the fifteenth day of January to the first day of September, under a penalty of $40 for each moose and $20 for each deer so killed. No person not an inhabitant of this State shall, at any time, hunt or kill any moose or deer except on his own land, under the same penalties as above provided. Any person may lawfully shoot or otherwise kill any dog found hunting moose or deer within the time or with the persons herein prohibited."

The aliens meant are undoubtedly Canadians, for summer travel had not then begun to any extent. But why prohibit hounding in close time only? This is covered by the prohibition to hunt at all at that season one would suppose. Park always declared that this point was "got up by Mann on purpose to annoy him." It must have been introduced by someone living east of the Penobscot, for those living where dogs were not used would have no interest in the matter. The still-hunters of the Union River would have been little likely to propose legislation on the subject; for they would have killed the dog that troubled them without waiting to have the law passed to permit them, and this law would not have protected them in the fall when they needed it most. Park always said that Mann was at the bottom of it. Note how this might have been.

Previous to the law of 1858, the law (E. S. 1840) had been:

"Any person who shall kill any moose or deer between the first day of July and the first day of November in any year shall forfeit or pay for every moose or deer so killed the sum of five dollars."

That is, close time previous to 1853 was from July 1 to Nov. 1, the very period when Park was hounding deer, for no one ever kept the law then. The line was too small to be a perquisite to anybody, as only half went to the complainant, so that Mann could have done Park no harm by complaining. But to allow the killing of dogs in close time—that is from July to November—would be the most serious injury possible. If Mann could compass that, he had abundant revenge.

Mann was not a representative at any time—"He hadn't education enough," said Johnson, his old rival, to me this winter. Whatever he did he must do through others. Supposing, then, that he argued with some representative the need of stopping hounding in close time, the advantages of killing dogs as the means of stopping it, and impressed on the legislator the fact that close time was the period of danger. When the close time is changed from the fall months to the winter and summer months, that representative is still acting in obedience to his constituency by urging that dogs ought to be killed in the new close time, while Mann, if he were guilty, loses the opportunity which he correctly sought, though gaining the letter of his desires. That this change in the game law which he could not help even if he had known it, should take place at the same time that he did desire a change is natural enough, while only such a desire as his could explain the singular provision which allows the use of dogs part of the year, but makes their lives a forfeit at the period when they were least likely to be used. For this is not aimed at crust hunting, as may be seen from the fact that moose may be killed with dogs until the middle of March. It was an unfeathered shaft that flew aslant.

Until a better explanation of the subject is given we may assume, as Park did, that the first law permitting dogs to be killed was framed from personal malice. Even if he were wrong, the history of the law would justify such a supposition.

Good it has never done, could not do.

The man who loses one dog will buy two more, and will forever hate the man who killed his pet and companion. If dogging is illegal, it should be stopped, but never by killing the irresponsible dog. Arrest the offender and fine him—he will submit; but any attempt to kill his dog will be resisted, and in one way or another will harm the cause in which it is done or the man who does it. The slaughter of dogs has caused deer dogging to thrive in this State. Doing it in the name of the law has merely brought the law into disrepute; for it is now and long will be considered a worse offense to kill a dog than to use him in running deer. To arrest the man brings credit to the law and little or no danger to the officer; to kill the dog has just opposite effect.

I will give three examples of the results of dog killing, selecting for obvious reasons some of long standing. In every case, I could give fullest particulars and could cite other parallel instances. In the first a woodchopper, hearing a hound, stepped behind a tree and cut out her shoulder as she ran past. He escaped with his life, but it was of little value to him for some time. The dog was owned by Louis Ketchum, the well-known Indian guide, who could give full particulars although at the time he was miles away, having lent the hound to those who had her.[131] The second occurred on Long Island in Bluehill Bay. There was a special law that no deer should be killed on the island, but an Indian named Joe Orons, whom I suppose to be dead, met there with companions to evade the law by driving deer into the water and shooting them from the canoe. He had just killed one in this way when a man, said to be named Henderson, shot his dog. The Indian instantly threw down the gun he had, thinking the range too long for the buckshot barrel, and seized a rifle lying beside him. Careless handling caused a premature discharge, which tore open his coat sleeve and burned his arm, but he once more changed guns and fired at the man before he disappeared. He then searched a house on the island to find him, and failing in this, was with difficulty restrained from doing great damage to personal property. Almost any of the Oldtown guides could give further particulars. Nor must it be thought that only an Indian would do this. A white man would do fully as much. I know of one man, now deceased, a selectman of his town for many years, a man honest and trusted and with a host of friends, who declared

---

[131] Louis (Lewey, Lewis) Ketchum. See chapter, *Spike Sole Shoes.*

that he himself had walked many miles and spent two days in trying to kill the man who shot his dog. Nor need reference be made to the two wardens who were killed for attempting to take a dog from its owner, in order to prove the hazard of doing it.

Not only is it dangerous to kill dogs, but of late this danger has been greatly increased because most of it has been done illegally. It is not lawful to destroy any dog not actually engaged in hunting, either on the track, or swimming after the deer, or holding it at bay. Yet most of the dogs killed here for some years have either been poisoned or taken from their owners and killed before their eyes. Need we cite the instances of three dogs taken from one canoe and killed, of four belonging to one sportsman, of one and two in many instances belonging sometimes to residents and sometimes to visitors, but in every case killed while not engaged in hunting? Nor has the least discretion been shown in the dogs selected. One well known and decidedly popular contributor to *Forest and Stream* has given me his own experience.

"When I was in Maine, Mr. H. and I had a narrow chance," he writes, "for the lives of two liver and white pointer dogs (which any person could tell were not hounds) notwithstanding the fact that we offered to show what they were by working them on game."

"Hounds and greyhounds, mongrels, spaniels, curs, shoughs, water rugs and demi-wolves," all that in the catalogue are clept[132] by the name of dogs, to misquote—have lost their lives or had them dangered by the law that however it has been enforced, says only:

"Any person may lawfully kill any dog found hunting moose, deer or caribou."

Nor has the poisoning been legal. Most of it has been necessarily laid out contrary to law prohibiting its distribution within five-eighths of a mile from "any highway, pasture, field or other improved land;" and anyone can see, that while hunting, the dog would not take poison—"unless he was a very poor dog," adds one hunter slyly.

-----

[132] Clept - obsolete use - past tense and past participle of clepe - to name or call.

True, the law does not prohibit poisoning dogs, but if they will not take it while hunting and cannot be killed when not hunting, there is barrier none the less strong for being unexpressed. If not killed in the act, the dog cannot be killed in any way, for he returns to his owner who becomes responsible according to the law which says:

"Any person owning or having in possession dogs for the purpose of hunting moose, deer or caribou, forfeits not less than twenty nor more than one hundred dollars," and "Any person may lawfully kill any dog found hunting moose, deer or caribou."

That is how runs the law; not a wise provision at best, but infinitely unwise as it has been administered. Consider the provocation that has been given, the illegality of methods used, the domestic animals killed and supposed to be killed by those engaged in this work, the peril to human life, that this work was kept up for three years in spite of all remonstrances, and it is not hard to see how murder grew out of it as the stalk from the seed.

Even if it had not been done by officials and under orders it would have caused trouble; but those set to protect and defend the law broke the laws, and disaster was inevitable. The Commissioners—that is Mr. Stilwell, who represents them here— had timely and frequent warnings of what would happen. It was not chance that caused the death of Hill and Niles; it was fate.[133] By the same work we shall have more of it unless care is taken. That murder was no surprise, but we expected it nearer home. It was in this way that I heard it—for I was out of the State that year and my father wrote of it to me:

"12 Nov., 1886.—Dear Fannie: I send two dailies. You will see by reading, that as Meg Merrilies told Dirk Hatteraick, 'It is sown; it is grown; it is heckled; it is twisted.' [134] What I have so long

---

[133] The two murdered wardens; covered in the next chapter.

[134] Here Manly is quoting from the novel, *Guy Mannering or The Astrologer,* by Sir Walter Scott, first published anonymously in 1815. The full line is, "It's sown, and it's grown, and it's heckled, and it's twisted."

expected and foretold has come to pass, and in the way I predicted—
by killing dogs. I went to Stilwell twice last month to talk to him
about this very thing.[135] He asked me only a short time ago [if] I
really believed any man was bad enough to kill another. I told him
I did not think, I knew it, and it would be done if he kept such a set
of men as wardens and allowed them to do such things. I do not
know any of the parties. They may all be angels for all I know. I
know the place exactly, as I have slept on the very same spot."[136]

The original of this, with other important documents published
and unpublished, is in the hands of the editor. On receiving it, I
formed the resolution which I have held to ever since, not to stop
until the time came to prevent worse evils by showing up these.
Unknown to me, my father had decided to do the same, had written
to the editor of this paper about it and then (had it) withdrawn
because the danger was not then pressing, and the Commissioners
needed what support could be given.

The danger is here again. We have a new set of laws yet untried,
and worse conditions than at first for enforcing them. In giving the
results of years of study of these matters, it must again be stated that
there is no personal advantage to be sought; no desire to present
more than can be proved, but the necessity of saying less; no hatred
to any class, for none have injured me; no wish to bring our wardens
into disrepute, for some of them could not well have blacker
reputations than they now wear; no wish to disparage the
Commissioners, for their works are their judges; no thought to stir
up trouble—for there is more abroad at present than most realize.
To prevent trouble, to save respect for those broken laws before it
gets too late, to diminish the danger to human life—that of these
wardens and of better men than most of them—is the only possible
advantage.

Fannie Pearson Hardy

---

[135] Manly Hardy had several times given warning on this topic.
[136] This letter was used in developing the conversation Manly Hardy
had with the game commissioner in the novel, *I am Penobscot*.

# IX. AN ASPECT OF THE GRAVES CASE

## June 11, 1891

The murder of the two wardens, Niles and Hill,[137] by Calvin Graves, in 1886, was the means of calling forth a sympathy for the latter which to those not intimate with all that had preceded must have seemed unaccountable. I do not refer to the reckless talk of desperadoes and malcontents who delight in upheavals; but sober-minded men of character and good repute, who disapproved the act, felt and still feel a sympathy for the actor. Anomaly as this is, it is what has happened before often enough when the side which wielded authority did not do it according to justice.

Of course, this murder has been extenuated in every possible way on the one hand, and been intensified with equal ingenuity on the other. It is beyond the province of this paper to enter into any discussion of the case—whether it was in self-defense or otherwise, provoked or not, deliberate or the impulse of a fiery moment. It was done—double murder. The courts have investigated all the facts pertaining and by their sentence expressed unqualified disapproval. There can be no reason for seeking to differ from their decision and to discuss the case here or seek extenuations would virtually be doing this. Yet, there is an aspect of the case which did not enter into the trial in court that has had weight in producing the sympathy which I find exists toward Graves.

The trial was for murder. It did not therefore concern itself with questions whether Graves at the time of committing this act was engaged or purposed to engage in breaking the game laws. An authority so high that investigation of the records seemed needless after his statement, has told me that no evidence was brought on to

---

[137] Wardens Charles Niles and Lyman Hill.

show that Graves was hounding deer. The only testimony on the point, he said, was that McFarland, his companion, went away with the dog and returned with it about noon tied to his belt. The keen eye of the public took note of this fact and the attempt has been made, on Penobscot waters at least, to show that Graves was the one attacked. Without in any manner pretending to settle the point, indeed without considering it important except as producing sympathy for Graves, we may examine the grounds of this claim:

The place at which this deed was committed is a peculiar one. Five lakes of the same chain—First, Second, Third, Fourth and Fifth Lakes Machias—are arranged almost in a circle, the head of Fifth Lake lying very near to First Lake, with Fletcher Brook cutting off half of the remaining distance, the whole inclosing a piece of land nearly, if not quite, thirty miles in circumference. This unfits it for hounding, because the deer when pursued are quite as likely to run into one of the other four lakes as into the one which is watched. All who are experienced in the use of hounds declare that it is one of the poorest places in the State for that work. There are deer enough within this region, but they cannot be obtained with hounds.

Yet, Graves and McFarland were hunting here on Nov. 8. Either they were not hounding deer or they did not know their business, say those who know no more of the circumstances than was published in the newspapers. Not only is this section entirely unfitted for the use of hounds, because it is so surrounded by water and devoid of natural runways, but there are no boats on any of the five lakes, except such canoes as the Shaws of Lower Dobsy own and keep for their own use on the further side of Fourth Lake. It is well known that Graves and MacFarland had no boat. This greatly diminishes the probability that they were hounding. They were in a county where deer could not be dogged successfully, where they had not the ordinary means for pursuing them in the water, where there was little chance that they could be posted so as to shoot at a deer on the land because most of it is too flat to afford runways, yet they had a dog with them.

It is well known here that there are dogs, rarely, but yet sometimes found, which are trained to keep close to their masters and by whining when they catch the scent of a deer direct the attention of the hunter to the right point. When the deer is wounded, they will keep the trail when otherwise the animal might be lost. These dogs are sometimes owned and used by still-hunters here, but the practice is not general. Because the location in which Graves and McFarland were hunting was so unfavorable to the use of hounds in the usual way, because also when they came back after an unsuccessful hunt the dog was with them, which would hardly have been the case if he had been put out after a deer and lost him, it has been supposed by those willing to put the matter in as good a light as possible that the dog was one trained to aid in still-hunting and that the men were not engaged in hounding at the time. If this is true—and it is purely a supposition—sympathy with the accused would be the natural consequence; but it would follow equally if the supposition were merely a probability.

Having seen enough of the ground myself to judge the matter, and having conversed with those who knew it thoroughly and also knew about hounding deer, there seems to be nothing inconsistent in the theory, though has probably nothing more than an ingenious explanation of what might have been true if events had been different. No confidence need be placed in the truth of this supposition, for its influence lies in its existence and the absence of known facts to disprove it. It throws the burden of the crime upon the wardens and partially exonerates Graves, which is all that is desired. For, if this is true, though when strictly construed such a use of a dog might be found illegal, it is so different from ordinary hounding that no one here would consider it a violation of the law. Then to the illegality of attempting to take a dog from its owner instead of fining the owner, is added this still further complication of taking a dog which was supposed to be used in a way not contrary to the statute, when the owners, by the testimony given in court, were attempting to carry it off to avoid a quarrel which the wardens themselves provoked.

I give this not because it has any value as fact—probably has none—but because it shows how keen people have been to discover extenuating circumstances, how they seized on the absence of evidence to construct a defense, how they have not ceased to continue to do this. How prevalent this sympathy may be I cannot tell, having deemed it unwise to discuss the matter more than was necessary; but I never heard a woodsman or back-settler speak upon the subject who did not feel less severe in his judgment of the doer than of the deed.

On Machias, where the event occurred and the men are known, a very different sentiment may prevail, but on Penobscot, where personalities do not enter into opinions formed and the knowledge of the facts is very likely limited, there is a sympathy felt and expressed which must be recognized. If the reports which I have received at second hand are at all correct, the feeling is not by any means so limited in its extent.

Although not bearing directly upon the subject in hand, I have deemed it important to speak of this sympathy with Graves and this tendency to find excuses for his deed, because a timely recognition of it is needed. The excuses may be flimsy fabrications, but the sympathy is a fact which must not be denied, and I do not find that in the records that I have kept for the four years past there is any material abatement of it. It is a dangerous element in the present status—dangerous because the feeling is divorced from the ethics of the case, and exists side by side with condemnation of the act, dangerous because it does not stand as staunchly by the decision of the courts as it should, and also because it is shared by honest law-abiding men with the dishonest and lawless. Yet, it is the inevitable result of certain given conditions.

The representatives of the law had been acting unlawfully and had alienated from their support a large body of people. Some of them had gone so far that their lives were in danger if they went beyond well understood limits of both territory and action. The provocation was great and long continued, of a kind very often most difficult to prove, highly exasperating to public feeling, and yet not sufficiently damaging to property to warrant recourse to law in the cases where proof could be obtained. Appeals to have the wrong suppressed were made and the petitions were disregarded. The dangers feared with sufficient evidence of what occurred under less irritating conditions were detailed and rejected as visionary. There was no redress of the wrongs, but they could not go on much longer without being avenged, and it was only a question of circumstances sufficiently provoking, and a man whose judgment or self-control had deserted him, to decide where the inevitable event would occur.

It came like a great shock to one-half of the State, but to another part it was an arrow sped, which slacks the tension on the bowstring and brings the bow back to its shape. The hunters, the back-settlers, the people of the smaller towns of eastern Maine were relieved from future fears and a sympathy with the one who had removed from them what might well have happened nearer home was natural. That the deed seemed not to be prompted by personal malice or premeditation removed much disapproval which would otherwise have been felt. That so good excuses as the one already given could be constructed without violence to any known facts, was considered an additional reason for allowing the impulse to get the better of the judgment.

I would not wish to over-estimate either the amount or the extent of this feeling, too common anywhere, far too much so on Penobscot.[138] It will do no harm at present, but with the recurrence of conditions similar to the old ones its power will be felt as a serious obstacle to the course of justice. Just how this will occur need not be described, but there is a way already suggested by some which makes it seem better to avoid than to incur the risk. For this danger to the laws and their action seems to me a more serious evil than the loss of life which is also to be feared. Concerning the latter there will be differences of opinion; but the ones to underrate it will be those who know least about it; and those who know most will not be likely to tell all they know. In eastern Maine there is continual risk that a repetition may recur, and there is a fear and distrust lest the old conditions may be renewed, thus precipitating the danger.

It is not expedient to say why it seems necessary to speak of this sympathy for Graves further than what has been said, but I have heard too much on the subject without seeking it, and been forced to read too far between the lines sometimes when little has been said, to consider the matter one of light import. If local, restricted to

---

[138] Meaning of anywhere along Penobscot waters and territory of Penobscot County.

comparatively narrow limits, it will spread fast enough; if of wider range it is still worse: but as a fact it must be faced and considered. There is no excitement on the subject now, and this is the time to prepare for the eradication of such a sentiment as this and the protection of our higher forms of administering justice, by a just and equitable enforcement of the game laws by men who will be respected for their personal worth as well as for their office. Otherwise, there is danger.

A careful study of sociological conditions here and a good acquaintance with the history of the woods for the past sixty years have left no doubt in my mind that murder has been historically much more common than most suppose; that it still is likely to occur at any time when personal revenge or a rude but extra-legal sense of justice demands satisfaction; that it may be committed by men who are not dishonest and who would scorn to do a mean act, and that if the man who does it has borne a fair reputation previously and acts in a way for which any possible justification may be found, he will obtain a sympathy which will hinder the cause of law or largely annul the effect of the sentence.

Under our game laws, administered as they have been for the past few years, this is sure to happen in event of another Graves case; for the public conscience has gone wrong and we who have grown up under this strained and distorted condition where officers of justice have been unjust and rights have been made wrong, hardly know what right is and what wrong is in game matters.[139]

Fannie Pearson Hardy

---

[139] The editor will remind the reader that these essays were written by Fannie Hardy in early 1891, when she was twenty-five years of age. She was a young woman writing in *Forest and Stream*, the leading outdoor magazine of the time, and what she covered took a good deal of courage.

## Editor Note

In 1948, *Ridge Runner–The Story of a Maine Woodsman*, by Gerald Averill was published. Averill was raised in the small village of Frankfort, Maine along Marsh Stream that runs into the Penobscot River near to where the river entered Penobscot Bay. Records show he may have been born July of 1898. He died in 1946 at the age of 47. In his memoir, he hints toward the end of an illness, during which period of his life he spent writing the book. Over the course of his life, he became proficient at hunting and later worked in lumber camps as a clerk.

In October of 1933 he became a Maine Game Warden. From then until 1944 he was assigned to various locations across the state, including the area of Nicatous Lake.

He was later assigned the district around North Berwick, Sanford, and North Shapleigh. In his book he writes of dealing with dogs in this location. He writes: *"This business of dogs killing deer is something that most wardens find very unpleasant to deal with, especially if they happen to like dogs. Despite a very rigid law which states that an officer may kill any dog that is found in the act of chasing deer, a great many dog owners profess to be ignorant of it."* Averill describes instances where he killed dogs, wild and domestic, who were nuisance animals caught chasing deer.

As of 2023, the Maine law states:

### Maine Title 12: CONSERVATION
### Part 13: INLAND FISHERIES AND WILDLIFE
### Subpart 4: FISH AND WILDLIFE
### Chapter 921: WILDLIFE CAUSING DAMAGE OR NUISANCE

Title 12 §12404 - Specific animals
6. Dogs. This subsection applies to nuisance dogs.

A. A game warden may kill a dog outside the enclosure or immediate care of its owner or keeper when the game warden finds that dog:

(1) Chasing, killing, wounding or pursuing a moose or deer at any time;

(2) Chasing, killing, wounding or pursuing any other wild animal in closed season; or

(3) Worrying, wounding or killing a domestic animal, livestock or poultry.

B. An owner of domestic animals, livestock or poultry, a member of the owner's family or a person to whom is entrusted the custody of domestic livestock or poultry may kill any dog killing or attacking the domestic animals, livestock or poultry.

C. A person having evidence of a dog chasing, killing, wounding or pursuing moose or deer or any other wild animal in closed season may present that evidence to the commissioner or any game warden.

(1) The commissioner or game warden shall give notice in writing to the owner or keeper of the dog, stating the acts committed by the dog.

(2) After the owner or keeper of the dog has received written notice that the dog has committed any act prohibited by paragraphs E-1, E-2, F and G, anyone may kill the dog when it is found committing any of those prohibited acts.

maine.gov/ifw/fish-wildlife/wildlife/living-with-wildlife/avoid-resolve-conflict/laws.html

and

mainelegislature.org/legis/statutes/12/title12sec12404.html

Cited February 2023.

# X. THE JOCK DARLING CASE

## July 2, 1891

**No game case** of this State has enjoyed the notoriety of the Jock Darling case,[140] and none seems to have been less generally understood. Did it check hounding? Did it crush Darling? The full force of the negatives can be appreciated only by those very intimate with Maine game matters for the past year.

On account of the misapprehension which prevails regarding what was accomplished and the personal prejudice involved, it is of all the game cases on record the most difficult to explain. Few are so bound up in the personality of an individual, and few depend for their influence so little upon the facts and pleadings recorded by the court, so much upon what forms no part of the court record; for, as a legal decision, this case accomplished nothing of importance, but as a power to affect public opinion it had a weight entirely independent of and not commensurate with the court ruling. The case was decided in favor of the State, yet nothing that has ever happened in eastern Maine, not even the dog-killing, has done so much to hurt the Commissioners as the Darling case. The Hammond case, famous as it was, fell far short; for the injustice there, though flagrant, rested on a point of legal interpretation, while here it lay on an abuse of legal methods, for which, as the State was the prosecutor, the Commissioners were popularly held responsible.

The great interest which attaches to the case arises from the fact that with good ground for procedure, in a cause and against a man,

---

[140] Additional editorial details about Darling, along with photos, are included in, *Exploring the Maine Woods - The Hardy Family Expedition to the Machias Lakes*, and are not repeated in this book.

both believed to be in the wrong, the case could have been so handled as, against popular prejudice and an adverse court decision, to win to both the cause and the man more tolerance and good will than they ever had enjoyed before. How this occurred will be shown. For the rest it need only be said that the principal charge on which the case rested was nowhere denied or doubted, and the decision of the court was manifestly just.

Darling had for years been openly engaged in deer hounding. That he should be capable of overcoming the opposition which was very strong against him, of maintaining his insecure position and strengthening it, of winning good will which seems to be continually increasing, indicates an ability with which he is not popularly credited. It has been to his advantage that he has been under-rated by his enemies, but personal justification and personal conviction stand equally apart from the purpose of these papers. In speaking of Mr. Darling's character, it is enough to say that he is better thought of near home than away from it; that his candor and honesty are believed in by those who know him, and that he is not and never has been an outlaw as is so frequently declared. This being admitted, what follows will not be hard to understand. As a review of the principal facts of the case in hand, I will quote portions of two accounts published at the time in the newspapers.

* * *

"Bangor. Me., Nov. 4, (1889)—The officers say the arrest of "Jock" Darling, the Lowell outlaw, whose arrest for illegal hunting was reported in the Herald, is the most important capture made for years. Well-laid plans were made by Commissioner Stilwell and Detective William McNamara, of Boston. They claim to have secured enough evidence to prosecute to the full extent of the law."

*    *    *    *    *    *    *    *    *

"They were out each day with the dogs. "Jock" putting out the dogs twice each day for three days, the guides doing the business the other two days. They killed four deer, one each themselves. Darling one and a guide one. They came upon Darling after the dog had run the deer into the water, just after he had shot him. They heard the report of the rifle, which was still smoking when they came up, and the deer was still warm. McNamara says they were obliged to kill the deer to accomplish the purpose for which they went there."

\*     \*     \*     \*     \*     \*     \*     \*     \*

"As the offense was committed in Hancock County, they were obliged to go into that county to swear out warrants against Darling and his guides. The warrants were sworn out and assistants were obtained. On their way to Darling's camp, they met Darling in the town of Lowell and immediately arrested him. Jock wanted to go to his house to change his clothes and get his overcoat, which the officer consented to, but said one of them must go with him. But "Jock" insisted on going alone, which the officers would not agree to, and he was accordingly handcuffed, and Officer Davis volunteered to bring the old man to this city, while the others kept on to the camp in quest of the guides. Darling in some manner sent a warning to the guides, so they disappeared before the officers arrived. Darling had $770 with him when arrested. Darling is charged with hunting deer with dogs, keeping dogs for that purpose, and hunting and destroying deer on Sunday."

\*     \*     \*     \*     \*     \*     \*     \*     \*


The second, from the Calais (Me.) *Times*, gives some additional particulars. Both these extracts may be considered as official, since, aside from internal evidence, one comes from Bangor, the home of Commissioner Stilwell, and the other from Calais, the home of Game Warden French, who laid the plans, which Mr. Stilwell approved and McNamara executed. (The italics are not in the original.)

\*     \*     \*     \*     \*     \*     \*     \*     \*

"Darling's camp on Nicatous Lake is very difficult to reach, and is a sort of stronghold for poachers. It is fifty miles from any railroad station, and to reach it one must travel over a rough road. McNamara, accompanied by Swanton, of Milbridge, made their way to the camp with much difficulty, and engaged quarters with Darling. They hired his guides and dogs to hunt deer with, paying well for them. They remained five days. When McNamara and Swanton had obtained all the evidence they wanted, enough they thought to convict Darling on some twenty or thirty cases, they left the camp. As the offense was committed in Hancock County, they were obliged to go into that county to swear out warrants against Darling and his guides. Accordingly, they went to Bucksport, where the warrants were obtained. Constable George Davis and Sheriff James Swanton, with a formidable party, set out for Nicatous Lake. On their way to Darling's camp, they met Darling in the town of Lowell and immediately arrested him. Darling was arraigned at Bucksport, Monday, before a trial justice. The justice found Mr. Darling guilty and fined him $40 for the deer which it was charged he killed, *and $40 for each of the deer which the other parties admitted that they killed*. He was also fined *$50 a day* for keeping dogs to hunt deer two days, the whole making $250. On the question of costs there was some argument. Mr. Voss [Vose] suggested that the case of bringing seven men from Milbridge to Nicatous Lake to arrest Jock Darling be charged to the prisoner, to which Col. Hutchinson [Hutchings] objected, and said that any one officer could have arrested Mr. Darling without a bit of difficulty. The cost question finally went over for the counsel to talk over and see if they couldn't decide upon something satisfactory. The case was appealed and will come before the Supreme Court at Ellsworth on the 8th of April next. Other cases stand against Darling. The officers who went to Nicatous to arrest the guides found that they had taken the alarm and fled. They will be captured later."

\* \* \* \* \* \* \* \* \*

From these accounts it will be seen that a Massachusetts detective, not a Maine warden, was employed to collect proof, which of course was perfectly right; that this man then swore out warrants, which was not at all right according to our laws. Then seven men were sent all the way from Milbridge in the southeastern part of Washington county to Nicatowis Lake[141] in the northern part of Hancock County, via Lowell in Penobscot county—a long and roundabout journey, and expensive because train communication can be had only part of the way. What the object of this was it would be difficult to discover unless to add to the expenses and force the prisoner to pay them, as was actually attempted, for there was no possible good that they could accomplish. If the object was to arrest Darling's guides by force in the woods, there were not men enough sent; otherwise there were too many, since one unarmed man with a warrant could do more than a posse. If it was supposed that this number was necessary to overpower Mr. Darling singly, there was an entire misapprehension of his character. In like manner the use of handcuffs, though probably intended as an irritation, had no sufficient excuse. It was the officer's duty to keep his prisoner securely, yet in insisting on this point there was shown the same misunderstanding of Darling's position. Resistance to authority is no part of his plan, as lack of control is no part of his disposition. His word would have been the only guarantee needed; because had he attempted escape, he could have been held on a graver charge than the one for which he was arrested, and had he wished to make the attempt he could have done it as well with the manacles as without them. Finally, the refusal to allow him to change his clothes was either a piece of short-sightedness or another unnecessary annoyance. According to the report published at the time, from information which must have been derived from official sources, Mr. Darling had above $700 on his person at the time of his arrest. From a number of sources, I am informed that he offered to deposit this with the officers as security, if they would permit him to change his clothes. There is every reason for believing the statement. Without questioning the officers' reasons for refusal, it is none the less true that the favor might have been safely granted. Here was

---

[141] Hardy is using the original spelling of Nicatous; her explanation of the name derivation and corruption from Nicatowis can be read in, *Exploring the Maine Woods – The Hardy Family Expedition to the Machias Lakes*.

full indemnity to the State against personal loss, and no real danger of any loss. Darling knew that the charge was a violation of the game law; that the penalty could not be anything more serious than a fine. Even if he had determined to abscond, leaving his money, he would be doing it on uncertainties, since he did not know the specific charge, and would be making himself the outlaw he had falsely been declared to be, thus practically forfeiting his home and all his other property.

The indignity of this treatment, which had to be admitted, reacted strongly in Darling's favor; and his non-resistance and refusal to accept interference in his behalf left the officers to bear the odium of unnecessary severity. Then it was found that he was arrested on defective warrants, and on these warrants fined not only for keeping dogs and for killing a deer himself when in the employ of McNamara (though here the employer is always looked on as responsible for the action of the guide), but for the three deer that Swanton and McNamara killed themselves. This was outdoing justice's justice, even as we get it in Maine game cases.

But these were not all, nor even, the greatest of the indignities offered. I had heard from a number of sources the account of his arrest and trial, but this winter, wishing to get a continuous and accurate account, I wrote Mr. Darling about it. He also called during the winter, the first time I had seen him for many years. From his letter and oral statement, the following account is compiled. Full references were given me for substantiating the different points, and I believe the account to be correct.

"At the time Stilwell sent McNamara to Nicatowis Lake to get evidence against me," he writes, "I had a sick daughter in Massachusetts. I had been there to see her, and the doctors told me that she could not live but a short time.[142] The rest of my family was there, with her. I felt so bad that I could not bear to stay there. I went home and McNamara and Swanton

---

[142] Mary I. Darling Nov 11, 1889 (24 yrs. old). Darling's other children, Charles Leroy died in 1865 at under 3 years of age, and Emily E. Darling died in 1861 before she reached 2 years of age.

came to my house and wanted me to take them to Nicatowis, deer hunting. I took them to the lake and stopped one day. They hired each of them a guide and killed three deer. I killed one the day I was there. They killed two on Sunday and I went home Sunday. Before I went, I saw them from the house at the lake kill two. I sat on the steps of my door and saw them shoot them. McNamara stopped two days after I came down and hunted and then went directly to Bangor, etc., and swore out four warrants for me and several for other parties and then went to Milbridge and got a warden and seven men all told and started for Nicatowis. I was at home watching the mail and the telegraph, expecting any moment to hear of the death of my daughter, when those men came. They told me that they had a warrant for me for violation of the game laws. I told them all right and I wished to see it. They would not, and took out handcuffs. I told them that such things were uncalled for, but they told me to have them on."

In the conversation on the subject, Mr. Darling said that he wished to go to the post office to get his mail, being anxious to hear from his daughter. He was forbidden to have his mail at all. He insisted upon it, and at last was permitted to go, the officer of course accompanying. Some men about the post office wished to remove the handcuffs, but he refused. He did, however, ask one of them to go up to the lake that day, which was done.[143]

"They put them on," the letter continues, "and started me for Bangor with one man, and the rest went to the lake. When I got to Olamon, I demanded the warrant to read it. I declined to go further until I read it."

This of course was simple enough. Had he wished to do it, Darling could at any time have leaped from the open wagon, and the officer would have been unable to secure his prisoner again. At last, the warrant was given him.

---

[143] No doubt to deliver the message of his predicament.

"I read it. It was for killing four deer, and three of them was killed by them while with their guides."

At Olamon they stopped for dinner. Mr. Darling requested to have the handcuffs removed while he ate. The officer would not do it. He refused to eat unless it was done, and for the third time that day the officer yielded. Before this, however, a well-known man, whose name was given me, not a resident of the place, offered to cut the link with a cold chisel.

"But," writes Mr. Darling, "I wanted to let those men show themselves in full and I would not have them taken off, only when I ate dinner. I was taken to the jail in Bangor on Friday night and held until Monday, and then taken to Bucksport for trial, fined for killing four deer and keeping dogs in my possession, etc. I have forgotten the amount of the fine, costs, etc., but I appealed."

The confinement in the Bangor jail for two days was the worst part of the insult. Bail was offered by different men whom he named, and could have been had to any amount required; but it was refused. What possible excuse could there be for this? The charge was only a violation of the game laws; the fine at the most less than the amount of ready money which the officers knew Mr. Darling had in his possession; and unexceptional bail could have been obtained to any amount.

The fact that the State was the prosecutor did not improve the situation. Instead of prosecution, some declared that this was persecution. Of the foul condition of the jail at that time, the insufficient food, and the wretched quality of the same, and the exposure to contagious disease, Mr. Darling gave a full account, which has been fully confirmed by others, among them Mr. Robert Jordan, the secretary of the Bangor Y. M. C. A.

On Monday, Mr. Darling was taken to Bucksport, in Hancock County, for trial before a trial justice. Why this particular man was chosen, whether he was there at the time or not, I cannot say, but he was not a trial justice. He had been one formerly, but had lost his commission by moving out of the county, from Bucksport to Bangor. There is no doubt of this, as it was to have been one of the fundamental points of cases to be brought against Darling in the

Supreme Court. The quality of the justice rendered can be seen from the fines imposed for deer which Darling did not kill, but saw the officers themselves kill on Sunday, which being close time in this State, made them liable to the fine. The fines and the costs, I am told, were made to amount to over $600. In addition, as has already been said, the warrants on which this was done were worthless. McNamara was not a warden, and no one but a warden has the right to prosecute in a game case until fourteen days after the offense; according to section 18 (now quoted in the *Book of the Game Laws*):

"After fourteen days from the commission of any offense hereinbefore named any person may prosecute by action, complaint or indictment, unless such warden or deputy has prosecuted therefor."

Yet, McNamara swore out his warrants within a week of the time that he first reached Nicatowis.[144]

At the Supreme Court at Ellsworth four complaints were brought against Darling, one for using dogs and three for killing deer. The latter were not McNamara's original cases but others substituted for them. None of these were tried, two being nol prosed[145] and one quashed as defective. The dog case was tried and the verdict given in favor of the State.

Now comes the much vexed question whether Darling was fined or not. He paid $100, which is the sum set as the maximum fine for keeping or using dogs, but he paid no costs. The case was concluded on a Saturday, the other cases were to be brought up the next week.

---

[144] The reader may find authors who claim Eckstorm took the side of Darling's poaching and dogging. Eckstorm writes nowhere in this essay that she supported Darling's illegal dogging of deer. As in the prior essays, she is summarizing the account. Eckstorm, not trained in law, does a remarkable job of analyzing statute law against the evidence, testimony, the papers, and hearsay. Her point is, as in all these essays, to show why a good percentage of Mainers felt the way they did about the game laws, the wardens, the commissioners, and justice levied against those accused of crimes.

[145] Past tense of *nolle pros*; to abandon or dismiss by issuing a nolle prosequi.

Whether they would have gone in favor of Darling or against him, whether he would have begun action against his accusers for grounds which were certainly good, cannot be told; for the judge and the counsel on both sides after conference agreed to settle this case and dismiss the others on payment of $100 without costs. Mr. Darling rather reluctantly consented. He had two drives of logs which needed his attention, as this was in April, and though he wished to bring the matter to a decisive issue the loss would be more than the satisfaction to be derived. Mr. Darling himself claims, and all those not personally hostile to him grant, there was a settlement, not a fine proper. "It may be entered on the docket at Ellsworth as a fine," said his counsel, "I do not know; but it satisfied all the cases and did not include costs."

No game case that we have had, on which so much depended, ever was so indecisive as this. It did nothing. It is even a little uncertain whether Darling actually was fined. He was found guilty of using dogs which no one denied, but the possible effect of even this was neutralized by the part which McNamara played. He was to appear before the April term of the Supreme Court as the principal witness against Darling; but at that time there was some little doubt as to the value of his testimony. In February, 1890, he (McNamara) was tried at Ellsworth on the charge of perjury.

"In summing up the evidence he [Judge Redman] charged that McNamara was an unprincipled man working for money only and unless he were punished the life and property of any citizen was in danger. Judge Clark held that there was probable cause and ordered the defendant to furnish bonds in the sum of $800 for his appearance at the April term of the Supreme Court."

But if McNamara were convicted, Darling could not be; if McNamara were acquitted, unless by the fullest proof, his testimony, whether true or untrue, would fail to affect the public at large. Without entering into the details, it is enough to say that by a disagreement of the jury McNamara was qualified to be sworn as witness in the Darling case.

We need not review the various points already given, which combine to make this case unique among those that are monumental for their injustices. The effect upon a people who love to see fair play does not need to be described; but more than anything else, what affected those who had any interest in game matters, was that the same might be tried at any time upon anyone, whether innocent or guilty.

It was not Jonathan Darling who was ill-treated, but every man against whom there was ill will or from whom there could be any profit derived. Had it been a matter of interpretation, this would not have been so: the first case would be the last, and no one need fear; but this case was a precedent of the sort to be dreaded, a menace that the same might at any time be repeated.

Fannie Pearson Hardy

---

## Editor Note

Jonathan "Jock" Darling fought the charges brought against him for eight years from 1889 until in January 1897, when the case was ultimately dismissed. Darling died the following January of 1898 (age 67).

In the midst of his ongoing court cases, Darling became a Maine Game Warden. The following letter, from himself, was published in The Bangor News on September 17, 1891 (a month after Eckstorm's final game law essay).

\* \* \*

## Game Warden Darling - Sept. 17 , 1891

The *Bangor News* asserts that Maine has few more energetic or more honest game wardens than "Jock" Darling and prints this letter from him:

### To the Editor of the News:

I have recently received letters from hunters and guides asking for an explanation as to why I have accepted an office of a game warden: and one sends me a clipping from a Bangor paper which reads: "Maine's notorious game warden. Set a thief to catch a thief, etc." and says that "Uncle Jock has long set the game laws and wardens at defiance, and openly advocated the dogging of deer in various publications over his own signature, etc."

I will give a partial explanation. I advocated dogging deer during the open season, as my long experience told me, with few exceptions, they could not be had any other way, and that my belief was the most of the deer doggers would help enforce the law in close time. I fought the law or rather the wardens when I believed that they were the law breakers, and I went to our Legislature and did all I could to amend the game law by repealing a portion of it, and I did it alone. Not a hunter, guide or sportsman helped me to a cent or lifted a hand to help me. On the other hand, many of the guides that I had given employment that put many a dollar into their pockets, did not appreciate the favor, and worked against me in many ways.

And now they can take their turn, if they want to fight the law, they have the field, and if they want the law amended or repealed, they have a chance to see what they can do.

Our judges will tell the jurors in their charge to them that the law may be wrong or obnoxious, but as long as it stands on our statues it must be regarded as law, and that they must decide according to law and evidence.

Years ago, I killed hundreds of moose and used to get every pound of meat out of the carcass, until I found that the other hunters, mostly Canada Indian, were bound to kill them all just for their hides, and to get my share I took a hand in it, at the same time believing it to be wrong.

I have given some of my reasons for accepting the office of game warden, and, as I have accepted it, I shall try to protect and preserve the game when it should be.

And I will say to the hunters, guides, or poachers, that I don't want to catch them breaking the fish and game laws. I shall not try to induce anyone to break the law for the purpose of catching you to get your money. I don't want you to kill game when you are not allowed to do so by law; but I do say if you keep on or do kill, as some of you have in years past, I shall catch a few or more of you.

I shall make it a point to see the hunters, guides, etc., and talk the matter over with them and try to persuade them not to kill the fish and game in close time, and if I am successful in this I shall think I have done a better work than I should if I had arrested them and put them to trouble and costs.

J. Darling.
Lowell, Mass., Sept. 7, 1891

**Editor Note**

*The *Bangor News* had typeset Darling's town at the end of the original letter, as *Lowell, Mass*. Darling's home was in Lowell, Maine, in Penobscot County. Darling, along with his wife and three children, is buried in Tannery Cemetery in East Lowell, Maine.

The tiny town of Lowell is along the Passadumkeag River, with easy access to the water route through Saponac Pond and on to Nicatowis Lake, where Darling had his lodge. The fall of 1890 Hardy canoe trip down the river and to Darling's hunting lodge is described in detail by Eckstorm in, *Exploring the Maine Woods – The Hardy Family Expedition to the Machias Lakes.*

# XI. THE ONE BEFORE THE LAST

## July 16, 1891

**The** time has come to close this series of papers. Unforeseen circumstances have delayed their preparation, and other causes equally unforeseen have altered their original plan, so that they are widely different from the first design. It is therefore impossible to draw conclusions or to sum up in any orderly fashion what has been said. But there are a few additional points to be touched upon and some probable consequences—which may a better ordering of affairs avert!—that need to be set forth; and just a word may be said of what was intended but was not accomplished.

In the beginning a state of feeling was described in which a bitter and unreasoning resentment must have seemed predominant. It was planned to account for this, to show how it arose and why, and what were the principal local modifications of it with their local causes. The plan has been carried out only in part. What was said of the waste of game and non-transportation in open season applied with varying force to all the counties and has been influential in all to produce the present state of dissatisfaction. But what has been said of deer hounding and killing dogs pertains only to the southeastern counties of the State. Nothing has been said of Piscataquis and its interests, nor of Aroostook and Aroostook affairs, although the plan was to illustrate and explain the causes which had operated in these to produce a feeling substantially the same, but differing in its degree. A change made last March in the law permitting the destruction of dogs, bringing new and unexpected dangers close upon us, as it was feared, caused the abandonment of the original design and a fuller treatment of topics relating to deer hounding than was at first intended or deemed desirable, while in consequence the other sections had to be slighted.

I have said that it was not the intention to speak of deer hounding at such length. There were other topics equally interesting which did not have the peculiar disadvantages of this, namely, that whoever would speak of abuses connected with its suppression must consent to be accused of favoring the practice. Now, the practice cannot be defended in this State.[146] As a method deer hounding may be the best or the worst, the most humane or the most cruel way of getting a deer—that is a matter of opinion; as a *practice* it is illegal and should be stopped. Yet it is of supreme importance that the means of suppression shall be such that those who wish to see the law enforced can honestly defend the means taken to enforce it. Who could do this of the poisoning and dog killing of years past? The extraordinary abuses connected with these methods of procedure have put them into such disrepute that neither of them can ever gain any measure of popular support. Yet this spring the law has been changed so that the killing of dogs is encouraged by the new license granted, even if it is not intended, as has been feared, to make it an official feature of the campaign this fall. Nothing could be more fatal than this. These practices may be legalized, but such is the odium attaching that they will injure the cause in which they are employed.

The reaction against the last attempts has been very strong. Nearly, if not quite twice as much deer hounding was carried on last fall on Penobscot and Union River waters as ever before. Deer were dogged more or less regularly on some thirty ponds and lakes which I could name, and at Chemo Lake,[147] only about fifteen miles from Bangor, they were run all the fall. Hounds used to run deer are openly kept in Bangor and vicinity. Men go from Bangor and surrounding towns to places where deer are dogged, the papers tell

---

[146] Incorrect and inaccurate references can be found which state that Eckstorm came out in support of those who hunted by deer-hounding with dogs, and also that she stated that the state had no right to pass laws about game. Here, in these papers you have read her own words and know she supported the game laws.

[147] Pronounced, Chee-mo, the ch soft as in *cheek*.

where they have gone, and what they bring back, and the deer, shot in the back of the head, are openly exhibited.[148] There is no secret made of it.

What is more, men who a few years ago strongly disapproved the practice, now favor it more or less openly. Whoever would stop hounding must overcome an opposition which did not exist a few years ago, and this can be done only by the use of fair and legal methods. Fine the men who engage in it, but give us no more Darling cases and no more dog killing. To repeat the proceedings of the few years past would give us not only more murders, but would be the speediest way of creating a general demand from this section to have a law permitting hounding.

It was planned, among other things, to speak at some length of the illegal sale of fish and game, of the number of prosecutions brought and fines collected, of certain cases tried and minor untenable interpretations of the laws, of the character and efficiency of the wardens now in the service; and facts were collected for this purpose, which the change of plan already spoken of has made it necessary to set aside.

However, that the case may not seem to go by default, we will have a word upon some of these points.

Game and fish have been illegally sold this winter, and not by any means in lone and sequestered spots. It has been done in our largest cities and in the markets, so openly that strangers have commented on it. Not to speak of what has been done nearer home. In Augusta, game and fish both were sold contrary to law; and at the very time that new trout laws were under discussion, togue were openly sold in the city and were served under the name of trout on the table of the hotel where many of the senators and representatives boarded. Complaint was made but no prosecutions followed. Without discussing where these fish were taken, it was directly

---

[148] The point here is when hunters returned with their deer on display, the wound location most certainly indicated the shot was taken at close range; the implication being the hunter was illegally assisted by dogs hounding the deer to the water.

contrary to law to sell them, and yet while the sale was permitted in Augusta, in the eastern part of the State, Pete Newell, an Indian, poor undoubtedly, ignorant very likely, was fined for selling trout.

Regarding the collection of fines and their disposition, little can be said in little space. But the aggregate of fines paid in to the treasuries is not what might be expected. In Penobscot it is too small to make any account of. From Jan. 1st to the middle of April of this year only $40 was paid in from nearly ninety towns and townships which are included in this county. The sum for any year is very small. This would not be a disadvantage if the violations of the law were few, but they are numerous and open. Some cases come up in the higher courts of Penobscot, but very few appear in the lower courts of Bangor. The clerk of the municipal court who has been in the office many years could show me papers pertaining to only two cases, which he said were all that he distinctly remembered. One was the voluntary complaint against himself of a gentleman who killed a moose last September; the other a case against a man for netting fish last October, ending in an appeal.

Some cases come before trial justices outside the city. There are a few justices in this and other counties to whom game cases are frequently carried, or who are carried to the cases, whence the nickname of "pocket justices" sometimes applied to them; and there is some particularly edifying history connected with the cases which come up before these men. The aggregate of game cases in eastern Maine for the past few years has been small when we except the seizures illegally made under the transportation fiasco and what has been done on the seashore.

Concerning wardens, we will say as little as possible. It is not fair to speak disparagingly of a whole class without bringing forward the proof. Yet it is true that after much inquiry I have found many poor wardens and only two that could be called good ones. Good men there may be, undoubtedly are, among the hundred and fifty who are employed as wardens, but unless they live in the western part of the State or upon the seashore, they must be scarce. The majority of the more prominent wardens of eastern Maine are not only bad wardens but bad men. There is full proof of their unfitness for the place. I was intending to bring forward enough to show the kind of men into whose hands the execution of our game laws has fallen, but it would take too long to do the subject justice, and we may leave it with Charley Utter's benediction, "May the Lord think well of you"—and its logical inference.[149]

It is of more importance just now to know that some of these men have been reappointed not once, but some times more than once, in spite of repeated protest. We have been told that nobody was responsible for this. The change of the law this year which requires the approval of two of the Commissioners before a warden will be given an appointment, is a great improvement. It makes the Commissioners personally responsible for the character of the men employed, and the improvement of the service by the substitution of better men for some of those now in the service may be expected. We have been told that heretofore men had been selected for their strength and ability to shoot quickly. The authority for the statement was high, yet this may not be the real ground of selection. At any rate these would be merely imaginary advantages for an active warden. Strength may make an arrest, but it will not take a man out of the woods, and the ability to shoot quickly is merely a negative advantage, since an officer cannot use firearms except as a last resort. Plain, old-fashioned honesty is the best qualification a warden can have, and with it a man can go safely, when without it he would run considerable risk. The second-best recommendation to the position should be a thorough knowledge of woodcraft and the ability to go alone through the woods instead of along highways and frequented routes.

One change in the laws this year requires some attention. Henceforth wardens may make arrests without the use of a warrant. This will be a great advantage in securing the arrest of offenders, but visitors and residents alike will need to be on their guard against those who pretend to be wardens and extort fines on false pretenses. In years past this has been done more or less frequently. I know of

----

[149] Reference to Charlie Utter (1842-1915) a figure of the American Wild West and friend to assassinated Wild Bill Hickok (1837-1876).

three cases, one of them occurring this winter, where the attempt has been made by men who were not wardens, and I have been told on good authority of another where a fine was paid only this winter to a man who was not a warden, for fishing pickerel, which it is legal to fish at any season. It is well for everyone to carry a copy of the latest issue of the game laws, so that he can determine for himself just what the law is and whether he is guilty. There are many points where by mistake or evil intention a person not perfectly sure of his rights can be intimidated and made to pay blackmail by those who are not officials and have no right to interfere. How many who come here know that Sunday is close time on game but not on fish? Or that until this spring deer could be legally shipped from the State provided the legal number was not exceeded, while partridges could not be?[150] Or half a dozen other points on which a case could be made or lost?

The wise man, if detected in an offense against the laws, will, if possible, stand trial. He never will pay anything to settle a case, nor pay a fine to anyone without taking a receipt for it. If in any case he should pay a fine to anyone whom he does not know personally, he will at the expiration of two months write to the county treasurer of the county in which it was paid, to find whether it has been paid to the county, that being the limit of time which any justice or receiver of fines can keep them without incurring heavy fines. These are suggestions merely, but they are made to the wise. Never pay anything to anyone who may not be an official. Never pay without taking a receipt in full. Never fail to see whether that money was paid into the treasury at the proper time unless there is no room for doubt.

The next paper, which will be the final one, will take up some of the more general evils which will follow if something is not done to improve the present conditions here. They are too serious to be neglected and should receive thoughtful consideration of both residents and visitors who are interested in the welfare of this State. It is not the game alone that makes a trip here pleasant—the game

---

[150] 1891 references. See current Maine Game Laws.

and fish are the least part of it to many who come here, and certainly are not greatly esteemed by the residents. There are other interests upon which both can unite, which now, if not actually imperiled, are at that point where the future danger can be most easily averted. It is for what will be said in this final paper, however simply and unemphatically it may be put forth, that this whole series, with all the labor and unenviable notoriety it involves, was undertaken.


Fannie Pearson Hardy

# XII. IN CONCLUSION

August 6, 1891

**A Careful** observer may soon satisfy himself that the prospects for fish and game in Maine are not growing better. The fishing in some of the best places is deteriorating, and the game, though still abundant, has been mercilessly slaughtered, while the season for killing it grows yearly longer. This year the work began the first of June; and next year we expect it to open in May.

The summer killing is increasing continually, and the number of sportsmen grows larger every year. It is impossible for the natural increase of the fish and game to keep pace with the demand.

What then?

What happens when there is not enough for all?

At the same time, it is undeniable that no effort has been made to stop the summer killing, that the game laws have been very ill-enforced at the best, and that outrageous injustices have been committed in their name—the laws having been executed as they have been, what then!

What happens when the lowest ebb has been reached?

After the ebb, the flood; the highest tides follow the lowest. In the nature of things, there will be a reaction which will give not only a stricter enforcement of the laws we have—we want that, the sooner the better—but if the delay is long, a change of laws with heavier penalties, increasing in proportion as the reform is deferred.

The longer the inaction, the greater the reaction. On the other hand, when there ceases to be game enough for all, the effort will be made to secure it for the few. The nonexecution of the law diminishes the amount of game and hastens the day of game preserves; the establishment of the latter tends to increase the penalties and severities of the law; the very neglect of the laws at present inclines to the same end.

Great evils may hang upon the adjustment of these points. We fear them. We know that there has been a call for the increase of penalties and that there is a constant pressure to secure the establishment of game preserves. For the former, read our Game Commissioner's reports for the past few years—the last, however, is a commendable exception—and see how strongly they have urged to add imprisonment to *all* game law penalties; for the latter, follow the quiet but active endeavors to secure possession of land that is now open to the public. It is something not chronicled in the newspapers, but it is here.[151]

Of course, there is no immediate prospect that any considerable portion of Maine will be closed to the public. It is still what may be called a far-off danger; but our lumbermen and landowners could tell of a very decided trend in that direction. Nor does it by any means need that a very considerable portion should be so held in order to accomplish what seems now to be a great evil. Closing half a dozen well-located townships and making it trespass to camp or hunt upon them could be made a very great annoyance. There are a few townships which, for ease of approach, excellence of hunting and fishing grounds and beauty of scenery and camping places, are worth to the sportsman forty times as much as others somewhere else. Who wouldn't prefer the snug chance we all know of, which is open to us now whenever we choose to go, to—well, to a dozen townships around Baker Lake at the end of the nine-mile carry?[152]

---

[151] Game preserves for paid hunting exist in present day Maine.

[152] Baker Laker is in township T7 R17 WELS. In her father's hunting days, he would trap in the Allagash Lake region and no doubt had told her about the Baker Lake region, as did other woodsmen.

We do not speak with any hostility to anyone who prefers not to have the whole world use his land as an excursion ground. It is his own and he has a right to do with it what he pleases. But the principle of a game preserve is different. It is closing the land to enclose game and fish which were not bought, which are not property and to which there is no title. (Stocked ponds and preserves are not meant.) It is using a right to compass a wrong. Now this is very hateful to the mind of the average Maine man. To tell the truth our lumbermen and landowners have a little (or a good deal) spoiled us by their generosity; and, quite aside from the question of game as property, the invariable custom of leaving all land open to the public has led us to regard it as a right.

I well remember my own rebellion when I first went into a country where blueberries were private property and trout streams were posted. There is a strong objection here to closing land because the custom of sharing all the minor products is so nearly universal.

But it may be said that closing the land is not necessary; that some of the best preserves require scarcely more than respect for the State game laws. These favors are appreciated, and yet so captious is the public at present that even this would fail to disarm suspicion on Penobscot.

"The whole thing was free to them before, without costing. They didn't need only enough for their shanty. When they get good and ready they mean to shut down on us."[153]

The presence of private wardens to enforce State laws would be taken as an affront. Indeed (to show the feeling), the private rewards offered last winter by non-residents, whatever might have been their effect in the western part of the State, were bitterly resented here as unwarrantable interference.

The amount of it is that our landowners and lumbermen are wholly trusted. They are the most popular class of employers in the State. They wear the homespun in speech and manners and have immense personal popularity. Some of them merely on the strength of this popularity could muster a regiment to work for them or to

---

[153] No name or reference given on the quote.

fight for them. The land they own cannot be transferred in any quantities from their hands to strangers, without creating the feeling that it has gone from the control of friends to that of aliens, who may be never so worthy but are not the same. It is like seeing the old homestead change hands.

> Home was home then, my dear, full of kindly faces;
> Home was home then, my dear, happy for the child.[154]

That is the feeling we have; and no game preserve can be purchased here for some years at least without buying with it also a sub-acute hostility—home no longer being home, happy for the child.

Nor is this the sole cause of prejudice. The owner of a preserve may be the pattern of all moral excellence, but to those used to different customs he seems a dog in the manger, guarding what he cannot use and thinking to growl away those who have at least as good a right there as he. This antagonizes the woodsman at two points.

He will not take a dare and he hates selfishness. A body of gamekeepers signifies defiance; the effort to hold wild game on wild land is (to him) a meanness almost incomprehensible. Now the punishment of some sins is reserved for God alone, but (according to the Maine dictum) stinginess may be punished by God and the neighbors.

There is not the slightest doubt that the establishment of preserves, or even the purchasing of land for them at the present time, would result in burning the country.

How to express the certainty of this I do not know, nor that stern approval which it would meet from a large following; but I know only too well the kind of resolution which blows up the magazine

---

[154] Lines from *Home No More Home To Me, Whither Must I Wander*, a poem by Robert Louis Stevenson. Note, Eckstorm also used these lines in her story, *The Sheriff of Shottingham*.

and garrison (not always by their leave) to avoid surrender to the enemy.

If anyone doubts the outcome of preserves here let him ask the larger lumbermen and landowners and the best guides. What a hundred years will bring forth none can tell; whether ten years will produce a change of feeling these men would know better than I, but I am inclined to think that ten years will not do it. Changes occur slowly here, and as I showed in the beginning, the love of freedom so outweighs the love of money with woodsmen that it seems not improbable that the opposition to preserves will strengthen as the demand for them increases.[155]

We need not dwell upon the value of the lumbering interests to Maine, especially to the working classes who find employment by the thousand in the lumber camps, on the drives, in sawmills, in pulpmills, loading vessels and making them. Except farming no one occupation employs so many men as lumbering and its dependent trades. The people are dependent upon it, and those who try to teach us that the game and fish are worth more than all the lumber get laughed at for their pains. Then, again, the water powers are directly dependent upon the forests. This is especially true of the Penobscot, which rises in swamps and bays and little streamlets. Destroy the forests and the water powers are gone. And after the forests are gone come the floods and freshets. It is imperative that the forests should be saved from fire.

But could game preserves do this damage? Probably not. The opportunity will not be given. The chances are that the first preserve on Penobscot waters will be burned at once—there is an old saw about fighting fire with fire—and heavier conflagrations saved in later years when the system should gather force. For it would tend to heavier penalties; they would produce crime and the fires would follow. If the means of prevention cannot be commended, it must be admitted that is one of the ways in which the many instinctively

---

[155] As of 2023 there are several privately owned game preserves within the state, some holding species not native to Maine.

protect themselves when their well-being is imperiled for the pleasure of the few.

The second danger is to fish and game. I said that last summer's waste was responsible for last winter's killing. This was the beginning of retaliatory measures which will be kept up.

"It isn't fair that they should have and waste what we can't have to eat," is the complaint.

The fate of the game in this State depends very largely upon the good will of the rural classes. Sportsmen may be able, as has been boasted, to pass any reasonable laws here, but the veto power lies with the people, and unacceptable game laws will be destructive to the game. This is something worth remembering. People will, not stand today what they would a few years ago, and suspicion which was formerly quiescent is now fully alert.

The question is considered not one of game and who shall have it, but one of rights. The determination is to insist on fair play, to refuse to sell a birthright for any amount of pottage. Hence, any law that, for instance, cuts off December from the open season to open September is regarded with extreme disfavor. There is little likelihood that we shall have game dinners of the same order as the Boston tea party, for people are opposed to waste; but any attempt to introduce hunting licenses, for example, or leases of lands and waters, or to favor sportsmen more than residents would destroy the major part of the game in a very few years. There is, indeed, little danger of this being done with game, but at any time pickerel may be put into trout waters.

The sporting papers have had a great deal to say about the destructiveness of winter trout fishing, but they do not know that this is all that secures any trout fishing. The people here will have some kind of winter fishing, and if isn't trout it shall be pickerel. It is true that there is a strict law against the introduction of pickerel, but there is absolutely no means of enforcing it. I suppose that it is generally known that a pickerel may be frozen stiff, kept so for days and afterward resuscitated. The experiment is simple enough, for it only needs that the fish should be caught on a very cold day, frozen immediately and packed in snow, afterward thawed slowly in cold water. Anyone who tries it, as I have done, will be satisfied that pickerel could be transported in this way anywhere and that no law could be framed to prevent their introduction into the best trout waters.[156]

This is an absolute check to all attempts to take away the winter trout fishing. Had it been my purpose to deal with fish laws I could have made it plain that once already this danger was pressing and was avoided by the "one line for citizens" law, which no one ever kept. The change this winter permitting five set lines (this is practically an unlimited number, the real limit to the fishing being the law forbidding transportation of above a certain amount of fish)—this change was a wise and specific measure, which removes to some extent the danger to trout waters.

We come at length to the question of adding imprisonment to penalties. May the day of it long be averted! I know that some of our people, seeing the inequality of the money penalty, have advised it, but without due forethought. Of all bad things that can happen to us through the wretched possession of a little game, this would be the worst. "It would fill these woods full of outlaws," said one guide in gloomy anticipation. To add imprisonment to all our game-law penalties, as our Commissioners have urged, as others will be sure to urge in coming time, would be to put a premium on crime.

In the first place, the majority of all our game-law violations are committed by people called "sportsmen." This a safe estimate for game-law violators; the guides will put it higher. Now, none of these men, if they have any ready money, need ever suffer imprisonment unless their sense of honor be fantastically nice. To give an extreme instance, let us suppose that the recommendation of the Commissioners' Report in 1886 had actually become law, and that "a penalty of $500 and six months' imprisonment [was] the mildest punishment for killing a cow moose at any season." This would not save the cow moose. They would still be killed unintentionally, for

---

[156] Such arguments are as old as outdoor writing. David Stone Libbey penned an article, under his pen name of Penobscot, titled, *Do Pickerel Destroy Trout?* (*and other topics*). The essay may be read in, *David Stone Libbey – He Was Penobscot*, (2022).

half the time at least it is impossible to tell the sex of the animal shot before the chance is gone; and they would be killed intentionally also to spite the law. But with such a law, unworthy officers and justices would procure appointments and connive together (as has actually been done) to make the most they could out of offenses, real or trumped up. Certain justices would have the majority of the cases and have their price. But, supposing the case a good one, who would not pay $500, or even twice that, if a busy man, in order to escape six months in the county jail? As a matter of fact it would not cost so much. Rather than have the case appealed they would come down some on their prices.

The poor man, who would be some farmer, trapper or hunter, and who could not pay their price, must appeal. Now, in the higher courts both men would stand alike, or, indeed, the poor man would have the better chance; for a jury would not convict on any such case if there was any possible escape. But, as a matter of fact, not very many cases would go up to superior courts. Both would take their chances of being found out; the wealthier man would know his grounds and perhaps make it all right beforehand, while the poorer man if caught in the act would settle it on the spot or as soon thereafter as possible. That law, had it been made law, would have put a premium on murder. The suggestion was well intended, but it was not wise. It is to the credit of the Commissioners' judgment that they ceased to urge this, and have of late not proposed the addition of imprisonment. But the suggestion has been made and it cannot be forgotten. We fear that it would almost inevitably follow the establishment of an extensive system of private preserves. "It would be like it is in England," writes one hunter.

No better illustration of the iniquities of preserving the pleasure of the few by arbitrary enactments against the rights of the many can be given than in quoting what Hugh Miller, the Scotch geologist, wrote nearly fifty years ago concerning the English system and its results.

The extract is from his *"Crime Making Laws,"* in *Essays Political and Social*; but others of his papers are equally profitable and equally apt. There is, in these papers, the weight of righteousness nobly indignant and the weight of experience which overbears all theories and theoretical objections:

## Crime Making Laws - Hugh Miller

"If there was a special law enacted against all red-haired men and all men six-foot-high, red-haired men and men six-foot-high would in a short time become exceedingly dangerous characters. In order to render them greatly worse than their neighbors, there would be nothing more necessary than simply to set them beyond the pale of the constitution by providing by statute that whoever lodged informations against red-haired men or men six-feet-high should be handsomely rewarded, and that the culprits themselves should be lodged in prison and kept at hard labor on every conviction from a fortnight to sixty days. The country would at length come to groan under the untolerable burden of its red-haired men and its men six-feet-high. There would be frequent paragraphs in our columns and elsewhere to the effect that some three or four respectable white-haired gentlemen, varying in height from five feet nothing to five feet five, had been grievously maltreated in laudably attempting to apprehend some formidable felon, habit and repute six-feet-high; or to the effect that Constable D., of the third division, had been barbarously murdered by a red-haired ruffian. Philosophers would come to discover that so deeply implanted was the bias to outrage and wrong in red-haired nature that it held by the scoundrels even after their heads had become bald and their whiskers gray; and so inherent was rufiianism to six-feet-high men that though four six-feet fellows had for the sake of example, been cut short at the knees, they had remained, notwithstanding the mutilation, as incorrigible ruffians as ever. From time to time there would be some terrible tragedy enacted by some tremendous incarnation of illegality and evil, who was both red-haired and six-feet-high to boot."

With exquisite humor, Miller traces the gradual abolition of the enactments. He also draws a vivid picture of the former prevalence of highway robbery and murder in England. He continues;

"And so highway murder has become one of almost the rarest offenses in the criminal register of the country. Very different is the case, however, with murders of another kind.

"Within the last few years there have been no fewer than twenty-five game keepers murdered in England. The cases were all ascertained cases: coroners' juries sat upon the bodies, and verdicts of willful murder were returned against certain parties, known or unknown; and these were, of course, but the murders on the one side.

"Be it remembered, too, that the peculiar barbarism of the modern period is greatly more a national reproach than that of the ancient. The old enormities were enormities in spite of a good law; the newer enormities are enormities that arise directly out of a bad one. There is sound sense as well as good feeling in the remark of Mrs. Saddletree on the law, in Effie Dean's case, as laid down by her learned husband the saddler. 'The crime,' remarked the wiseacre to his better half, 'is rather a favorite of the law, this species of murder being one of its own creating.' 'Then, if the law makes murders,' replied the matron, 'the law should be hanged for them; or if they would hang up a lawyer instead, the country would find nae fault.'

"All the twenty-five ascertained murders to which we have referred, and the at least equally great number of concealed ones, were crimes of the law's making, murders which as certainly originated in the law, and which, if the law did not exist, would as certainly not have been, as the supposed crimes of our illustration under the anti-red-hair, anti six-foot-high statutes. No murders arise out of the killing of seals and sea gulls; why should any murders arise out of the killing of hares and pheasants? Simply because there is a pabulum of law in the one case, out of which the transgression springs, and no producing pabulum of law in the other. There can be nothing more perilous to the morals of the people than stringent laws—that is, instead of attaching their penalties to actual crime, and having, in consequence, like the laws against the housebreaker and the highwayman, the whole weight of the popular conscience on their side, *create the crime which they punish*, and have thus the moral sense of the country certainly not for, mayhap against them. They become invariably in all such cases a sort of machinery for converting useful subjects and honest men into rogues and public pests. Lacking the moral sanction, their penalties are neither more nor less than a certain amount of peril, which bold spirits do not hesitate to encounter, just as a keen sportsman does not hesitate to encounter the modicum of risk which he runs from the gun that he carries.

"And such is the principle, when the law, equally dissociated from the promptings of the moral sense, is not a law of accident, but of the statute book. Men brave the danger of the penalty, as they do the peril of the fowling piece. But there is this ultimate difference, without being in any degree a felon by his own conscience, the traverser of the statutory enactment becomes legally a felon; he may be dealt with, like the red-haired or six-feet-high felon of our illustration, as decidedly criminal.

"Few of our readers can have any adequate conception of the immense mass of criminality created yearly in the empire by this singularly deteriorating process. In the year 1843 there were in England and Wales alone no fewer than 4,589 convictions under the game laws. Forty of that number were deemed cases of so serious a nature that the culprits were transported. In all the other cases they were either fined or imprisoned; the fines taken in the aggregate averaging two pounds sterling, the imprisonments seven weeks. And it is out of this system of formidable penalties that the numerous murders have arisen, and that the game laws of the country have, like those of Draco, come to be written in blood."

## END OF QUOTED ESSAY

The future of the game and fish of Maine, the pleasure of sportsmen, the property of residents, the safety of some, the morals of many, are jeopardized by the feeble and unequal enforcement of the game laws of which we have been conscious for three years, which has in reality existed much longer. We need a prompt reform in the equitable enforcement of those laws (which are good) by competent and incorruptible officers. We need efforts to prevent infractions of the law as well as to punish them.

We need the cooperation of residents and sportsmen. To secure this on the part of the rural population, the movement toward reform must be begun in the summer months—in July instead of January; otherwise they will not believe in its honesty; we have always had something done in the winter, because "it costs less."

When they can feel confidence in the officials and their justice, the inhabitants will take an interest and a pride in their work, and local matters will right themselves, and the better class of sportsmen by extending their influence, as they can do, will accomplish more than we can to restrain and discountenance the misdoings of those who have brought disgrace upon the name.


Fannie Pearson Hardy

# AND TEN YEARS HENCE, 1901

Letters on the Maine game laws would continue to be published in Forest and Stream in nearly every issue in the decade following Eckstorm's series. While she herself ceased to contribute on the topic, ten years after Eckstorm's final game law essay "Special" had this to say on the state of affairs.

## The Maine Game Law
### January 5, 1901

What changes there will be made in the Maine fish and game laws this winter is much in doubt. The legislature assembles Jan. 1, and the game law matter will be one of the most important. The semi-annual report of the Commissioners is out. In itself the report is highly congratulatory and self-assuring. The code of game laws is already almost perfect. The Commissioners recommend a few minor changes of little importance; otherwise, the laws should stand as they are. The September license law is almost perfect and should stand. It has caused no forest fires; has prevented many, on the contrary. The Commissioners still admit their inability to enforce the game laws when they again assert that fewer deer are killed under the September license law than would be killed without it.[157] They do not refer to the slaughter of deer that has been

---

[157] The September license law was added in 1899, allowing hunting for one deer in September for a fee. This was a trial at adding licenses. During that time, two deer were still permitted in the rest of the open season, for no fee. The pay-to-hunt was unpopular and it was abolished shortly after. Hunting and fishing licenses would

going on by guides and everybody in Maine that can shoot, and sending the game to Boston for sale by anybody that will take charge of it. Will anything be done to stop this shipment? The Commissioners' report mentions accidental shooting, and says that there have been ten cases of such shooting during the past open game season. Regrets are expressed, but no remedies are suggested.

The report suggests that registered guides are universally in favor of the September license law; that from many replies received from these guides it appears that that no forest fires have resulted from the law. Why should not the guides favor such a law? Why should they admit forest fires have resulted from it? The law is a source of extra employment to them, and can they be expected to testify against it? I have a letter before me from a gentleman in Maine who is thoroughly acquainted with several of the best hunting and fishing sections in that State. The letter says that the Fish and Game Commissioners' report does not express the sentiment of those most interested in the game of the Stare, such men as have a right to be heard. The true sentiment is against the September license law, and this sentiment is bound to be heard at Augusta, unless the influence of the Commission is strong enough to shut of all sentiment or opinion outside their own. There is danger that such may be the case, since Commissioner Carleton is himself a member of the coming Legislature. Editor Bracket, of the *North Woods*, is also a member of the House, a man who has given great energy to blowing for the Rangeley fish and game region for many years. Such men ought to have the best interests of the fish and game in Maine at heart and ought to be willing to see if the September license law is not a dangerous one, and one most ridiculously abused. Then the matter of indiscriminate shipment of deer, and even moose to Boston by both citizens and guides, through pseudo sportsmen, should be thoroughly gone over.

---

be required in the coming decades. In 1919 the resident lifetime fee was 25 cents each for a hunting and fishing license.

Neither should the tremendous slaughter of fish at the Rangeleys and in other waters last season be lightly brushed aside and buried under a mass of figures concerning restocking with landlocked salmon. The trout of the Rangeley waters, the finest in the world, are gone if they continue to be drawn upon as they were last year. The Commissioners may answer that more trout and salmon were taken at the Rangeleys last year than ever before, but will they please take into consideration that there were more fishermen after them, and will they please note the great improvements in deadly tackle that have been introduced within a few years? If they will make inquiry, they will find that the record of trout taken at the Upper Dam, strictly on the fly, was smaller last year than for many years.

Special

# EDITOR CONCLUDING COMMENTS

There are two comments to make about this 1901 letter from "Special." First, "Special" had been passionate about the topic of the Maine game laws for more than three decades. Second, many of the same issues covered by Eckstorm, are mentioned in his letter. One must ask then, had there been any progress on the game law situation?

Eckstorm by the publication of Special's 1901 letter had been married, her and her husband had two children; she had lived between Maine, Chicago, Oregon, and Rhode Island. Seven years into her marriage she was widowed and moved back to Brewer, Maine. She never again published a paper on the game laws in *Forest and Stream*.

In 1904 when she published, *The Penobscot Man*, there was barely a mention of the death threat from Jack Russell, the poacher she named in her 1891 essays. But it was plain to see, she hinted at it and those who knew understood the meaning behind the dedication of the book. She told of the rifle the guide carried along at Ripogenus for what was her shooting expedition—only she was not shooting a gun, she was there to take pictures of the river-drivers on glass plates. Unknown to the girl during the early days of that trip, her life had been threatened, and her guide Wilbur Webster had also become her bodyguard.

Eckstorm had moved on in her life's work. I find no writings or evidence she herself ever hunted. Not one note have I seen in her journals on such; in contrast to her father's journals where he catalogued most every animal taken on his trapping trips.

The daughter was involved in studying the ways of the river-drivers, and was deeply involved in educating the young through field work suggestions, as is apparent in her books, *The Bird Book* and *The Woodpeckers*. Following these woodsmen and nature projects, she continued to document Maine Native American history and placenames. In a parallel path to the lumbermen history, she and co-researchers documented the ballads of the lumbermen and the seamen. Her study of the early game law issues must have been a taxing research project, and it appears it was a step along her development in the exactitude she would use in all her writing endeavors.

The game law essays in this book provide the reader and researcher with easy access to these pieces written by Eckstorm. These are her own words about the game laws so her position can be well understood and quoted correctly.

The writings of Eckstorm may tell of the lumbering and river-driving days, of woodsman and woodcraft; she may explain the details of batteau designs, or the use of the broad-axe; her explanations of statute law are clear and level-headed; the essays she writes on birds can near make the reader hear the bird singing. It seems she is at home in the woods under a canvas tent, as she is behind the keys of her typewriter. Yet, one needs only to look at a few of her pieces in aggregate to know her real subjects.

**"After all, the best thing to see in the Maine woods is the woods, unless you are able to go straight to the hearts of the people in them, which is better yet."**

**Fannie Hardy Eckstorm**

Tommy Carbone
Greenville, Maine
2023

# APPENDIX

Included here are several letters from the pages of *Forest and Stream* about the Maine Game Law situation in the late 1800s.

## PROFESSIONAL MEN AND GAME
*Eight Years Prior to Eckstorm's Essays*

### Letters of "Olibo" and J. F. SPRAGUE – 1883

For reference, this letter is an exchange on the game laws and the sentiments of 'professional men' and 'sportsmen' between *"Olibo"* and J. F. Sprague[158] appearing in *Forest and Stream* in <u>1883</u>, eight years earlier than the Fannie Hardy essays. It should be understood that when these exchanges were occurring, the term 'sportsmen' was applied in many cases referring to a class of hunters or fishermen who came merely to kill game, out of season, with no intention of eating the meat, or making use of the hides; even if it were a small percent of them whom were acting in this fashion.

In the current day, someone under the term of 'sportsmen' would be held in high regard as someone who is upholding the laws and

---

[158] J. F. Sprague wrote considerably about Maine outdoor matters. He was born in 1848 in the town of Sangerville, Maine. Later in life he lived in Monson, Maine. He was the editor and publisher of Sprague's Journal of Maine History. Eckstorm herself was a contributor to that periodical; her most famous essay was her 1926 analysis of Chadwick's Survey (*History of the Chadwick Survey from Fort Pownal in the District of Maine to the Province of Quebec in Canada in 1764*). Sprague praised Eckstorm with the words, "The Journal has been exceedingly fortunate in securing the services of Mrs. Eckstorm, one of Maine's talented writers, herself a lover of Maine's ancient history and a historian and research worker, faithful and efficient."

acting ethically. Changes in the meaning, or interpretation of words is nothing new. In the 1800s it was not unusual to have signs posted at the train stations or lodges stating, "*Welcome Nimrods.*" Imagine the thought on seeing that greeting on your arrival today when the word is taken to mean, informally at least, 'a foolish person.' Whereas, in earlier times it was an indication of being a mighty hunter after Nimrod, in the Book of Genesis.

Here, Olibo argues that it should be allowed for 'gentlemen' to go into the woods in close season and take what they need, because they are so important in their worldly affairs of business, that during closed season might be the only time they can get away from their most important duties. That he writes this in a leading magazine, is evidence of the attitudes of the times, and fully supports the observations Eckstorm was arguing on behalf of the farmer-hunter class in terms of what they saw as illegal activity and unequal enforcement of the laws.

## Editor Forest and Stream:

You seem strongly inclined to make use of the sad accident, by which my lamented friend, Prof. Stuart Phelps, lost, his life, "to point a moral and adorn a tale." In your issue of September 6, you class him—and possibly deservedly—among the thousand-and-one ignoramuses who do not know how to handle a gun, and in last weeks' issue you arraign him as a breaker of the game laws. If he could wield his caustic pen, he would, I am sure, send you something on both these points which would be well worthy of your consideration, but unfortunately his hand is still, and his friends must speak for him.

For three successive seasons—in '79, '80 and '81—it was my privilege to be with him in the woods, and I had abundant opportunity to observe him in all the phases of camp life. He was an enthusiastic and well-trained sportsman, thoroughly familiar with the use of weapons, and habitually one of the most cautious men in handling them I have ever known. I never saw him, for instance, put a loaded gun into or take one out, of a boat, or carry one into a tent, and when we were on the trail, he was always careful to hold his weapon in such a way that, in case of accidental discharge, it could not possibly injure himself or anyone else. No one knows precisely how the fatal accident occurred; it is evident, however, that in this instance he was disregarding consciously or unconsciously a rule which he considered "imperative," and which, so far as my observation extends, he habitually observed. Many surmises on the subject may be made, but, of course, speculation is useless. For my own part, I am content to regard the sad event as one which may happen to any person who uses a gun, as a providence for which there is no satisfactory explanation in this world.

You state editorially, that at the time of his death he was engaged in violating the game laws, and there at your editorial hands are lifted in holy horror over his new made grave. I am able to say on the best authority—that of the gentleman who was with him when the accident occurred—that he was standing on the shore of the lake, and was in the act of putting a gun into his boat. If the relation of professional men to the game laws is to be discussed, and I hope it will be thoroughly, I think that as Prof. Phelps, whatever his intentions may have been, was not actually in pursuit of game, his name ought, in all fairness, to be left, out of the discussion. On the general subject—the attitude of professional men toward the game laws—I am well aware there is much to be said on both sides, and I have read attentively all you have published hitherto. I frankly confess, that as the laws now stand, I much prefer to be classed among the breakers, than among the makers, of them. Laws which fail to secure the approbation of one of the best, and in general, most law-abiding portions of the community, may be safely set down as practically obsolete from the day of their enactment. The class of men to which I have the honor to belong are gentlemen; many of them are accomplished sportsmen; none of them are trout-hogs, or game-hogs. All they ask is what everybody else enjoys, or may enjoy, viz., the privilege of taking enough fish and game to eke out such supplies as they can conveniently take into camp. They could safely be trusted to kill no more game, than is necessary, and their number is not so large that they would make any serious inroad on the supply of game. Surely a law might be framed which would permit them, on presentation of proper papers to the game commissioners of any State, and perhaps on payment of a fee, large or small, to take what they need. But it is scarcely reasonable to suppose, whatever others may think, that professional men whose duties are such, that if they go into the woods at all, they must go during the close season, and to many whom a trip to the woods is literally a new lease of life, will respect a series of statutes enacted by the average State Legislature, the majority of whom, to judge them by their work, do not know the difference between trout and tomcod, or caribou and 'coon.

Olibo. - New Haven. Conn. Sept. 18, 1883

## J. F. Sprague Responds
### *Forest and Stream*, Oct 11, 1883 (pg. 203.)

### Editor Forest and Stream:

It would usually seem that whatever opinions we may have entertained of a man's acts while he lived and breathed among us, and was able to defend himself, that after he had "gone to that bourne from whence no traveler has ever returned," the least we can do is maintain a respectful silence in deference to the solemnity of the occasion and its circumstances.

The sad occurrence in the wilds of Northern Maine which railed forth the letter of "Olibo" in your last issue would have gone into oblivion without any public comment on my part, if he had not chosen to open the subject himself, and had not invited the discussion of this topic. He says, in referring to the late casualty in Maine, "I am able to say on the best authority—that of the gentleman who was with him when the accident occurred—that he was standing on the shore of the lake, and was in the act of putting his gun into the boat." And yet his gun was loaded with heavy buck shot while he was on a fishing excursion. Why was this? I will answer this query myself, "The gentleman who was with him" told several reliable persons at Mt. Kineo and Greenville, who related the same to the writer, that only a few moments before the accident occurred, they (Messrs. Smythe and Phelps) had been firing at a caribou and failed to kill. Besides this, an efficient State detective had previously been on the trail of this same party, knew their whereabouts, understood their intentions and was aware of their every movement, and he avers that such was the fact. It is useless to deny that they were openly and notoriously making an attempt to violate the game laws of Maine.

But, "Olibo" prepares himself for proof of their guilt by denouncing the law. There is an old maxim which says: "Those who do not preserve the law of the land, thence justly incur the ineffaceable brand of infamy."

The man who "prefers" to be classed with the "law-breakers" rather than the "law-makers" and law-abiding citizens, arrays himself upon the side of the lawless, espouses the cause of poaching, law-breaking, and violence, whether the law is right or wrong.

But upon the question of the merits of the game laws of Maine, "Olibo" is entirely in error. He claims that they fail to "secure the approbation of one of the best, and in general, most law-abiding portions of the community." No statement could possibly have been written that would have been further from the truth than this one.

If he refers to "professional men" or to the "sportsmen" in general who visit Maine during the season for fishing and shooting, I deny that assertion most emphatically.

For many years past I have resided in this portion of Maine, near the region which was the scene of this fatal and lamentable accident, and where thousands annually congregate during the summer months to enjoy the charms and attractions of these northern forests, lakes, ponds and streams, and during the time I have come in contact, become associated with and formed the acquaintance of many of these people who are denominated "sportsmen," and who represent the professions and various other avocations of life. They come from almost every Northern State, but more especially from New England and the Middle States. They are, as a rule, gentlemen, and law abiding, respectable citizens.

From what knowledge I have of them, which is based upon a close observation for ten years past, I believe that not five per cent of their number are violators of, or are in sympathy with, any infractions of the Maine game and fish laws.[159] On the other hand, they are usually among the most ardent and enthusiastic supporters of the idea of protection to our fish and game, and their influence with the guides, their intercourse with our own citizens of Maine during their summer visits here, have had much to do with creating the wholesome public sentiment that now prevails in favor of these laws throughout the entire length-and breadth of the State.

Instead of these laws failing to secure the approval of this class, they have ever been their truest and most staunch and reliable friends, and in more than one instance these "professional men" from other States have inspired or originated the acts which are now the very laws so despised by "Olibo."[160]

"Olibo" further says, in support of his denunciation of the game laws, "All they [the tourists] ask is * * * the privilege of taking enough fish and game to eke out such supplies as they can conveniently take into camp." The midnight assassin and the "gentleman" who robs banks could with as much reason make the same argument and appeal for their "rights." When the lone squatter upon the shores of Moosehead and Chesuncook lakes, and the hardy pioneer at the outposts of civilization, require game during the prohibited season for the purpose of satisfying the hunger of himself and his family, there might be, viewing his case from a purely humane standpoint, some plea in justification of the warden who refrains from enforcing the extreme rigors of the law upon him

---

[159] While this letter is from 1883, Sprague, in 1891 would take offense to what Fannie Hardy writes about the 'sportsmen' violators. Yet, like Sprague, Eckstorm did not condemn all the visiting sportsmen by any means, and certainly it was a small percentage whose violations were garnering so much attention.

[160] And here Sprague is proving Eckstorm's entire thesis of her essays. She does not condemn all of the sportsmen-tourists. She points out it is a small percentage, as does Sprague. And on the same hand, she highlighted how men from other states influenced the wording of the laws, just as Sprague admits. Seems they had more common ground than Sprague was willing to see in the article he wrote in 1891 to the editor replying to her essays.

when he exercises the "privilege of taking enough fish and game" to his meager and dreary cabin to prevent starvation. But for the professional—whether he be clothed in clerical robes, receiving a munificent salary, and living on the "fat of the land," or whether he be the luxuriant lawyer, endowed with a rich clientage—to claim this favor has not the merit of good sense.

The man who can afford to travel three or five hundred miles by rail, put up at first-class summer hotels, and employ guides in his tours, is able to supply himself with all the necessaries and luxuries of camp life without killing deer moose, caribou, or game birds in close time.

I do not say that the poor man should have the right to violate the law, but I do claim that if either of these classes are *(not)* to be condemned, it is in every sense more proper, fitting and Christian-like that it be him, rather than those represented by "Olibo."

As I have never been a member of the Legislature of Maine, I do not take any special umbrage, at his gentlemanly ideas in regard to the Maine law "makers." Generally speaking, they have been those who were amply able to defend themselves. But they have been "gentlemen" who have had convictions that the fish and game of our State belong to the public, and not to a privileged class or a favored few, whether they be men from the classic walks of professional life, owning Government securities, and living in palatial residents, or the backwoodsman of the forests owning a hundred acres of land and living in a log house, and they have enacted laws which protect and preserve this game for the whole public, and their laws are now being sustained by the most intelligent and influential of Maine's citizens, as well as by nearly all of those from the cities and towns of other States, who favor us with their presence during the summer months.

J. F. Sprague
Monson, Maine, Oct. 1, 1883.

# MANLY HARDY AND "SPECIAL"

## April 2, 1891, Manly Hardy

### Editor Note

In this same issue of April 2, 1891, in which the prior essay from Eckstorm appeared, Manly Hardy included a response to the correspondent who signed his name "Special." This contributor. "Special" had contributed to *Forest and Stream* over the years. It appears from Hardy's response that he was aware of who "Special" was and that he was not from Maine. The exchange looks to have started months earlier as Manly calls out "Special" in an article in the February 26, 1891.

Of particular interest for these essays, are Manly's own words about how he was a follower of the Game Laws. His position was also evident in, *Exploring the Maine Woods - The Hardy Family Expedition to the Machias Lakes.* That trip took place from the end of September into October of 1890. On a weekday during the latter days of that trip, guide Jot Eldredge and Manly shot a deer. The exact dates in the essays are not clear, but based on both Manly's writing, as well as his daughter's, it is safe to consider that the killing of the deer for their meat took place in the open season of October. It is likely their trip, and the dates into the open season week, was part of their strategy to secure the meat to take home with them. The deer was shot on the way out of the woods, close to the trail where they would be picked up again by carriage to be transported back to the station. Manly, Fannie had written, had a rule for carries, and that was to carry the least amount. This also applied to game. She wrote, "Father has been so much with the Indians that he is learned in their philosophy and never lugs an extra pound on a carry. Had he met a nine-prong buck on the Machias end of the Gassobeeis Carry, it would have been quite characteristic for him to request the buck to step across to the

Gassobeeis end, because he always preferred to shoot his deer at Gassobeeis and save lugging them across the carry."[161]


## THE OTHER SIDE - MANLY HARDY


### February 26, 1891
### Editor Forest and Stream:

In the war time we had two kinds of war correspondents—one followed the army, was present at the engagements and wrote the truth, the other stayed at home and manufactured their news. Your correspondent "Special" evidently belongs to the latter class. We Maine people would prefer to have the truth told about us. Said a leading Bangor physician to me last week: "It makes me mad every time I read one of 'Special's' articles." This voices the feeling of most who read them. Probably no ten men who write on this subject have done so much to make people hostile to the laws, and their enforcement, as he has by his wholesale denunciation of our land holders and people generally.

In his article in *Forest and Stream* for Jan. 16 he says: "As near as I can learn a movement will be made to repeal all fish and game laws. The movement will come from the lumber interest, and it is to be hoped it will acquire no force." Again, in *Forest and Stream* for Feb. 13, he says: "The opposition to opening the month of September for deer hunting is stronger among the lumber land holders than I had imagined. They will oppose such a measure with all the power they can bring to bear. * * * They are obstinate to pigheadedness about the matter and can see no difference between the true sportsman who would as deeply regret a forest fire as themselves and the worthless, thieving poacher of their own State."

---

[161] In, *Exploring the Maine Woods - The Hardy Family Expedition to the Machias Lakes*.

Now, who are these "pigheaded" land owners who are thus held up to public infamy? They are the men who own a body of land more than twice as large as the State of Massachusetts, worth millions of dollars, and who for a score of years have allowed hundreds of non-residents to roam over it at pleasure, to catch the fish, to kill the game, to use all the wood they needed for campfires—in fact to use it as if it were their own with no restrictions whatever. These visitors are mostly here to kill game in direct violation of our State laws, and yet these same land owners have kept quiet. I doubt if "Special" can find an article by one of them proposing to curtail any of these privileges. I showed his article to the largest land owner in the State and he pronounced his statements in regard to lumbermen false, as also his statement of the purchase of the dam and right of flowage at Rangeley Lakes.

These land owners employ tens of thousands of our men the year round in the woods, on drives and in mills. They do more for the interests of our State in one year than all the "true sportsmen" ever will in ten eternities. Would it be very selfish, when the prosperity of our whole State depends on the preservation of our forests (for our water powers and farming interests depend on their preservation), if these land owners should wish to take means to preserve them?

And who are these true sportsmen who are so careful of our property? They are the men who for years have come here in June, July, August, and September, who have killed large game and left it to rot by every stream and lakeside in our northern woods. "Special" speaks of our thieving poachers. How does it happen he has never heard of Prof. ----, of Yale College, who, with his companions, killed in September six moose, besides caribou, and left them to rot; and the next year killed a moose and caribou in close time besides another moose in October and had the horns seized? It is no secret; Mr. Stilwell can tell him. If he wishes to stir this thing up, I will give him names of some of his near neighbors. I can give him a list of some twenty moose killed this very fall near Chesuncook by these same "true sportsmen" and left to rot; I can give the place where each lies, and deer without number have gone the same way.

He speaks of the young man shot in Waltham and slanders the people of three counties—Penobscot, Washington, and Hancock—on his account. Generally, when a man dies even his enemies let his faults die with him; but ghoul-like "Special" takes delight in telling all he knows and complaining of not being able to find out more. We Maine men have not done so by your true sportsmen killed in this way. "Special" has probably heard that a few years ago a Massachusetts professor, hunting with a noted Connecticut clergyman, was shot with a charge of buckshot, in August, 1883. Out of regard for his friends our Maine papers said nothing about the facts. I know the guides and the whole story; if "Special" wishes it, I can give the bottom facts.[162]

The majority of our land owners and the men in their employ have favored observing our game laws. I have seen beef hauled seventy miles when there were moose yarded within three miles and plenty of snow for killing them; and those moose were saved—for what? The very next fall a Boston sportsman, by the help of Indian guides, killed two (his guides say three) at the same place, and refused to sell the meat as it lay for less than ten cents a pound to Mr. Rod Sunderland, the same man who had saved them, who having salt and barrels there wanted to get the meat for his lumber crews. Most of it was left there to rot.

Year after year our people have seen our game killed and wasted by the ton in close time by rich men, who, belonging outside the State, readily make their escape before their deeds are known—men who do more than the French and Indians of Canada, for these do save hides, while the others often leave hides and all, or at best give to the guides the hides they dare not carry home. "Special" may call our people all the names he pleases, but we have no class of our people who will kill for mere sport; such men come from outside.

---

[162] On the topic of the letters between Olibo and J.F. Sprague.

My candid opinion, based on facts in my possession, is, that up to this year, more large game has been killed in close time in Penobscot County by parties (from) outside the State than by the inhabitants. The visitors killed in warm weather and wasted; the inhabitants ate all they killed. This year sees a change. Finding that there was no use in saving game only as an inducement for more to come in close time to waste it, by common consent our people in the woods have killed what they needed. As far as I can learn they intend to keep on doing so.

For years the sporting papers have been accusing our lumbermen of doing that of which, as a class, they were innocent, and have been shielding the real offenders.

Now, these same men who have so willfully maligned us, can thank themselves for this state of affairs. The fact lies just here: keep your true sportsmen out of our woods in close time and our own people will respect the laws; but if these gentlemen sportsmen see fit to keep on doing as they have done, and have a man like "Special" to charge their sins to us, they must not blame Maine people if we join with them in killing in close time.

Manly Hardy.

## THE MAINE GAME QUESTION - "Special"

### March 19, 1891
### Editor Forest and Stream:

It is with considerable reluctance that I take up the task of replying to a letter of Mr. Manly Hardy in the *Forest and Stream* of Feb. 26, 1891. In the outset, permit me to say that I dislike a controversy in a newspaper above all things, and am well aware that the readers thereof share in my dislike. Indeed, were it not that a principle is involved, that the principles of *Forest and Stream* itself are involved in having published "Special's" articles for six or eight years, believing them to be the truth, that personal attack upon "Special" would never have been replied to by me.

In the first place, it may be well to state that I am convinced that Mr. Hardy is honest in his opinions; indeed, that he is an honest man, and, so far as his knowledge extends, he would not knowingly mislead the readers of the *Forest and Stream* in regard to the situation of game protection in Maine, the way to do it, or any of the affairs of the State immediately connected with that subject.

So far as Mr. Hardy's knowledge is concerned, so far as he has thought, he is right in regard to "Special." He evidently supposes him to be a writer in Boston or somewhere else, writing about Maine game affairs like a long-distance war correspondent. But it would perhaps surprise him to know that the writer behind the nom deplume of "Special" was born in Maine, in a back town (he is proud of it), schooled in one town in Maine, fitted for college in another town in that State, college-trained in another town, now a city, began newspaper life in yet another town, only removing to a larger New England city for the sake of the better opportunities offered. "Special" also visits Maine twice annually for the sake of the dear old hills, the woods and waters, and the little share of fish and game that is left to him after the legal open seasons commence. That "Special" is in daily contact with "sportsmen" and tradesmen who visit Maine, and goes there himself as often as occasion or business requires is another fact that Mr. Hardy should understand, lest he make another mistake; also that he is fully aware of the number of deer being shipped to Boston commission houses in the close season, and at a time when the city sportsmen are certainly at home.

That certain of the lumberland owners of Maine would willingly see all the fish and game laws of that State repealed is capable of proof, and that they would try some such action before the Legislature of that State this winter was communicated to me by men in whom I have confidence, need not be repeated. One of the largest land owners in Maine has told me himself that he should be glad of any form of law or any means whereby fishermen and hunters could be kept away from his lands.

"We don't want them there," he said, "we are afraid of their fires." Mr. Hardy must also be aware that the present game laws of his State were left in their present ineffective condition for the simple reason that a lumberland owner proposed the amendments that weakened these laws at the very last hours of the session two years ago, and at a time when the friends of the laws as proposed had all gone home.

Mr. Hardy objects to "true sportsmen." I do not. By the term, I mean a man who will not kill game in close time. There are many such who go to Maine. I can give Mr. Hardy some of their names. Some of them own camps and cottages on lands leased of the lumber land owners, costing thousands of dollars. I have in mind one such gentleman, who rowed three miles in an open boat himself one night, to try to extinguish a fire that some campers had left burning. He could not even wait for a man to come to row the boat, though he had several men at work not far away, who would be in at nightfall. The fire was set by some native hunters, and it could not be extinguished for several weeks, though it was kept in check by the efforts of crews of men from the camps in that region, till the fall rains came. True sportsmen will not kindle fires in the forest, neither will they kill game out of season, even at Nicatouse,[163] where, it must be admitted, the love of the game laws is at low ebb.

But Mr. Hardy should not for a moment imagine again, from the above, that I stand up for either the hunter from Massachusetts, New York or Yale College, that goes to Maine to kill deer in close time. If he does again allow himself to so think, I shall be obliged to accuse him of not having read my letters carefully. I defy him to produce either word or line that I have ever written for the *Forest and Stream* defending the killing of game out of season in Maine or any other State. The files of the *Forest and Stream* for all the time I have written for it are at his service; for if he does not have them at hand I will forward them to him, express paid. I shall expect that he will show some words from me defending those

---

[163] Now Nicatous Lake. Eckstorm provided the original spelling as, Nicatowis, in *Exploring the Maine Woods - The Hardy Family Expedition to the Machias Lakes.*

from outside of his State who have killed game out of season, or I can with justice claim in the *Forest and Stream* that the principal accusations in his letter in that paper of the issue of Feb. 26 have fallen to the ground for lack of truth.

I am also here obliged to ask him if he will kindly point out a single paragraph wherein I have denounced anybody, either citizen of Maine or any other State, except the enemies of the enforcement of the game laws of that State as interpreted by its able and honest commissioners. I shall be obliged to request him to refer this paragraph to those commissioners and ask them if I have ever denounced any other citizen of Maine. With replying to the accusations of Mr. Hardy I am done, except that I must request him in his careful perusal of what I have written in *Forest and Stream* to carefully note the many times I have openly denounced the carrying of guns into the Maine woods by anybody in the close time for game; to note where I say in substance that if anybody does this and gets shot, why, I am simply glad of it. Something like this idea he will find in connection with the shooting of the son of the Massachusetts professor, with the noted Connecticut professor, the announcement of which piece of news was made by me in the *Forest and Stream* at the time, or as near to the time as the news got out. Will he also carefully note the condemnation that I gave in the case where a New York sportsman got a charge of shot in his side, I think it was, at Seven Ponds, a year or two ago, while attempting to jack a deer in close time. Then there was the case of the son of a Boston gentleman, who was shot by his own rifle, in a Maine camp, last summer, or a year ago. He will find the case if he reads the back numbers of the *Forest and Stream* carefully. There I say in substance that the boy had no business with a rifle in camp in close time, and that if he was killed his parents had only themselves to blame. The editor of *Forest and Stream* will tell Mr. Hardy that I have very often scathed the breakers of the Maine game laws—several of the very ones that Mr. Hardy mentions in his letter—so severely in my articles that he has been obliged to soften and tone down the language, lest it might appear that I were altogether too severe.

With answering the attack of Mr. Hardy the above must suffice, but he will permit me to submit a proposition to his judgment. I desire him to answer it through the *Forest and Stream*. Now, suppose that for some cause or other it should happen to become the thing to do for about all of the vacationists of the country to burglarize houses in Boston. Indeed, allow that the desire for robbing houses in Boston had greatly increased during a few years; that even Maine visitors to the city had grown to have a passion for this thing. Now we will suppose that the Maine visitor does not even know the streets of Boston: does not know the location of the house he desires to rob, but that there are a set of men in Boston who are ready to guide him to the house for pay. Nay, they will even furnish the conveyance and "holdup" the place while the Maine "sportsman" you may call him, if you desire, does the robbery—brings off the trophy. House robbing becomes very common; even the "guide's" themselves are at it. Now it is necessary to enforce the law of Massachusetts against burglary. Where shall the officers begin? Shall they rush to a "newspaper and complain of the Maine "sportsmen," and claim that the "sportsmen" from Maine are altogether to blame; that the Boston "guides" have become disgusted with the robberies committed by the Maine visitors? Shall they say, "Keep your Maine sportsmen out of our city and the robberies will cease?" Has Mr. Hardy never heard about such a thing as an accessory in a crime? Don't the Maine laws have something to say about an accessory before the fact, where a "guide" writes letters telling thieves where the booty lies, when to come, etc.? Suppose that it was almost impossible for the visitors to find the particularly desired booty in the great city; that the visitors are not experts at stealing; yea, even that it would be almost impossible for these visitors to get the booty unless guided by experts, where would Mr. Hardy begin to enforce the laws of Massachusetts against this stealing?

I think that Mr. Hardy will reply that I have put the comparison in too strong terms. Please remember that I have drawn no comparison. I have not even mentioned the other side of the comparison. I have left that for him. He may say that I have put the case too severely; that shooting deer in close time is not a crime against society, and that housebreaking is; that the illegal killing of game is only a crime against the State. Well, then, put it in a different form, if you please. Suppose that it was the thing for Maine visitors to do to pluck the flowers from the Public Garden, or from private yards and greenhouses. That these visitors had to be guided by Boston "guides" in order to know where the flowers were; indeed, that they would not succeed in getting a flower once in a dog's age, unless assisted by a Boston "guide," where should we begin to enforce the law? Stealing flowers before the owner is willing that you should gather them is scarcely worse than shooting game in the legal close time.

Now let Mr. Hardy tell the readers of the *Forest and Stream* squarely whether if Maine people universally stood by their own game laws and refused to assist "sportsmen" from other States in the illegal killing of game, if the whole work would not be done; then take the last sentence in his own article in that paper of Feb. 26, and see again how it sounds: "The fact lies just here: keep your true sportsmen out of our woods in close time and our own people will respect the laws; but if these gentlemen see fit to keep on doing as they have done, and have a man like 'Special' to charge their sins to us, they must not blame Maine people if we join with them in killing in close time."

Special.

## MANLY'S REPLY TO "SPECIAL."
### April 2, 1891

I wish to thank "Special" for stating that he believes me to be honest. It is what I have always endeavored to be.

His statements as to who he is occasion no surprise, as I know far more about him than he supposes. It is on account of this knowledge, corroborated by the statements in his last, that I have written. I do not question his knowledge of Boston markets, or that he visits Maine occasionally, or that he sees many from there. I said he was a stay-at-home correspondent, and I still say so. I do not question his good intentions, but I do say that he gives statements as authoritative on many points of which he has a very limited knowledge. That he intends to state facts is no excuse for stating things to be so which are not so. I did not question the many correct statements; I challenged the incorrect ones regarding our land owners. By an official report to the *Boston Journal*, March 17, our wild lands are given as containing 9,260,836 acres, valued at over $19,000,000, and the tax for 1891 is $52,743. Is it wise to antagonize the owners of this property by making statements about them which cannot be proved? "Special" stated that they were "obstinate to pig-headedness" and would oppose a certain measure "with all the power they could bring to bear." In his article of March 19 he says truthfully, "There was not much opposition to the amendments," and his silence regarding land owners shows he was mistaken. I asked him to quote any article a land owner had ever written proposing to curtail the privileges of sportsmen. He has not done it. Instead of this he speaks of one who wished that hunters and fishermen could be kept off their lands for fear of fires. This, I think, is no unreasonable wish. If "Special" were a land owner he would wish the same.

He mentions a praiseworthy case where a gentleman tried to extinguish a fire which "some camper had left burning." If there had been no campers there, there would have been no fire. He complains of land owners because "they can see no difference between the real sportsman who would as deeply regret a forest fire as they would themselves and the worthless, thieving poacher of their own State." Now, the fact is that it is the guides, who belong to the class "Special" calls names, who really preserve our lands from fires. They choose the camping places, they build the fires for the sportsmen, whether real or sham, and they put them out on leaving; were it not for our guides the State would have been burned over long ago. A man may be a perfect gentleman and obey all laws, and yet be very careless with fire. I can give names of three Bangor men who set three separate fires in past years—all first-class men, but careless. To imply that a gentleman will not carelessly set a fire, and that those who do are poachers and thieves is absurd.

"Special" says that I object to "true sportsmen." That is his statement, not mine. I object to no man, white man or Indian, who kills no game and catches no fish to waste. A good many such come here to fish; a very few to hunt. All such men are welcome. What I do object to is having anyone calling the men who leave our trout in piles to rot on the banks, as I have often seen them, and who kill our game in summer and waste it, "true sportsmen," and calling other as good men "thieves and poachers," if later they kill what they need to eat. I do not believe in calling anyone hard names. It never does any good to the cause of the one who uses them; but I believe in fair play. "Special" says in the *Forest and Stream*, Jan. 13, 1887, page 487:

"I have heard a gentleman say within a couple of days, and I know him to be a true gentleman, notwithstanding he has been in disgrace in Maine for shooting game out of season, for which shooting he has paid his fines—I have heard him say that if Maine changed her game laws so as to give September as part of the open season on her larger game, that he should do all in his power toward helping the Commission."

Now if he means to say that a man who has killed game in close time is a true gentleman because he has paid his fines, why is not Jonathan Darling, after he has settled his fine, as much a gentleman? Darling wants September opened for dogging deer, and this man wants it opened to kill them after his own fashion. Wherein is the difference? What I wish him to see is that by making class distinctions, by keeping silent about the rich who come to waste and berating those of our State who kill to eat, such a state of feeling has been made to exist as "Special" at his distance knows nothing about. He hears one side and gives that as he hears it; there is another side of which he knows little and which I feel would modify his tone were he more fully informed. My daughter is writing a series of papers on Maine game which may place some things in a different light from what they have been viewed. "Special" doubtless knows more of the Rangeley region where he visits than I do; I make no pretensions to knowledge of that country; but of the country east of the Kennebec from the sea to the boundary lines, I have a knowledge such as he will never have.

"Special" asks me to find a line he has written defending the killing of game out of season. I have never stated that he defended it; what I do say is that he condemns one class and keeps silence about the other. He will remember that our close time extends to Oct. 1. He knows that fully three-fourths of our hunting visitors have finished their hunting before that; of the remainder I think a fair statement would be that at least half go to different points, where deer are dogged to hunt in this way. I think "Special" would be fair if he knew the facts, but our local papers rarely expose visitors, while they do give some cases of violations by our own people, and at his distance he repeats what he reads.

As to shooting cases, "Special" says: "Note where I say in substance that if anybody does this and gets shot, why, I am simply glad of it." I freely acquit him of partiality; but how any man can say he is glad when a man is killed or wounded and a home is left desolate, is beyond my comprehension; but that is his funeral, not mine.

A large part of his article is given to "submitting a proposition to my judgment," and to bring it down to my comprehension he has kindly restated it in simpler form. When I first read it over, I thought it sounded familiar and at once turned to Mark Twain's first interview with Artemas Ward. I quote a part of it, as I think anyone reading the two will at once see the similarity in directness of style:

"Now, what I want to get at is—is, well, the way deposits of ore are made, you know. For instance: Now, as I understand it, the vein which contains the silver is sandwiched in between casings of granite, and runs along the ground and sticks up like a curbstone. Well, take a vein 40ft. thick, for example, or 80 for that matter, or even a hundred—say you go down on it with a shaft, straight down, you know, or with what you call 'incline,' maybe you go down 500ft., or maybe you don't go down but 300—anyway you go down, and all the time this vein grows narrower, when the casings come nearer or approach each other, you may say—that is, when they do approach, which of course they do not always do, particularly in cases where the nature of the formation is such that they stand apart wider than they otherwise would, and which geology has failed to account for, although everything in that science goes to prove that, all things being equal, it would if it did not, or would not certainly if it did, and then of course they are. Do not you think it is?"

\* \* \* \* \* \* \* \* \* \* \* \* \* \* \* \* \* \* \* \* \* \* \* \* \* \*

And then I said aloud: "I—I—that is—if you don't mind, would you—would you say that over again? I ought—"

\* \* \* \* \* \* \* \* \* \* \* \* \* \* \* \* \* \* \* \* \* \* \* \* \* \*

"Now, don't you be afraid. I'll put it so plain this time that you can't help but get the hang of it. We will begin at the very beginning. You know the vein, the ledge, the thing that contains the metal, whereby it constitutes the medium between all other forces, whether of present or remote agencies, so brought to bear in favor of the former against the latter, or the latter against the former or all, or both, or compromising the relative differences existing within the radius whence culminate the several degrees of similarity to which—"

I said, "Oh, hang my wooden head, it ain't any use—it ain't any use to try—I can't understand anything. The plainer you get it the more I can't get the hang of it."

"Special" sums up his proposition by asking me "squarely to tell the readers of *Forest and Stream* whether if Maine people stood by their own game laws and refused to assist 'sportsmen' from other States in illegal killing of game, if the whole work would not be done." I answer squarely, no. Only the year before last a New York gentleman whose name I have, left here threatening to bring his guides and boats from the Adirondack County. I say that if our people all stood by the laws to a man, these men would come as long as they knew that by paying a fine, light to them, they would still be considered gentlemen in other States. They care no more for our laws or our State than the Boston liquor dealers do; what they want is the game. "Special" has unwittingly showed where his sympathies are. He has proposed for the whole people of a State to keep the laws and to keep any of their number from being hired by outsiders to help them break the laws, before he proposes to help us. Did he ever know any State, city or town, where no one could be hired to break laws? If that is the only condition on which he proposes to give us any moral support, we will "paddle our own canoe." To expect the people who own the game and the land it is on, to stand by year after year and see it wasted, with rewards offered by outsiders for their conviction if they break their own laws, and no rewards for non-resident violators, and no word of encouragement for those who do well, but only opprobrious epithets hurled at those who follow bad examples, is too much to expect even of Maine.

Manly Hardy

**Manly Hardy**
**1832 – 1910**

# About Maine Author Tommy Carbone

Tommy Carbone lives in Maine and spends a wicked amount of his time exploring the waterways and trails of the north woods. He has a Ph.D. in engineering but has closed his spreadsheets, databases, and modeling software and now writes from a one room cabin, on the shores of a lake, that is frozen for almost six months out of the year, and moose outnumber people three to one.

His first novel, "*The Lobster Lake Bandits – Mystery at Moosehead,*" has made those 'from away' want to visit Maine. It's a big state – come explore.

**www.tommycarbone.com**

# BOOKS FROM MAINE'S NORTH WOODS

## A Maine Novel

The first novel in the

*Moosehead Mystery*

series.

Poachers, game wardens, and unknown characters roaming the Maine woods make for a suspenseful assignment for New York writer Sarah Molloy.

The second novel in the

## *Moosehead Mystery*

Series.

Game Warden Henry Ford, Joe Parker, and Sarah Molloy get mixed up in a crime that brings to the small town of Greenville a mystery man who may be up to no good.

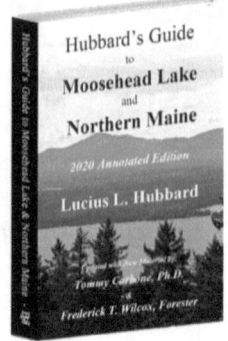

Hubbard's Guide

to exploring

Northern Maine.

Annotated Edition

Hubbard's

adventure through

Maine to Canada.

Annotated Edition.

*Thomas S. Steele's*

*Maine Adventures.*

Two book collection.

Annotated Edition

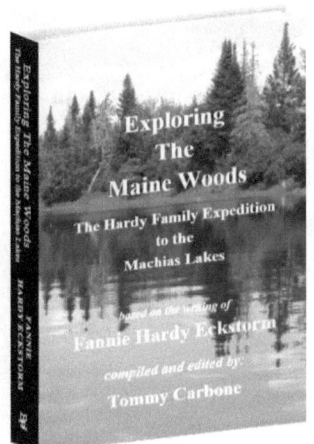

Based on the writing of
**Fannie Hardy Eckstorm**
this memoir is a wonderful tale
of the Maine woods and history
from the 1800s.

An annotated edition of
additional stories from:
Fannie Hardy Eckstorm
Manly Hardy
&
Other writers on Maine

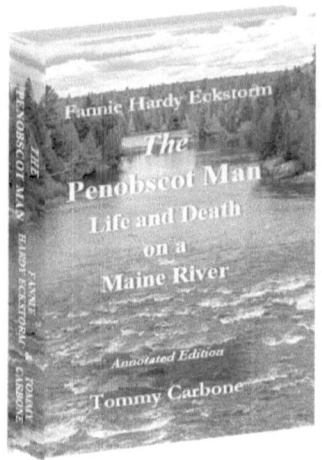

**The Penobscot Man**
**Life and Death**
**on a Maine River**

An updated and annotated
edition of the 1904 classic.

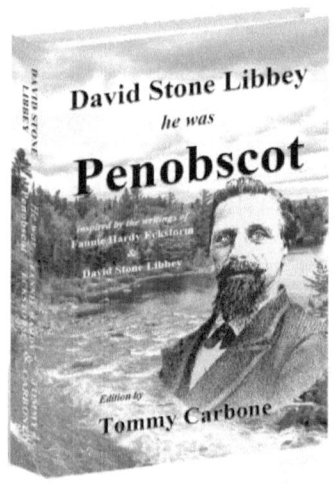

The journals of river-driver and
writer, David Stone Libbey, as
compiled by Fannie Hardy
Eckstorm are now updated with
his own writing in this
annotated edition.

# I Am Penobscot

## A Novel

The characters in this historical fiction novel are based on the Mainers of Eckstorm's writings. Eckstorm herself plays a key role in this story. Without her documenting Maine history as she had done, this story would not have been possible. Names you've read in this book—Manly Hardy, John Ross, Commissioner Stilwell, Dan Golden, Jock Darling, Jack Russell, Wilbur Webster, James White, David Stone Libbey and more are all characters that take to adventure in the Maine woods. For the setting is the woods, but the story is about the people.

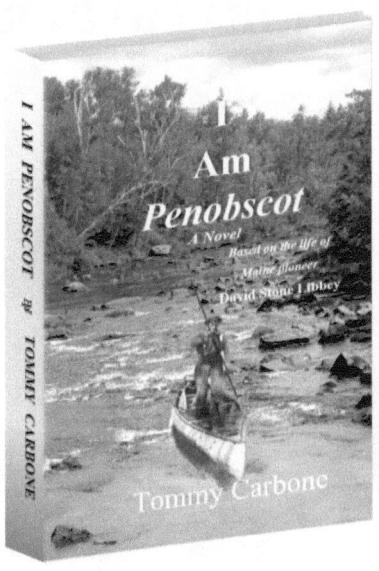

For more stories and pictures from the

Maine coast to the north woods,

find Tommy at:


**www.tommycarbone.com**

www.ingramcontent.com/pod-product-compliance
Lightning Source LLC
Chambersburg PA
CBHW021703120626
46545CB00004B/1371